Doing Recent History

Doing Recent History

On Privacy, Copyright, Video Games,
Institutional Review Boards, Activist Scholarship,
and History That Talks Back

EDITED BY
CLAIRE BOND POTTER
AND RENEE C. ROMANO

The University of Georgia Press
Athens and London

© 2012 by the University of Georgia Press
Athens, Georgia 30602
www.ugapress.org
All rights reserved
Set in Minion by Graphic Composition, Inc., Bogart, Ga.
Manufactured by Sheridan Books
The paper in this book meets the guidelines for permanence
and durability of the Committee on Production Guidelines
for Book Longevity of the Council on Library Resources.

Printed in the United States of America
16 15 14 13 12   P   5 4 3 2 1

Library of Congress Cataloging-in-Publication Data

Doing recent history : on privacy, copyright, video games,
institutional review boards, activist scholarship, and history
that talks back / edited by Claire Bond Potter and Renee C. Romano.
    p. cm. — (Since 1970 : histories of contemporary America)
Includes bibliographical references and index.
ISBN-13: 978-0-8203-3467-7 (cloth : alk. paper)
ISBN-10: 0-8203-3467-7 (cloth : alk. paper)
ISBN-13: 978-0-8203-4302-0 (pbk. : alk. paper)
ISBN-10: 0-8203-4302-1 (pbk. : alk. paper)
    1. United States—History—20th century—Historiography—Methodology.
    2. United States—History—21st century—Historiography—Methodology.
    3. Historiography—United States—Sources.
    4. Historiography—Methodology.
    5. Historiography—Technological innovations.
    6. History, Modern—Historiography—Methodology.
    I. Potter, Claire Bond, 1958– II. Romano, Renee Christine.
E175.7.06 2012
973.072—dc23   2011044423

British Library Cataloging-in-Publication Data available

Contents

Acknowledgments

IT IS COMMON IN ACKNOWLEDGMENTS for authors to thank their editors. But in our case, we owe more than a debt of gratitude to Derek Krissoff, our wonderfully supportive editor at the University of Georgia Press. The Since 1970: Histories of Contemporary America series was really Derek's idea. What about a book series that published only works of recent history, perhaps those that focused on events since 1970? he asked Renee at a history conference a few short years ago. Begun in a conversation over drinks, then a set of notes that became a proposal, the series was launched last year. This anthology is among the first works published in that series. So first and foremost, we would like to thank Derek for his intellectual insight that this was a project whose time had come; his belief that we were the people who could do it; his enthusiastic support for both the book series and this anthology; and for his skills in seeing a volume through to publication. And, of course, we need to thank him for all the subsequent drinks we have imbibed and meals we have eaten at history conferences while talking about the book series and this anthology.

Renee would most like to thank her coeditor, Claire Potter. Claire has been a mentor and friend for more years than I care to admit, and it has been a highlight of my professional career to have the opportunity to work with her closely on a collaborative project. I moved to a new institution, Oberlin College, just as the Since 1970 series was getting under way, and I am blessed to have wonderful colleagues here who have been supportive of this project and of my work more generally. Finally, I would like to thank my family. My husband, Sean Decatur, has been his usual supportive self, cheerfully listening to me talk through my ideas and challenges related to this work, while my children, Sabine and Owen, proved willing conspirators whenever I needed a break.

Claire is indebted to Renee Romano for her shrewd intelligence, her ability to keep things moving, and for being the colleague and friend with whom everyone would like to work but is rarely able to. This series, and the book, are a small piece of the story of what I have learned from her and what we have accomplished together. By imagining this anthology, and bringing her experience editing another book to the collaboration, she ensured that our friendship would more than survive her move to Oberlin: it would flourish. It has been a particular pleasure to work with Derek. I first met him as a seminar student at Wesleyan University a very long time ago, and he has long since established himself as a friend and colleague. When Renee led me over to the University of Georgia Press booth at a conference to sketch out a couple of ideas, it was clear that the three of us were a match.

At Wesleyan, I would like to thank all my colleagues at the Center for the Americas for their constant encouragement; the Colonel Return Jonathan Meigs First Fund and history department colleagues for a grant that paid for research cited in my own chapter; and Academic Affairs for the travel and grant money it has devoted to this project. Although e-mail and cell phones have sped up collaborations dramatically since Arthur Schlesinger's day, sometimes an airplane and a hotel room just work better. In the final days of preparing this manuscript, Lila and Harry Jacob opened their beautiful home in Ely, Minnesota, to a historian who needed only peace, quiet, and good cheer to make it to the finish line. Most important, I would like to thank my partner, Nancy Barnes, whose energy, affection, advice, and editorial skills always make things so much better than they would be if I tried to do them alone.

We would also like to thank Estelle Freedman and Susan Ware. As dissertation advisors, Estelle and Susan were the first to introduce us to the methodology of researching and writing history. We are indebted to them for pushing our work while we were in school and for their continued support ever since.

Finally, we look back over our shoulders at two years with the authors in this volume. Their hard work, vision, and willingness to push just a little harder to get things right made this book happen. Thank you.

Oberlin, Ohio
New Haven, Connecticut

Doing Recent History

INTRODUCTION

Just over Our Shoulder

The Pleasures and Perils of Writing the Recent Past

RENEE C. ROMANO AND CLAIRE BOND POTTER

RECENT HISTORY—THE VERY PHRASE SEEMS like an oxymoron. Yet historians have been writing accounts of the recent past—of events that have occurred in their own lifetimes and that they perhaps participated in only a few years previously—since printed history acquired a modern audience. As early as 1614, Sir Walter Raleigh noted that his *Historie of the World* might have "been more pleasing to the Reader, if I had written the story of *mine owne times.*"[1] That Raleigh was, at the time, imprisoned in the Tower of London for having participated in a plot against King James I speaks to the political investment he might have had in telling that story—and inciting an audience to ask for it. Today, while wrestling with a scholarly environment that has sometimes become just as political in exhilarating and disquieting ways, a growing number of historians seem to be gravitating toward writing the very recent past, a turn that may well be broadening the audience for our work.

The past few years have witnessed the publication of a significant number of contemporary histories by well-established and widely respected historians. In the field of political history, key works include James Patterson's *Restless Giant: The United States from Watergate to Bush v. Gore* (2007), Sean Wilentz's *The Age of Reagan: A History, 1974–2008* (2008), and Thomas Sugrue's *Not Even Past: Barack Obama and the Burden of Race* (2010). Social, cultural, and economic historians have turned their attention to very recent topics in numbers too great to cite here, responding to a demand for critical historical reflection on phenomena such as AIDS policies, the Internet, neoliberal economics, feminism, and the rise of evangelical Christianity as a political and social force.[2] As Julian Zelizer has noted, the claims of many of these latter accounts on traditionally dominant fields like political, military, and diplomatic history have been so powerful that they have pushed scholars to redefine their craft. Arguably, in an increasingly mass-mediated world, no historical category in the recent past can remain wholly untouched by another. Bethany Moreton's *To Serve God and Walmart: The Making of Christian Free Enterprise* (2009), Jeffrey G. Madrick's *Age of Greed: The Triumph of Finance and the Decline of America, 1970 to the Present* (2011), and a special issue of the *Journal of American History* (September 2002) on the terrorist attacks of 9/11, published a year after the event itself, all demonstrate that recent history not only is here to stay but is making aggressive claims for the relevance of history to understanding ongoing events.[3]

Yet as both of us discovered when we embarked on research in contemporary history, despite a rich tradition and a burgeoning present, there has been remarkably little discussion within the field about methodological issues related to writing the recent past. We connect this to historians' more general ambivalence about discussing their methods. In a set of reflections that has been useful to both of us, John Lewis Gaddis has observed that, unlike scientists and social scientists, historians are often perversely invested in concealing from the reader any methodology or theory that they might have knowingly employed.[4] Furthermore, as both of us found out the hard way, there is a difference between researching topics that took place centuries ago and those that took place only years ago. The more we shared our challenges, the more we thought it was time that someone scrutinized this exciting practice a little more closely.

The essays collected here seek to provide advice and guidance to historians who are contemplating the study of subjects located in the recent past. Arthur M. Schlesinger, Jr., a renowned practitioner of recent history whose three-volume tome, *The Age of Roosevelt*, was completed within a quarter century of Roosevelt's election and the implementation of the New Deal, described his project as writing a history that was "just over our shoulder." The perspective of any historian who tries to write about such recent events, he suggested, was not unlike being in the exciting and dangerous hollow of a wave: "Not until we reach the crest of the next one can we look back and estimate properly what went on before." He acknowledged that the historian needs to be fully aware of the "inadequacy of the present moment for any sort of lasting judgments."[5]

Reviewers of Schlesinger's *Age of Roosevelt* focused on some of these inadequacies, articulating criticisms about which any of us might be concerned were they leveled at us. Although the trilogy was hailed as a "major work of recent history," many reviewers expressed the same concerns that the authors featured in this volume address. For example, some saw it as a liability that Schlesinger could consult few other historical works to support and contextualize his research.[6] Other reviewers felt that Schlesinger's bold arguments about the transformative importance of Roosevelt's vision and New Deal policies themselves were premature, as he was writing too soon to understand the full impact of these events. Not only would new evidence surely emerge that might call Schlesinger's interpretation of the period into question, but Schlesinger's insistence that the Age of Roosevelt represented a "watershed" in the history of the nation seemed precipitous.[7] As W. R. Brock of the *Historical Journal* commented acidly, didn't it seem a "little premature to discover a watershed in history among events which began twenty-four and ended thirteen years ago?"[8] Finally, reviewers questioned whether Schlesinger, or any historian, could really be objective and unbiased in writing a history of recent events that continued to resonate in present politics. Some suggested that Schlesinger's obvious political bias— he made no effort to disguise his admiration for Roosevelt or his disdain for the business community—must be due to writing about events that were simply too present and thus were unavoidably politicized. "Perhaps good contemporary history must always be" partisan, one charitable voice remarked. Another mused that it was "probably still too early to expect an objective appraisal" of the transformation from an "old order" to the New Deal order that Schlesinger described.[9]

Yet Schlesinger himself insisted that writing so soon after events occurred presented its own advantages and pleasures, in particular the opportunity to do oral histories and thus to ensure the survival of information and perspectives that might otherwise be lost. He was, he said, willing to take his chances on writing a history from a "zone of imperfect visibility."[10]

So are we. This book grapples with exactly the same problems that Schlesinger and these reviewers identified: the challenges of trying to write histories of recent events where visibility is inherently imperfect, hindsight and perspective are lacking, and historiography is underdeveloped. To that end, we define "recent history" as histories of events that have taken place no more than forty years ago, although some contributors to this volume, such as Eileen Boris, Jennifer Klein, Renee C. Romano, and Julius H. Bailey, write about events that are less than a decade old. Others, such as Alice Yang and Alan S. Christy, examine histories and interpretive frames that begin with World War II but have not ended to this day. As we came to understand, different scholars need to think about the recent past for different reasons. Many scholars writing contemporary history focus their research exclusively on very recent events. Others, often at the urging of editors who have their eye on an audience of educated, nonacademic readers, try to bring their narratives up to the present to assert the relevance of a much further past.

Although recognizing the problems that we as historians might face when we undertake to shift the boundaries of what constitutes a legitimate topic for historical study, we also insist on the rewards and the potential methodological innovations that result when one of us turns our gaze on that history "just over our shoulder." As the essays in this book make clear, historians who take up the challenge of writing about recent events find themselves forced, for various reasons (not the least of which is retaining our identity as historians!), to think critically about our own methodologies and stances. We have the opportunity to blaze trails that have not yet been marked in the historical literature. We have access to sources that simply do not exist for earlier periods: in addition to living witnesses, we have unruly evidence such as video games and television programming (which has expanded exponentially since the emergence of cable), as well as blogs, wikis, websites, and other virtual spaces. Our work, moreover, has the potential to complicate political or cultural discourses about urgent contemporary issues—war, work, memorialization, and the economy are but a few represented in this volume—that might otherwise lack sufficient historical context or understanding.

Neither the project of writing recent history nor criticisms of that project are new, as the work of a historian such as Schlesinger attests. So why have we chosen to produce a volume like this now? Why should historians care about the potential pitfalls and promise of studying events that have taken place in the past four decades?

We believe that there are at least three important reasons that the writing of the recent past requires our scrutiny, other than the fact that our colleagues—and particularly young scholars joining the profession—are doing it in increasing numbers and will continue to do so even if we censure rather than support them. First, and most prominently, historians' lack of attention to the methodological issues related to studying contemporary history is likely to have consequences. As Renee C. Romano's essay in this collection asserts, the existing literature rarely even acknowledges that studying a past that is, as she calls it, "not dead yet" might be a different project than researching and writing the comfortably dead pasts on which most graduate schools focus their training. As our authors demonstrate, among the fundamental questions that need to be revisited are positionality, the difficulties of crafting narratives in the absence of any clear moments of closure, and the specific challenges that arise when working with new kinds of sources that are available for students of the past twenty or thirty years but have not been available to their mentors. These issues have not been explored systematically elsewhere, and we think it is time to start that discussion.

As the essays collected here make clear, we believe as a group that the methodological challenges involved in doing recent history are matched by the rewards: exploring untouched archives, establishing new fields and topics, and having an intellectual platform from which to speak about history as it happens are but a few. Reflecting on those challenges not only offers an arena for a discussion about what constitutes best practices for recent historians but also helps shed new light on some of the long-standing theoretical and methodological issues related to the discipline of history more generally. Reflecting on recent history, then, offers an important lens through which to explore historical practice, especially as it is shifting in the twenty-first century to include more interdisciplinary approaches and to embrace technologies that offer challenges to interpretation and sometimes—as Jeremy K. Saucier notes in his essay on using video games as historical evidence—to the basic skills sets any of us might bring to research.

A second reason to pay careful attention to the particular challenges of recent history stems from what we believe are increasing pressures on scholars from publishing houses to do more contemporary work and from the troubled academic job market to do more startling, interdisciplinary, or topically new work. At the very least, scholars of twentieth-century events are often urged to connect scholarship on a distant past more directly to contemporary concerns. By doing so, editors hope to lure that audience of educated, nonscholarly readers who have made scholars as different as Schlesinger, Richard Hofstadter, Sara Evans, and George Chauncey into best-selling authors.[11] As recent PhDs in all fields know, it is becoming increasingly difficult to find publishers for the narrowly specialized monographs that are valued by dissertation and tenure committees. The changing nature of academic publishing suggests that historians may well feel compelled to undertake work that can be framed as being "relevant" to an audience, even if the scholar's original concerns, and the focus of much of the book, is far more traditionally "dead." While studies in any field and from any period can potentially speak to more contemporary concerns, to do it well—and to ground those connections in empirical evidence—may mean learning unfamiliar and nontraditional research skills, as well as accessing archives that are neither neatly packaged nor fully accessible. Many scholars, and several who are represented in this volume, are drawn to recent history for their own reasons. However, we believe that established historians as well as graduate students may feel increasingly pulled by market forces to focus on pasts that (accurately or not) might be deemed more relevant by readers who are more interested in the events that have affected their own generation.

Moreover, the mark of many an established scholar's success has been, like Schlesinger, to become an engaged public intellectual speaking with authority to newspaper, television, magazine, and Internet audiences who might not be interested in reading books at all. Market-driven publishing means that a featured article in a mainstream publication, an op-ed, or a particularly provocative blog has, for many, led back to book contracts that ask scholars to parlay a more conventional reputation into work that blends historical scholarship with commentary. The research trajectories of established scholars such as Sean Wilentz, Jill Lepore, and James Kloppenberg—who began their careers with monographs in early America, colonial history, and late nineteenth-century history and have now all published historical works focused on very contemporary events—attest both to the lure of the recent past and the desire of a general readership for accessible, intelligent scholarship that explains the changes people are experiencing in their lives right now.[12]

While the forays of these prestigious scholars into more recent history have produced rich and thoughtful work, these same books also suggest that there are issues related to doing this kind of research that need to be considered more systematically. For example, in the introduction to his book *The Age of Reagan* (2009), Wilentz writes about his decision to forgo interviews, in part because there were too many living witnesses to the events he was describing. "More importantly," he writes, "I am suspicious of interviews as a reliable source for historians, especially political historians." Interviews might be necessary for journalists, who must "establish basic facts" as events are unfolding, but historians "run the risk of being manipulated by informants" and are better off relying on "the kinds of sources historians have traditionally interpreted."[13] But what is the nature of this manipulation? Has the historian no defense against it? Wilentz does not say.

Even as we admired the book's accomplishments, we could not help but wonder: was this decision impelled by Wilentz's greater comfort level with the more traditional sources that he used in his earlier studies and a lack of familiarity with oral history methods and practices that might have given him some guidance about when the task was complete? Essays in this volume by Martin Meeker, Willoughby Anderson, and Claire Bond Potter attest to the difficulties historians of the recent past must grapple with in undertaking interviews but also argue that they can be overcome. Potter, in particular, addresses the questions of interpretation that might create conflict between a living subject's story and the historian's conclusions. But these three authors also insist that oral histories offer an avenue for enhanced access to the past that not only is a fruitful archive but also helps scholars rethink their own research design, arguments, and perspectives. While an absence of oral histories probably did not affect Wilentz's excellent synthesis of the thirty-five-year "Age of Reagan," it would probably be remiss of a historian working on a more specialized political topic not to seek the testimony of at least a few key witnesses. Not all of us can have the specialized training oral history requires, but a historian might nevertheless need to develop new methodologies and, as Meeker notes, learn to navigate the ethical rules governing those methods.

Questions of rhetoric may also be important, as is the capacity of the historical establishment, or politics, to strike back when new interpretations in the field become available to a mass audience.[14] Did Kloppenberg anticipate, as he put the final touches on a manuscript that would go to press in 2010, that his characterization of Obama's political sensibility ("any defeat can be redeemed, and any triumph lost in the next vote") would become a gut-wrenching reality as a newly formed conservative coalition that called itself the Tea Party pushed candidates, the electorate, and the Congress to the right in the November by-election? Did Lepore imagine, as she wove relatively commonplace observations about female citizenship and the status of race in the Founding Fathers' vision into a book about conservative appropriations of the revolutionary past, that an eminent colleague in the field would link her position as "a staff writer for the *New Yorker*" to his own view that she was less a historian than a "partisan" who was "an expert at mocking" Tea Party activists' need for selective memories that reinforce their fears about the present?[15]

Finally, we believe that this volume is timely because we are living in an age of incredibly swift technological changes that have immense implications for all historians, not just those who study the recent past. These changes—whether in something we take for granted, like television, or something relatively new, like the Internet—are sources of rich evidence and difficult interpretation that the profession has only just begun to consider seriously. On the Internet, for example, even as far more evidence becomes available, we fear that much of it will eventually disappear. The desire and resources for archiving commonplace communications such as e-mails, wikis, and blogs lag far behind our social shift away from paper documents.[16] We are living in a moment when new technologies might not only create an entirely new terrain for our research, as the essays here by David Greenberg and Jeremy K. Saucier explore, but could also reshape our sense of historical practice itself. Simply put, we might have to steel ourselves to learning how to do more: for Saucier, that means playing video games with fingers that have never done more than tap a keyboard; for Greenberg, sifting through hours of TV footage for evidence that cannot yet be processed or catalogued by an archivist. The Internet, blogs, YouTube, Twitter, and webcams hold great promise for historians who are teaching and doing research on all kinds of topics, especially those related to more recent pasts.[17] New digital technology makes sources much more readily accessible while at the same time inundating researchers with more material than they could consider in a lifetime. A focus on recent history offers a site for a thoughtful appraisal of these changes, and an assessment of what we can bring to them.

Historians of the far past have sometimes been challenged by the paucity of their source material, the fragility of documents, and eyestrain (Potter remembers the wave of relief that passed over her in an earlier project when an archive folder revealed the purchase of a portable typewriter by a nineteenth-century intellectual with copperplate handwriting.) But those of us who study more recent periods encounter what some scholars have called "info glut."[18] That challenge forces us to find systematic and legitimate ways to sift through the enormous amounts of material available on many topics and to make good decisions about what needs to be ruled out of bounds if the book is ever to be published. We need to consider the ways in which search engines and databases can shape our research, asking the same critical and creative questions about the nature of electronic archives that we have long asked about more traditional ones.[19] We must develop practices related to the credibility and use of new kinds of electronic writing (whereas eighteenth-century anonymous authors were often not actually anonymous, blog commenters and wiki writers can be untraceable), and we must learn how to use sources that we may not know how to "read," such as television programs or video games.

The nature of new technology, which is making all kinds of material so much more accessible than before, has other implications that historians must take seriously as well. Contributions here by Laura Clark Brown, Nancy Kaiser, and Martin Meeker attest to the ways in which the easy accessibility enabled by the Internet is placing new pressures on archivists around issues of privacy. When collections are placed online, they circulate beyond a small circle of professionals and specialists and therefore raise more pressing concerns about the protection of individuals discussed in them. But traditional paper archives pose their own challenges. Archivists Clark Brown and Kaiser warn that if historians don't find new ways to work with special-collections departments to respond to privacy concerns, archives might choose to close collections until they are seventy years old, a decision that would seriously hamper many of us from gaining access to far less delicate material, so that documents that raise the most pressing concerns can be sequestered.

Like other aspects of doing recent history, the new age of digital technology offers both potential peril and great promise for historians. Schlesinger's determination to reach a mass audience has new implications when we think about the ways in which the idea of the book itself has been transformed by new media. The Internet has created global audiences for local histories, as well as for intercultural and transnational historical phenomena, in the 1990s. Yet those who theoretically make up a "global" audience do not always have equal access. In perhaps the most sweeping assessment of the potential for new technology to pioneer methods for the recent past by rethinking the ways historians have traditionally studied, archived, written, and disseminated the far past, Alice Yang and Alan S. Christy's essay makes a powerful case that properly designed web tools might enable historians to take up the challenge to do transnational and translingual research in much more effective ways. They, like other contributors to this volume, suggest that new historical practices may develop as we begin to understand more fully the nature and implications of the technologies that have become commonplace in the past ten years.

We have organized the essays in the anthology into five thematic sections, although we are pleased to observe that many of the articles raise similar issues from different vantage points and some offer important commentary on essays grouped by other themes. In the first section, essays by Renee C. Romano and Shelley Sang-Hee Lee provide an overview of some pitfalls and rewards of researching and teaching recent history, a project Lee aptly describes as similar to "working without a safety net." Both of these essays point to some of the significant methodological challenges of writing and teaching about events since the 1970s, including the lack of an established historiography to frame an interpretation, the dilemma of crafting a narrative of events that have no clear end and can be ongoing, and the vexing problem of how one can achieve a historical perspective on events about which we have little hindsight.

Romano turns to theoretical and philosophical writings about history to sort through her own anxieties about whether research on the recent past is properly historical. Paradoxically, the challenges she has faced in her own work on the recent past illuminate long-standing methodological and epistemological historical debates. They are, she concludes, better thought of as opportunities rather than limitations. The difficulties of crafting a narrative when events are ongoing can serve as a reminder that all narratives and endpoints are constructed to some extent, chosen by the historian in ways that affect interpretation. To return briefly to Wilentz's volume, one might ask: why structure a forty-year political narrative as the *Age of Reagan*? Might Reagan's more jovial conservatism not have been a prelude to the gloves-off right-wing Republicanism in an Age of Bush? One might also conjecture that, by turning the focus away from the president himself and toward the executive branch as a whole, it was the Age of Cheney or Rumsfeld.

Like Romano, Lee finds teaching the recent past to be a fraught, but highly rewarding, task that can capture students' imagination and lead them into study of the far past. Her essay recounts experiences in the classroom and how being forced to teach in the absence of accepted historical narratives and interpretations—working without a script, as she puts it—has provided an excellent way to teach students about the nature of the discipline. Furthermore, the imaginations of the young are more easily captured by histories that offer some explanation for family experiences that shaped their lives but that relatives may be reluctant to discuss. In some fields students can be lured into researching difficult historical problems with the promise that a family member's experiences, or even the entire family's historical trajectory, will be better illuminated through their own scholarly investigations.

The other four sections of the book expand on some of the themes raised in the first two essays. In the second part, Laura Clark Brown, Nancy Kaiser, and Gail Drakes address some of the challenges that may befall historians of the recent past when they attempt to access archives that are newly deposited or located in private collections. As it turns out, the traditional paper archive can also be fraught. Clark Brown and Kaiser, archivists at the Southern History Collection at UNC, offer a detailed and eye-opening discussion of the complications that ensue when archives collect materials covering recent years that necessarily involve living subjects. Their concern is the tension between access and privacy for collections that contain the records of living people or family members of the dead who might have a strong investment in suppressing personal information about medical or psychiatric histories, sexuality, or other intimate details that might revise a reputation. Archivists also face ethical, and sometimes legal, quandaries. They must decide whether and how to restrict collections that could reference personal information about a third party whose interests are not protected by the scrutiny of the donor, or federally protected information about a student, patient, or employee who would be difficult or impossible to contact for permission. As an alternative to closing collections until such materials can be vetted—a nearly impossible task—they propose a partnership with us, by which historians learn to identify such documents on our own and agree to the subject's privacy in some matters in exchange for access to the whole collection.

Gail Drakes addresses a radically different barrier to access: copyright protections and the passing of critical historical documents into private hands through sale on the open market. She provides a chilling account of the ways in which new laws and court rulings have expanded copyright protections over materials, such as television programs, films, and news broadcasts, that are vital to understanding the recent past. Just as problematic are private collectors who may seek to use historical sources for their own profit or be invested in a particular representation of a subject, restricting the use of materials in their possession. Drakes points to the ways in which private ownership and estate sales have already limited historians' access to vital sources related to important national figures such as Martin Luther King, Jr., and Malcolm X. In this way, not only do letters,

manuscripts, photographs, and ephemera become difficult to locate and access, but entire collections are broken up and scattered among people who
have no obligation to share them with researchers and who may view them
only as objects of personal sentiment.

The three essays in the third section of the book explore an issue that
frequently recurs among those writing about the recent past: the challenge of working with living subjects. While historians have long engaged
in interviews in the course of their work, as a field, history seems to lag
behind anthropology and other social sciences in theorizing the ethical
and practical problems that arise when those who experienced an event
or participated in making history are key sources for a study. Indeed, as
Martin Meeker's essay in this section wryly notes, professional historical
associations seem to have spent more energy on having oral history defined
as not "generalizable knowledge"—and thus not subject to the scrutiny of
human-subject research protocols—than they have on considering the ongoing development of methodological practices for historians conducting
fundamental research through interviewing. These essays, then, explore
some of the ethical, practical, legal, and methodological issues that arise
when, as Claire Bond Potter puts it, history can "talk back" to the historian.
As Willoughby Anderson argues, even subjects who wish to cooperate fully
with a researcher sometimes live in a further iconic past and are reluctant
to discuss recent events about which there is no community consensus. All
three essays suggest that those who study a more recent past may have to
develop different historical methods and practices as they navigate the challenges presented by the living.

Even established practices like oral history can be perilous when the historian is in uncharted methodological territory. It is not uncommon for a
historian of the recent past who is entirely untrained in oral history to do
a few interviews, and then find that for legal reasons the research cannot
be used. Meeker argues that historians who are creating their own archives
by undertaking oral histories must think more systematically and critically
about their practices and methodologies and the conditions under which
those might change. His essay documents a long debate about whether oral
historians should need to get approval from Institutional Review Boards, or
IRBs, for their research with human subjects. This conversation accelerated
dramatically in the 1990s and became the object of negotiation between
the historical profession and the federal government. Professional historical
associations have long sought exemption from oral history projects on the

grounds that IRBs are designed more for medical or large-scale sociological studies, but Meeker argues that historians make a Faustian bargain when they insist that oral history should be exempted from IRB review because it does not constitute "research" under the guidelines established by the National Institutes of Health (NIH) in the wake of revelations about abuse of living subjects in syphilis research.[20] Insisting that oral history should be considered research—and especially, that it should be defined as a practice distinctly different from journalism—Meeker calls on those who do oral history to engage with their campus IRBs to ensure that they follow the most ethical course for working with interviewees.

While Meeker's essay explores the need to rethink the practice of oral history as a systematic form of research that the university has a stake in, Anderson's essay about her research on Birmingham, Alabama, explores how doing oral histories about the recent past forced her to rethink some of her other core assumptions about what "history" is. Anderson asks how historians can research and write accounts of recent events when a celebrated past is so dominant that it shapes the historical scholarship as well as the memories of participants. The 1963 demonstrations in Birmingham, with their famous photos of police dogs and fire hoses, have become part of a powerful and dominant narrative, both about the changes that Birmingham has undergone since those violent days and about the important role those demonstrations played in changing the national conversation about civil rights. For Anderson, who hoped to study a process of school desegregation in Birmingham that took place some time after 1963, the iconic power of that historical moment became a barrier to the research that she wanted to do. The unfinished nature of desegregation ensured that all subjects had a strong political investment in these iconic moments, stronger than anything that happened after 1963. In doing this work, she was forced to confront her own position in relation to her research: she could not be simply a scholar looking in from the outside but had to understand the ways in which she was participating in shaping the historical record through the process of doing oral histories. Ultimately, these challenges led her to reshape her methods. She had to broaden her scope to consider not just what happened, but the way participants told the story, how the past shaped their contemporary identities, and how their outlook affected interactions with her as a researcher.

In the final essay in this section, Claire Bond Potter suggests that historians who use interviews to reconstruct a controversial social-movement history might want to take an "ethnographic turn." Like Anderson, Potter recounts a struggle to come to terms with her position as a feminist scholar and an academic among the prominent feminist activists who have a strong stake in a particular story about the past. In her research, oral history confers a dual responsibility: to represent participants in antipornography activism from the 1980s in a way they would recognize and to tell a story that incorporates perspectives and insights that might complicate activists' accounts. The struggle among feminists over the meaning of pornography played a traumatic role in the trajectory of late twentieth-century feminism, a history that, as Potter notes, remains emotionally and politically charged for actors from all sides. Initially naive about the particular ethical challenges posed by working with living subjects on a controversial topic, who trusted her to tell "their" version of the story, she describes how adopting a position of empathy toward antipornography activists in particular—a group who has often felt misrepresented and maligned—has enabled her to not just better understand the sex wars and but also to perceive why all the aspects of this story have been so difficult for others to write. Questioning whether, at least in this case, scholarly detachment might be detrimental to historical understanding, Potter suggests that working with sources who "talk back" has given her new insights and tools as a historian that she can apply to textual sources as well.

The essays in the fourth part of the book focus on the ways in which the project of writing recent history is influenced and enhanced by the evidence contained in different forms of technology. The first two articles, by David Greenberg and Jeremy K. Saucier, appeal to historians to pay more attention to and make more use of two relatively new kinds of sources: television broadcasts and video games. Although television cannot be classified as a "new" technology, historians have not yet tapped its full potential, Greenberg, a political historian, argues. Although television programming offers historians a multilayered source for studying the past and provides an intimacy with a historical moment that a printed text cannot, the use of television broadcasts as sources for political history is rare, even though historians use iconic televised moments to drive their narratives.

Video games are the opposite of iconic; they are ephemeral and require special skills to access and understand. Saucier, a cultural historian, insists that in the twenty-first century, video games are vital cultural and political artifacts that demand historical attention, particularly as their formal links to the political sphere become more pronounced.[21] Video games, he argues, have narratives embedded in them—not unlike films—and they are not only enormously successful corporate products but are increasingly being used by groups like the military to facilitate recruiting. Both authors recognize the challenges of using these kinds of sources, from the small numbers of archives that collect televised programs and video games to the sheer number of hours it would take a researcher to watch nightly newscasts or to master a video game. But both Greenberg and Saucier insist that these visual and interactive sources offer fresh and important new ways for accessing the past, and both provide something of a "how-to" guide for historians who would like to try using television programs or video games in their own research.

In the third essay in this section, Alice Yang and Alan S. Christy describe the new technologies they are developing to help historians engage in more informed, more collaborative research on the recent past, and especially on historical memory. In their essay, they make a powerful case that the new web tools they are developing to better research different national memories of World War II can provide solutions to two challenges that many historians of the recent past face: an overabundance of sources and the difficulty of transnational and translingual research. In recent years, groups such as the Organization of American Historians (OAH) have called on historians of the United States to take a more transnational approach in their research, to explore the ways in which many historical events, processes, and ideas have—or have always been—global.[22] Yet despite the importance of projects, such as the September 11 Digital Archive, that embrace multiple communities, the barriers to access are real when the obstacles to technology and to translation cannot be surmounted.[23]

As the harsh critique of Jill Lepore that we cited earlier demonstrates, historians of the recent past also risk encountering embedded and often politicized commitments to a further past that are being deployed for contemporary purposes. Yang and Christy suggest that, at least in the case of World War II memory, approaches that restrict themselves to the discursive field of a single-nation state are likely to be limited, if not misleading. Cognizant of the enormous difficulties and expense of undertaking transnational research, they argue that new digital technologies may offer a way to overcome some of these barriers by promoting the "far more robust habits of collaborative work" that will be necessary for historians to adopt in the age of info glut. In an innovative and ambitious web project, they are developing tools to enable scholars, war survivors, activists, and the public to share information and ideas about World War II artifacts, in multiple languages from the vantage point of many different countries, building communities of interest and intellectual exchange across national and linguistic boundaries. Undertaking truly transnational histories, they suggest, requires a "fundamental shift in the norms of practices in the field of history." The new web technology they have developed offers one approach toward developing those new norms and practices.

The two essays in the final section of the volume foreground complicated problems of narrative, perspective, and positionality for historians who are working on recent topics. Both explore in more depth critical questions that earlier essays raise. When does the story end, Eileen Boris and Jennifer Klein ask of a labor history that began to shift its meaning even as they had hoped to send their book to press. Julius H. Bailey, in his research on new religions, addresses the problems that arise for historians of religion when journalists and contemporary critics define new communities of faith as cults. His essay illustrates the challenges of trying to craft a historical interpretation in the face of powerful, but problematic, paradigms articulated by the media and other contemporary observers.

Boris and Klein write about how developments in the present led them to question the narrative they had developed about the past, in this case, about their history of home health care. Their nearly complete book on the topic framed this history as a victory for a new kind of unionism that had achieved a major triumph when more than seventy thousand health care workers voted to join the Service Employees International Union (SEIU). But when that union began disciplining locals, insisting that smaller locals merge into megalocals and making backroom deals with corporations, Boris and Klein came to question the arc of their narrative, finding, as they reconsidered the story, that "ongoing events have a way of destabilizing neat historical trajectories." In choosing to embrace this disruption, Boris and Klein went back to their archive, reconsidered their reading of the sources, and undertook new research. They found that the evidence that explained these unexpected events had been there all along but that because they had focused on a particular community they had not understood the forces that would come to bear on the organizing strategy that threw the SEIU into turmoil by 2009. The end result was, they believe, a better history that offers not only a more complicated portrait of the past but also a better understanding of the present political moment.

Julius H. Bailey describes a different relationship between present and past in his essay on the challenges of studying new religious movements. For Bailey, a presentist impulse to label most new religious groups as "cults" poses a challenge to historians who seek to understand these movements and what they mean to their followers on their own terms. Part of that challenge is the hierarchy of values that articulates older supernatural experiences as "real," because of a religion's long past and consequent social respectability, while labeling newer experiences, beliefs by breakaway sects, or recently articulated structures of faith as delusional and odd. That challenge is only further complicated by the researcher's tenuous position in relation to a new religious community that may well feel threatened and seek to shield its traditions and sacred practices from public scrutiny. How, Bailey asks, can a historian achieve "insider" status or, at least, access to insiders, when that access is mediated by a group or public spokesperson? Without such status, can a historian hope to understand his subjects' worldview or to make sense of claims that may seem contradictory or paradoxical? As Bailey also points out, whereas for many historians in the far past, newspapers and court records may be critical to reconstructing a narrative, for followers of new religions, such accounts may be false or misleading.

Most of the contributors to this book study the history of the United States, and therefore they use U.S. history as the examples in their methodological discussions. Yet the issues discussed here are by no means unique to the United States as an object of study. These essays should prove equally useful for scholars who study geographic areas other than the United States, although surely historians working in other fields will find new ways to develop and refine the ideas in this volume. They will also have new questions. Recent revolutions in Tunisia, Egypt, Libya, Syria, and Bahrain, as well as ongoing resistance to totalitarian regimes in countries such as Iran, Myanmar, and North Korea, demonstrate that although the reach of technology is uneven, it is now one of the engines influencing history. Already an attempt to archive a revolution has produced Alex Nunn's and Nadia Idle's *Tweets from Tahrir* (2011), an instabook compiled from a fraction of the Twitter messages sent by activists during the 2011 Arab Spring. Who, we ask, will write a history of the revolution that toppled Hosni Mubarak, and how will that scholar access the vast social network archive on Facebook and Twitter that seemed to play such an influential role? Who will be the John Reed of Tunisia in 2011, cataloguing the 10 million Tweets that shook the world? We don't know. But we do know that there is little unique about studying recent U.S. history, and we invite historians outside the United States to join us in theorizing this exciting new work. Our particular research issues may differ, but all historians of the recent past face similar methodological challenges. We hope that this volume may serve as a first step toward opening fruitful conversations about both the difficulties and the rewards of writing contemporary history.

Notes

1. Sir Walter Raleigh, quoted in Beverly Southgate, *History: What and Why; Ancient, Modern, and Postmodern Perspectives*, 2nd ed. (London: Routledge, 2001), 143.

2. See, for example, Annelise Orleck, *Storming Caesar's Palace: How Black Mothers Fought Their Own War on Poverty* (Boston: Beacon, 2005); John D'Emilio, *The World Turned: Essays on Gay History, Politics and Culture* (Durham: Duke University Press, 2002); Alice Echols, *Hot Stuff: Disco and the Remaking of American Culture* (New York: Norton, 2011); and Susan Ware, *Game, Set, Match: Billie Jean King and the Revolution in Women's Sports* (Chapel Hill: University of North Carolina Press, 2011).

3. Julian Zelizer, "The Interdisciplinarity of Political History," *Perspectives on History* 49, no. 5 (2011), 17–18; Bethany Moreton, *To Serve God and Wal-mart: The Making of Christian Free Enterprise* (Cambridge, Mass.: Harvard University Press, 2009); Jeffrey G. Madrick, *Age of Greed: The Triumph of Finance and the Decline of America, 1970 to the Present* (New York: Knopf, 2011); "History and September 11," special issue, *Journal of American History*, 89, no. 2 (2002). For critical works that deliberately challenge the boundaries of traditional subfields, see Jennifer Brier, *Infectious Ideas: U.S. Political Responses to the AIDS Crisis* (Chapel Hill: University of North Carolina Press, 2009); Stephen J. Pitti, *The Devil in Silicon Valley: California, Race and Mexican Americans* (Princeton, N.J.: Princeton University Press, 2004), and Michael J. Allen, *Until the Last Man Comes Home: POWs, MIAs, and the Unending Vietnam War* (Chapel Hill: University of North Carolina Press, 2009).

4. John Lewis Gaddis, *The Landscape of History: How Historians Map the Past* (New York: Oxford University Press, 2002), xi.

5. Arthur M. Schlesinger, Jr., *The Crisis of the Old Order*, vol. 1 of *The Age of Roosevelt* (Boston: Houghton Mifflin, 1957), ix–x.

6. Robert Burke, review of *The Coming of the New Deal*, by Arthur M. Schlesinger, Jr., *American Historical Review* 65, no. 1 (1959): 150.

7. Florence Kiper Frank, review of *The Coming of the New Deal*, by Arthur M. Schlesinger, Jr., *Yale Law Journal* 68, no. 8 (1959): 1724.

8. W. R. Brock, "Review of *The Crisis of the Old Order*," *Historical Journal* 1, no. 1 (1958): 91.

9. Frank Thistlethwaite, review of *The Crisis of the Old Order*, by Arthur M. Schlesinger, Jr., *English Historical Review* 73, no. 287 (1958): 331; John B. Rae, review of *The Coming of the New Deal*, by Arthur M. Schlesinger, Jr., *Business History Review* 33, no. 2 (1959): 257.

10. Schlesinger, *Crisis of the Old Order*, ix–x.

11. Richard Hofstadter, *The Paranoid Style in American Politics* (New York: Knopf, 1965); Sara Evans, *Personal Politics: The Roots of Women's Liberation in the Civil Rights Movement and the New Left* (New York: Knopf, 1979); George Chauncey, *Why Marriage? The History Shaping Today's Debate over Gay Equality* (New York: Basic Books, 2005).

12. Sean Wilentz's first book, *Chants Democratic: New York City and the Rise of the American Working Class, 1788–1850* (New York: Oxford University Press, 1984), made his reputation as one of the leading historians of Jacksonian America. In 2008, however, he made a radical departure from this earlier work by publishing *The Age of Reagan: A History, 1974–2008* (New York: Harper, 2008), which he has followed up with *Bob Dylan in America* (New York: Doubleday, 2010). Jill Lepore's award-winning first book, *The Name of War: King Philip's War and the Making of American Identity* (New York: Vintage Books, 1998), focuses on events in seventeenth-century U.S. history. Her newest book, *The Whites of Their Eyes: The Tea Party's Revolution and the Battle over American History* (Princeton, N.J.: Princeton University Press, 2010), focuses on the Tea Party Movement since 2008. James Kloppenberg, an intellectual historian of the nineteenth and early twentieth century, has turned his eye to the election of the nation's first black president in *Reading Obama: Dreams, Hope and the American Political Tradition* (Princeton, N.J.: Princeton University Press, 2010).

13. Wilentz, *Age of Reagan*, 10.

14. The Wisconsin Republican Party's attack on American Historical Association incoming president William Cronon puts in stark relief the potential political consequences for historians who address contemporary issues. For an account of this event, see Anthony Grafton and Jim Grossman, "The Imperative of Public Participation," *Perspectives on History* 49, no. 5 (2011): 5–7.

15. Kloppenberg, *Reading Obama*, 2; Gordon S. Wood, "No Thanks for the Memories," *New York Review of Books*, January 13, 2011.

16. Jie Jenny Zou, "Old Dominion University Researchers Ask How Much of the Web Is Archived," *Chronicle of Higher Education*, July 6, 2011, http://chronicle.com/blogs/wiredcampus/old-dominion-u-researchers-ask-how-much-of-the-web-is-archived/.

17. "Because It Is Gone Now: Teaching the September 11 Digital Archive," *OAH Magazine of History* 25 no. 3 (2011): 31–34.

18. Kristin Luker, *Salsa Dancing into the Social Sciences: Research in the Age of Info Glut* (Cambridge, Mass.: Harvard University Press, 2010).

19. Siva Vaidhyanathan, *The Googlization of Everything: And Why We Should Worry* (Berkeley: University of California Press, 2011).

20. See Susan Reverby, *The Infamous Tuskegee Scandal and Its Legacy* (Chapel Hill: University of North Carolina Press, 2009).

21. P. W. Singer, *Wired for War: The Robotics Revolution and Conflict in the 21st Century* (New York: Penguin, 2009).

22. See, for example, the OAH report in 2000 urging historians of the United States to adopt a more internationalist approach. Thomas Bender, *La Pietra Report: A Report to the Profession* (Bloomington: Organization of American Historians, 2000), http://www.oah.org/activities/lapietra/final.html.

23. September 11 Digital Archive, Center for History and New Media, American Social History Project/Center for Media and Learning, 1996–2007, http://911digitalarchive.org/.

PART ONE

Framing the Issues

RENEE C. ROMANO

Not Dead Yet

My Identity Crisis as a Historian of the Recent Past

A COLLEAGUE RECENTLY STOPPED BY my office to express his concerns about a research project on racial politics in the late 1980s and 1990s that one of my students had proposed for his approval. The proposed research, my colleague feared, was not properly historical. How could this student write a strong history paper without more distance from the events she was writing about? he asked. Would there be any historiography that the student could consult to guide her research? Wouldn't the project become more of a politically driven reflection on recent events than a historical analysis?

While I gathered my thoughts to respond, I couldn't help but remember the many times I had faced similar questions about my own research. My first project, which began as a dissertation and became a book, was a history of black-white interracial marriage in the United States. The book opened in the 1940s and ended about a day before the manuscript went to page proofs in 2003. My current research jumps even more firmly into contemporary history, focusing on the prosecution of a series of civil rights–era crimes that didn't begin in earnest until 1994, trials that are ongoing and that may continue for some time. As a result, I have often heard concerns that my work might not be properly historical. Similar to my colleague, a few of my graduate school professors questioned whether my dissertation was really a legitimate topic, given the very limited historiography on the subject of interracial marriage available at the time. Over the years, I've heard more casual remarks that my work might be better understood as political science or sociology than as history; indeed, I was surprised to find my history of interracial marriage catalogued by bookstores as belonging in the sociology section, a move no doubt related both to the period and the subject matter.

But having double-majored in political science in college and having at least a sense of what sociological studies look like, I knew that I was writing history. I remained confident that I was, in fact, a historian, albeit one who was writing about quite recent events.

But my colleague's inquiry about this undergraduate paper still gave me pause. Are those of us who study the very recent past always engaged in the act of writing history? Am I really a historian? Trying to answer those questions has forced me to think more deeply than I ever have before about what exactly makes a study historical, about, in short, the methodology of the discipline of history.[1] Reflecting on this exchange with a colleague, I realized that my own identity crisis stemmed from four specific methodological or practical challenges that many historians of the recent past must grapple with and view as productive, if vexing, aspects of our craft. Despite the fact that I have already completed one book of this kind, I continue to worry that I lack access to the kinds of sources that have typically been deemed "most legitimate" by the profession, especially the archival sources that are the foundation of our work. Then there is the problem that few other historians have written about the events I research; the secondary literature on my topics is quite limited. I also have concerns about my inability to construct a historical narrative with any sense of finality, because the events I research are still ongoing and their effects are not yet clear. Finally, I wonder whether I have sufficient distance from the events that I write about—both politically and temporally—to offer meaningful interpretations of my evidence.

To help me navigate this identity crisis, I have turned not to a psychologist but to people who have thought deeply about the field of history and the nature of historical thinking: theorists and philosophers of history. What might those who have written about the nature of historical inquiry have to say about the place of studies of the recent past within the discipline that is constituted and described as history? And how might theoretical writings on history help me think through and about the specific challenges related to researching and writing contemporary history?

What I found is that most of those who write philosophies of history or methodological guidebooks have not spent much time considering what it might mean to write the history of the very recent past. Indeed, much of the theoretical and methodological literature defines history in such a way as to entirely exclude those who study more contemporary events. But I also found that the challenges I have encountered in doing recent history offer an excellent vantage point into the larger methodological and epistemological questions that philosophers and theorists of history have long grappled with. Those of us who are on the boundaries of the discipline, who are trying to forge a way for historians to engage with the recent past without losing our identity or credibility as historians, might have a useful perspective from which to consider the nature and methods of historical thinking and writing more generally.

This essay begins with a survey of when and how key thinkers and writers about the nature of history as a discipline have discussed the study of the recent past.[2] It then explores what this body of work—with its focus on historical method and form, the nature of historical thinking, and the problems of bias and objectivity—might offer us. While the theoretical literature on the discipline may not specifically address the issues attendant to recent history, it does offer ideas and insights that may prove helpful to those trying to find answers to my problems related to sources, historiography, narrative, and perspective. And while all of these challenges might be considered liabilities, I believe that, in many ways, they also present opportunities for scholars who are serious about that seemingly paradoxical project of writing a history of our own times.

But Is It History? Defining and Disciplining a Field

The idea of history is premised on the belief that there is a break between the present and the past, and that the past is a realm distinct from the present. In her 2008 presidential address to the American Historical Association, Gabrielle Spiegel noted that modern historical writing (here she is differentiating nineteenth- and twentieth-century historians from the ancients) stems from the concept of a "decisive differentiation between the present and past." The "basic principle" of modern historiography, Spiegel claims, is based on "the disappearance of the past from the present, its movement from visibility to invisibility."[3]

While philosophers and theorists of history differ on many issues related to E. H. Carr's seminal 1961 question, "What is History?," they readily agree that history is a study and a recovery of this "invisible" past.[4] Indeed, that definition is so basic as to be almost axiomatic. What is history if not the study of a past that we can distinguish from our present? As one of these works proclaims, "Everyone knows, of course, what history was and is: quite simply, the study of the past. . . . While other subjects like philosophy, physics, or geography, may include some consideration of the past . . . , history is differentiated by its nature of having the past as its exclusive subject-matter."[5] Historians, like all other scholars, might comment on contemporary events as public intellectuals, but we tend to agree that the past—and only the past—is the proper subject for our scholarship.

Although the works I consulted do not offer any precise definition of when a past suitable for historical study begins (thirty minutes ago? thirty hours ago? thirty years ago?), their rhetoric provides some not-so-subtle clues. Spiegel highlights an invisible past that has disappeared from the present, suggesting that the past worthy of study is the absent past. The language of absence—and of that ultimate absence, death—pervades descriptions of the suitably historical past and of the historian's task in evoking it. Historians, most of these works suggest, seek to bring back to life a past that is dead, to make visible and legible a past that has passed on into invisibility. Thus Spiegel, paraphrasing Michel de Certeau's *The Writing of History*, suggests that the practice of history requires opening a "dead corpse" to investigation; discourse about the past is, as de Certeau asserts, "discourse about the dead." Michael Oakeshott notes that historians turn to the past that has survived in objects and artifacts to attain their real goal: access to the past that has not survived. And both John Tosh and Peter Charles Hoffer task the historian with bringing a past that has not survived back to life. As Tosh writes in *The Pursuit of History*, historians must direct their imaginative powers to "bringing the past back to life—or *resurrecting* it," while Hoffer asserts, "Historians bring to life what is dead."[6] Historians, it seems, are part scholars and part saviors.

What, then, are those of us who study the recent past doing when we turn our attention to events that happened in our lifetimes, or even just a few years ago? "But I'm not dead yet!" we might imagine we hear our subjects protest, not unlike the hapless peasant in *Monty Python and the Holy Grail*.[7] For recent history, no matter what else it is, is not a study of a dead past; the pasts we study are still breathing and very much in living memory. And while Monty Python's peasant could be put out of his misery with a quick and comic hit on the head, we recent historians can't kill our own subjects so easily. All we can do, presumably, is wait for our pasts to become *dead enough* to be worthy of historical attention.

There are, to be sure, a few theorists who admit the possibility of a field of historical study focused on a more recent past. John Tosh even posits that studies of the recent past can be particularly useful. Tosh argues that the idea of the difference between "then" and "now" that lies at the foundation of the historical discipline can be found in a more recent past that is compressed into single life span. Citing as examples the cases of Nazi Germany and Stalinist Russia, Tosh argues that those who study more recent events can offer to their readers a "reminder of the deeply alien elements in our recent past." For Tosh, the recent past can be a subject of historical inquiry as long as that past is *different* enough from the present. Here, the extent of difference rather than the passage of time becomes the key factor that makes a past historical. In this light, the contemporary historian plays a role similar to a psychoanalyst who forces individuals to face the truth of their personal past: "so the contemporary historian helps us to face the present and the future by enabling us to understand the forces, however shocking, which have made our world and our society what it is." This language of shock implies that studies of recent events are legitimate only if they can claim to show great differences between the recent past and the present. In other words, as long as the past, even a recent one, is "a foreign country," as David Lowenthal has famously remarked, then it is worthy of study.[8]

But what if the pasts we study, like my work on interracial marriage and civil rights prosecutions, aren't all that foreign? What if they address a phenomenon that is still emerging and is provoking new conversations? Philosophers and theorists of history provide little guidance in such cases. Here, I can articulate my own identity crisis: I feel like a historian, I think like a historian, but my own work (given that I study a recent past that is neither dead nor all that foreign) is suspect given the boundaries of the discipline in which I am trained. Pushing back at and testing those boundaries requires, in my experience, that we take seriously some of the methodological challenges that can arise when we write recent history, including issues related to sources, historiography, narrative, and perspective, all topics central to historical thinking. Yet considering those challenges in light of the literature on historical methodology and philosophy that guides our practice more generally suggests that, although there are certainly problems particular to writing about a past that is "not dead yet," many of the issues that historians of the recent past confront have been the subject of long debate within the profession. We do have guidance. Moreover, having to face those challenges squarely and openly may well offer opportunities for enriching our scholarship and our historical understanding more generally.

The Problem of Sources: Archives, Glut, and Mastery

When I first began writing contemporary history, the aspect of researching a recent past that contributed most to my own concern that perhaps I wasn't a "real" historian was the nature of my sources. Although all good historians know that our goal is to find as many sources as we can from as many different vantage points as possible, my graduate training communicated very effectively that some kinds of research and some types of sources carried more weight than others in terms of legitimizing work as truly "historical." Thus, when I proposed a dissertation on interracial marriage, one of my professors protested, "You won't find any sources!" He feared, of course, that I wouldn't find any *archival sources*. (He was wrong, by the way, which is a struggle with which historians of race, sexuality, and women—all the fields I was working in—will be familiar from presenting proposals to doctoral committees.) But my mentor's concern was plain: if I couldn't do my research in the archives, no one would take me seriously as a historian.

Lesson #1 from graduate school: sources found in the archives, for some reason, counted more than others.

Sitting around the table in our graduate seminar dissecting the work of other historians conveyed three other subtle but unmistakable lessons about the relationship between research and archival sources: that the best research often involved a detectivelike hunt for that elusive document, or set of documents, that had rarely (if ever) been used before; that textual sources offered the most responsible and careful way of exploring the past; and that a historian must try to master as many sources as possible before sitting down to write. My own research process for both books has borne little resemblance to this ideal: most of my sources are not from the archives and a good number are not textual. I spend less time hunting for elusive sources than I do sifting through thousands of potential (although often repetitive) sources. Given the sheer volume of the available material, if I tried to consult every source available, I would never finish my project. My problem is less in finding sources than in deciding when it's time to stop researching and start writing.

Although these may not be the lessons conveyed in all graduate programs—I'm sure that some students may have learned more about doing oral history and using oral evidence than I did—I don't think my training, or the lessons it conveyed about sources, was unique. John Tosh notes in *The Pursuit of History* that since the age of Leopold von Ranke and the emergence of the modern historical profession, historians have placed more emphasis on textual than on oral sources and have confined most of their research to "libraries and archives."[9] Yet those of us who study recent history rarely find that our research conforms to the practices that earn the most favor and acclaim from our fellow historians. Some of us might be able to find information in archives, but they typically have fewer collections about more recent events, and those collections are more likely than older ones to be restricted by privacy and copyright issues. Government documents, moreover, are typically restricted or closed for at least thirty years after an event has taken place.

Instead, many of us turn to other kinds of sources, which present both opportunities and challenges. Unlike many of our peers, those of us who study more recent events can often speak with people who witnessed and lived through the past we are studying, an opportunity fraught with promise and peril. Looking back on my graduate education, I regret not having taken an anthropology class, where I might have gained more theoretical and practical insight into both how the position of the researcher can influence research with living subjects and how to research and write about events that I have witnessed. I am grateful that I have been present at some of the events I write about and that I consider historically important—a commemoration ceremony honoring civil rights martyrs, for example. On the other hand, I also feel keenly the challenge of trying to achieve enough critical distance to write about people I now know. I also feel both blessed and burdened to have so many nontextual sources available for my research. For many recent topics, nontextual sources, such as television news broadcasts, made-for-TV movies, YouTube uploads, and even video games, can be vitally important. Use of these kinds of sources, of course, is not restricted to scholars who are working on very recent topics, but those of us who do have little choice but to draw on media that we have likely not been trained to interpret in the same way that we have been taught to dissect a written text.

Yet the lack of more traditional archival sources, which I initially saw as a threat to my identity and status as a historian, can be reframed as an opportunity. Pioneering new sources allows historians of the recent past to challenge some of the disciplinary dogmas that have limited the range of legitimate historical subjects and historical knowledge in all periods. Those of us who study the recent past have the opportunity to continue and further the project begun by social historians in the 1960s, a project that challenges the supremacy of archival and textual sources and seeks out new sources that make previously invisible subjects and dynamics knowable. Making a connection to this project, while reassuring, also tarnishes our potential status as a methodological vanguard. Our fight began decades ago as scholars of the working class, of women, and of racial and sexual minorities sought to find ways to tell the story of groups who had been excluded from traditional histories. Scholars such as Lawrence Levine insisted that sources such as folktales, oral histories, songs, and material culture were as valuable as anything that could be found in archives.[10] Such work has helped to show the limited and constructed nature of archives, which typically have far more documentation about the lives of elites than of ordinary people. In other words, those of us who study the recent past have the opportunity to participate in an ongoing project of decentering the place of archives and textual sources in historical research and of making archival sources of equal, not greater, value than any other kind of source.

Studying recent history not only offers an important vantage point from which to assess and critique a continued bias toward archival and textual sources but also encourages a deeper reflection on the nostalgic desire of historians to equate mastery over a source base with absolute knowledge of every available source. Although works in the philosophy of history make clear that consulting every available source is an increasingly impossible project for modern periods, they nonetheless assume that good historians must strive to do so. John Tosh thus asserts that although the proliferation of sources in the nineteenth and twentieth centuries might make reading them all impossible, "mastery of all the sources must remain the ideal." E. H. Carr bemoans the plight of modern historians who actually have too much information at their disposal. Those who study ancient or medieval history, he suggests, should be "grateful for the vast winnowing process which, over the years, has put at [their] disposal a manageable corpus of historical facts."[11] Grateful that there are so few sources in one's field that I can read them all? No thanks, Professor Carr. I'll take my feast, however unruly, over that kind of famine.

As someone who studies contemporary history, I have had to come up with my own definition of mastery over my sources, one that recognizes that for many topics in our information age, and especially those in more recent history, there are simply too many sources to read all of them, even if we define our studies or our research narrowly. Yet we don't need to amass every single source to be able to offer a well-documented and compelling historical interpretation. In *The Landscape of History*, John Lewis Gaddis reminds us that pattern recognition is one of the "primary forms of human perception" and that all history draws on the recognition of patterns.[12] I know, after having read hundreds, if not thousands, of media articles on the civil rights trials I write about, what the patterns and trends are in the media coverage. We historians must immerse ourselves in our sources and read as widely as we can, but we must also be aware of diminishing returns. At a recognizable point in the research process, looking at more sources does not provide more insight. When we have consulted enough material to identify patterns and developments, then, I think it's safe to say, we have the mastery necessary to offer an interpretation of the past.[13]

The persistent nostalgia about consulting every source—as well as my own lingering doubts when I cannot—stems from a long-standing debate about the historical project that itself refuses to die: can historical scholarship offer the "truth" about the past? In *History: What and Why?* Beverly Southgate argues that despite the emergence of relativism and the general consensus that there is no such thing as a single objective "historical truth," historians still have a lingering sense that they can access some kind of reality of the past if they have the proper critical method.[14] The inclination to equate mastery with consultation of every available source reflects a stubborn belief that historians can find the "truth" of the past if they only try hard enough. This idea served as the foundation for the claim of nineteenth-century empiricists that history could be thought of as a science. According to the empiricists, Peter Hoffer notes in *The Historian's Paradox*, the library and the archive were their "laboratories," and historical evidence "rigorously tested and objectively presented could be used to prove, or disprove, hypotheses about the past." Indeed, the first seminar room in the first graduate program in U.S. history at Johns Hopkins University was "designed to look like a laboratory."[15] Research done properly and scientifically could, that original empiricist Ranke insisted, reveal to us "the past as it actually happened."[16]

This belief represents what David Hackett Fischer terms the "holist fallacy," that historians can't know anything until they know everything, a goal that is patently impossible for contemporary historians. "The whole truth, at any stage of an inquiry, is an ideal that ought to be abolished from historiography," Fischer insists, "for it cannot ever be attained." Historians are bound "to tell the best and biggest truths they can discover," but the "whole truth" does not and cannot exist. John Lewis Gaddis puts it even more starkly: trying to uncover the "truth" of the past is not only impossible but also not useful. Historians map the past, much like cartographers map a landscape. Recreating an entire landscape isn't a map; it's a reproduction. It's not useful to those who seek to use it and doesn't offer any manageable insight into that landscape. In that same way, history is only useful when it is a representation, not a reproduction; it must make the past legible to those who seek to learn something about it. As theorist Keith Jenkins reminds us in *Re-Thinking History*, "no historian can cover and thus re-cover the totality of past events because their 'content' is virtually limitless. One cannot recount more than a fraction of what has occurred and no historian's account ever corresponds precisely with the past: the sheer bulk of the past precludes total history."[17]

Those of us who write recent history are in a particularly good position to try to finally lay the holist fallacy to rest. Despite our often very extensive source base, despite the recentness of the events we write about, and despite the familiarity we have with those events, we—like other historians—cannot capture the truth of even a very recent past in its entirety. Redefining mastery over our sources as being immersed enough in those sources to recognize patterns and trends can serve to challenge the epistemologically problematic claim that historians can accurately recreate the past if they just dig deeply enough. Historians of recent events know full well that having access to an enormous range of sources does not mean having access to unmediated truth; our writings, like all historical interpretations, are partial and incomplete constructions of a past that can never be fully known, no matter how recent that past truly was. Researching recent history has helped me understand that and has made me more confident in asserting the importance of my findings as the "best truths" I can identify.[18]

Historiography: Finding Other Conversations

Anxieties about sources, of course, are not the only challenge for those of us who write recent history. I remember vividly when I first tried to do a literature review in preparation for my dissertation prospectus. I envisioned researching and writing a political, social, and cultural history of black-white interracial marriage from World War II to the present day. But when I went to survey the existing historiography, I found little that directly addressed my topic. A small body of work focused on legal histories of antimiscegenation law, a subject that I knew I would address but that I did not consider my central concern. Scholars had also written about interracial sex during the nineteenth century and about the historical construction of race and gender that made black-white sex so taboo. But I found only one historical work that addressed even a few of the questions that interested me. In short, despite an extensive sociological and psychological literature on interracial relations, historians had spent little time exploring black-white relationships in modern America.

Thus, as I began my research, I found myself lacking a historiographical literature that I could use to hone my thinking, sharpen my research questions, or provide a counterpoint to my own interpretations. Given that historians can never uncover the truth of the past as it actually was, history, Keith Jenkins explains, is better understood as a "shifting, problematic discourse" about the past produced by professional historians. Or as Peter Hoffer puts it, "History is always argument."[19] One of the fundamental contentions of the discipline is that historical experts will engage with one another's interpretations and that the ensuing conversation will contribute to greater understanding and new approaches. Historiography is that scholarly conversation; an existing historiography offers scholars a starting point for their own research, a guide to the key issues in the field, and a reference point for locating their own approach in relation to others.

Yet lacking a readily available preexisting historiography *doesn't* necessarily hurt or hinder historical scholarship. This is the surprising feature of studying the recent past, or of tackling any topic that has not been the subject of extensive historical scholarship (early writings in queer history or black women's history come to mind here). As I have discovered in my own work, the lack of a preexisting historiography can lead historians to openly acknowledge the limitations of our studies, to reach beyond easy categories when locating our own work, and to be especially aware of our own position and assumptions in relation to our research. And it allows us, at our best, to do something entirely new.

An existing historiography offers historians, particularly those at the beginning of their careers, a safety net that can be too safe. Professors often tell their students to read what others have written on a topic and then to fill the research gaps as their contribution to a framework that is already well established. Instead, those of us studying very recent events often find ourselves in the uncomfortable, but exhilarating, position of being the first historian (or among the first) to write about the events we study. Someone had to be the first to write the history on any given topic: why shouldn't it be you? Although it's hard to imagine today, someone had to write that first historical study of the Civil War (surprisingly, it was published to a wide commercial audience almost immediately after the Battle of Appomattox). Historiographies develop over time, so from one perspective, those of us writing about a recent past have the privilege of making what one hopes will be the first of many contributions to the historiography on a particular topic. This is indeed a daunting task, and not one that all might want to take on, because recent historians must be even more keenly aware than others that our interpretations are only a "first draft" of history that will certainly face revision and challenge.

An existing historiography also offers us a relatively easy frame of reference for setting conceptual limits to a project or argument. A historian might, for example, frame a study to explore a well-recognized historiographical question: how progressive was the Progressive Movement? Was the New Deal conservative or radical? How did slavery affect the structure of black families? These debates signal to our fellow historians that we are building on what others have found important in a field. They offer us a way to situate our own studies—either by participating in an ongoing debate or challenging the ways in which that debate has been framed. Without an established historiographical literature, it can be hard for recent historians to feel situated within a field. Yet lacking that sense of a field can also be liberating, because it encourages us to think broadly about the questions we ask of our area of study and about the contexts that will usefully illuminate our research.

We are, in short, forced to find, and even create, broader conversations in which we can participate. For example, in my current work on the contemporary prosecution of civil rights trials, the dearth of existing historical literature drove me to instead read widely in the larger field of post–civil rights racial history and in the interdisciplinary field of justice studies (exploring, for example, political theories about different types of justice). Of course, historians in fields with well-developed historiographies can always read widely in other literatures and can look beyond their own field for frames of reference. But for them it is more of an option, while contemporary historians have little choice.

Finally, perhaps the most important benefit of historiography is that it helps historians to locate and understand our own approach and position in regard to our subject matter. Keith Jenkins suggests that a vital aspect of historical studies must be what he calls the "historicisation of history." There is, he writes, "the need for detailed historiographical studies to examine how previous and current histories have been constructed both in terms of their method and their content." Historicizing one's own study, Jenkins insists, must be the starting point for any "self-reflexive" historian. As anthropologists know, understanding one's own position in relation to one's work is crucial. As Jenkins writes, it's fantasy to believe that anyone can write a "position-less" (or objective) history: "The only choice is between a history that is aware of what it is doing and what it is not."[20] Locating oneself in relation to the existing historiography is a key mechanism by which historians can become more self-aware of their positionality.

Yet we do not have to rely exclusively on comparing our work to the work of other historians to achieve such perspective. Delving into other intellectual interventions—journalistic accounts; sociological, anthropological, or psychological studies—provides insight not only into personal assumptions about our research but into the entire approach we might take as a historian. Reading psychological studies about interracial marriage, for example, helped me to frame my own research questions about the relative importance of and relationship between cultural depictions, structural constraints, and individual psychology in choosing a marriage partner. In other words, historians can draw on any number of fields to locate our own studies. We do not need to, and should not, limit ourselves to reading only scholarship by other historians.

Narrative: How Do You Write a Story When the Story Isn't Over?

If the lack of traditional sources or a well-established historiography were not enough of a challenge, those of us who tackle recent topics also have to contend with the problems posed by crafting a finite narrative when we do not know—and sometimes cannot even make a reasonable guess—about how the story might end. I remember this dilemma vividly when I was revising my dissertation for publication. The dissertation had been organized thematically, but my editor pushed me to instead tell a chronological story of change over time. That was all well and good until I got near the end of the book, when I realized that I couldn't make definitive claims about where the history I had been tracing was going. By tracking the history of interracial marriage up to what was then the present, I had no sure way to determine whether the trends that I believed were important (for example an increasing erosion of the taboo on black-white relationships) were in fact deeply rooted in U.S. society. I knew that twenty-five or thirty years in the future, the changes I had argued were meaningful might have played out quite differently. In other words, although I felt confident that I had identified some important historical trends, I could not yet assess the legacies and impacts of the changes that I traced.

Where, in short, was my closure? How could I craft a story with a clear beginning, middle, and end if I didn't know where things were going? How could I establish a narrative arc in the absence of a set end to my story? What if I was wrong?

This inability to feel confident about the accuracy of the stories we tell and the narratives we construct—because we know that they may well not stand the test of time—is perhaps one of the hardest challenges scholars of the recent past face. Historians have long prided themselves on crafting narratives, on offering interpretations that analyze change over time and making a case about the significance of the changes they have identified. There is no denying that we who write contemporary history must be much more circumspect in crafting our narratives, especially in making strong claims about the legacies of the developments we trace. We must write histories that do not in fact aim for or achieve closure. If our pasts are "not dead yet," we can't pretend that they are by tying up our stories with a lovely narrative bow.

Again, this might seem like a liability, but it also offers, even requires, recent historians to take seriously historian Hayden White's call to be cognizant of the constructed quality of all narratives. In several important works, including *The Content of the Form: Narrative Discourse and Historical Representation*, White has argued that the narratives historians develop and use are constructed fictions; they do not reflect any reality of the past because "real events do not offer themselves as stories." The dominance of the narrative form among historians, White insists, reflects a larger problem: our desire to make the past tidy and contained in a way that does not, and cannot, represent reality. By framing our historical interpretations as narrative, White charges, historians endow the past with a false sense of coherence. "What kind of notion of reality authorizes construction of a narrative account of reality in which continuity rather than discontinuity governs the articulation of the discourse?" he demands.[21]

Anyone who has actually tried to study the past knows that it is anything but tidy, and all of us who have written narrative histories know—even if we do not admit it—that we choose when to start and end our stories. Those beginnings and ends might seem natural (start with the Great Depression and end in 1941, start with *Brown v. Board of Education* and end in 1968), but they reflect choices that have serious consequences for our readers' understanding of the past. Indeed, many historiographical debates start as criticisms of narrative choices. For example, in recent years, the starting and end points historians have typically used to understand and explain the civil rights movement have come under closer scrutiny. A new body of work insists that starting earlier (e.g., in the 1930s instead of the 1950s) offers us a better means to understand twentieth-century black activism. These proponents of a "long civil rights movement" have also questioned whether histories of the movement should end in the 1960s or early 1970s, or whether, in fact, the stories we tell about black activism might look different if we carried our stories forward to the 1980s or beyond.[22] Civil rights histories that extend beyond 1968, for example, often offer a more complex picture of the ways in which change took root on a local level or, alternatively, was stymied and made less meaningful.[23] This work reminds us, as Hayden White argues, that the choice of narrative not only determines the form of the history but also affects its content.[24]

White argues instead for histories that avoid narrative closure and that highlight the contingency of the past. Critical of professional conventions that privilege narrative as a sign of a "proper history," White urges historians to find alternatives to narrative. He points especially to chronicle—a form marked by a lack of closure—as a useful alternative to the narrative. In a chronicle, historians offer an interpretation of the past but simply end the account when they reach the present. A chronicle, White explains, "does not so much conclude as simply terminate. It starts out to tell a story but breaks off *in media re*, in the chronicler's own present; it leaves things unresolved, or rather, it leaves them unresolved in a story-like way."[25] This is not a failed example of a narrative or an imperfect history, White insists, but a different conception of historical reality.[26]

In some ways, those of us who write about very recent pasts have no choice but to heed White's advice to avoid narrative closure. Although we might not embrace or even be aware of White's call to be chroniclers rather than narrative historians, we who write recent history are at least cognizant of the ways in which the past is chaotic and the endings unclear. And this lack of closure can also represent a form of freedom: if we are constrained by not knowing the long-term impact of the historical events we trace, we are also liberated by not knowing how the story ends, free to suggest a range of possibilities and to highlight the contingencies that always shape the past and the present. If we heed White, then the inability of historians of the recent past to determine the end of our stories is not evidence of the ahistorical nature of our projects; indeed, it might be considered one of their strengths. Rather than lamenting the contingency of the stories we tell, we should embrace our lack of narrative closure and challenge those who insist on closure as a requirement for legitimate history.

Perspective: What Distance Is Critical?

There is, however, perhaps one criticism leveled at the practice of researching and writing recent history that is harder to celebrate. I can happily claim legitimacy for my sources, argue for my own definition of mastery over them, insist that there are benefits to working outside of an established historiography, and highlight the ways in which the unfinished nature of the stories we tell can be a strength rather than a weakness. But the last, and perhaps the most fundamental, question raised about contemporary history—whether those who choose to write about recent events have the necessary critical distance from those events to do so well—offers more of a challenge.

What forms of distance from the topics we study are perceived as critical? Well, first, there is the well-worn charge that people who have some kind of political connection or ideological attachment to their field of study will be biased and might therefore choose their evidence to fit their agenda. There has long been the sense that historians writing about their own times are more likely to be swayed by such biases. As Lord Bolingbroke warned as early as 1752, a particularly contentious time in the political history of the British Empire, "contemporary authors are the most liable to be warped from the straight rule of truth, in writing on subjects which have affected them strongly."[27] Yet given that today few scholars contend that there is any such thing as an absolutely true account of the past, then the challenges that recent historians face in positioning ourselves in relation to politicized events are no different than those who study more distant, but politically charged, pasts. If, as Beverly Southgate argues, objectivity has been discredited and "relativism rules," then all historians—regardless of their subject matter—must be aware of the ways in which their work engages with contemporary political concerns. It is impossible, Southgate continues, "to write any history without *some* standpoint—and that means some philosophical or ideological standpoint. The only questions are whether or not we acknowledge that standpoint, and whether our not our choices have been *consciously* made." Our perceptions of the past, Southgate insists, always reflect "both upon our present position and upon our vision of the future."[28] Historical theorists have thoroughly critiqued the Rankean perspective that a history relevant to our own times is somehow illegitimate.[29]

Those of us who study more recent pasts, where it might be more likely that we will be caught up in or even seek to influence contemporary political debates, have therefore a pressing, but by no means unique, responsibility to be open about locating ourselves in relation to our work and to be mindful of the ways in which an ideological imperative might influence the stories we tell. Historians of the recent past aren't alone in having to grapple with the ways in which we, or our work, can be affected by our politics. However, as the culture wars of the late twentieth century (in which ownership of the historical narrative has played as central role) have perhaps underlined, we must be *especially* aware of our biases and of "the ease with which political commitment can slide into illogical argument."[30] By being careful to position ourselves in relation to our work, and being articulate about that without being defensive, historians of the recent past can reject the charge that we lack "sufficient detachment" to undertake our studies.[31] Such claims imply that we've somehow "lost" our sense of objectivity, when the truth is that we've instead rejected the lingering sense that any history can ever achieve objectivity.[32]

A second concern about critical distance relates not to political commitments but to more fundamental questions about historical consciousness. Some theorists imply that it is nearly impossible to have sufficient detachment from the recent past simply because we are too close to it in time; those who are caught up in events or who experience them firsthand cannot understand the larger processes at work at the heart of the historical enterprise. John Lewis Gaddis thus argues that historical consciousness "demands detachment from—or if you prefer, elevation above—the landscape that is the past." By elevating themselves above the past, Gaddis suggests, historians are able to achieve a wider view that enables them to see connections and patterns that people at the time didn't necessarily recognize. A time machine, if such a thing could ever exist, would not be particularly useful to a historian, Gaddis insists. Historians who could travel back in time might get a better sense of what a particular time or place felt like, but living in the past would not help them draw connections, identify trends, or develop interpretations. The "direct experience of events," he notes, "isn't necessarily the best path towards understanding them, because your field of vision extends no further than your immediate sense."[33] Someone who lived through a particular event, in other words, can know only what he or she experienced.

Other theorists label this expanded vision "hindsight," which they consider to be one of the historian's best assets. Hindsight can be defined as the "understanding of a situation or event only after it has happened or developed."[34] In other words, looking back on an event after it has happened confers a greater ability to understand it. Only by looking back on something can we see patterns and connections, theorist John Tosh asserts. Hindsight thus confers "a superior vision" on historians, Tosh argues, because "it is precisely our position in time relative to the subject of our enquiry that enables us to make sense of the past—to identify conditioning sequences for what they were, rather than what they were intended to be."[35] Keith Jenkins makes a similar case for the importance of hindsight. Through hindsight, he claims,

> we in a way know more about the past than the people who lived in it. In translating the past into modern terms and in using knowledge previously unavailable, the historian discovers both what has been forgotten about the past, and pieces together things never pieced together before. People and social formations are thus caught up in processes that can only be seen in retrospect, and documents and other traces are ripped out of their original contexts of purpose and function to illustrate, say, a pattern which might not be remotely meaningful to any of their authors.[36]

Those of us who study the recent past, these works suggest, won't have enough temporal distance from the events we write about to truly understand or explain them. We lack that greatest asset of any historian—hindsight.

The belief that proper distance from the past is necessary to see larger patterns explains why many theorists insist that the pasts and people suitable for historical study must be "dead." One could, I suppose, seek to dismiss this longing for patterns and connections as stemming from the dominance accorded to the narrative form. If we could free ourselves from what

White considers the tyranny of narrative, then we might better recognize that we are imposing whatever patterns we see in the past. But I refuse to believe that historians can't achieve some kind of wider view about pasts that are not quite so distant—we are not writing about these pasts as people who lived them, even if, chronologically, we did. We are writing about them as historians, undertaking a project of critical inquiry that, like all historical projects, seeks to discern patterns, causal relationships, and connections in sources from many different perspectives.

A metaphor that Gaddis uses throughout his work, comparing historians to mapmakers, offers a useful way to think about the project of writing recent history. The first maps of any newly discovered territories, Gaddis writes, "are usually crude sketches of a coastline, with lots of blank spaces. . . . As exploration proceeds, the map's features become more specific."[37] Although those of us who write recent history are doing much more than providing "crude sketches" of events, we must recognize that the passage of time does allow for a wider view of the landscape of the past that will enable more blank spaces to be filled in. But we should also recognize that those early mapmakers were still cartographers and their maps performed a valuable service, useful in their own right at the time and useful to those who later revised them and added to them. And while there is perhaps danger in being the first to draw a map—one could end up on the rocks—there is also opportunity and exhilaration in being one of the first to chart the important topography of a past event or phenomenon.

Every discipline needs to draw some boundaries—there is no sense of a discipline without what Beverly Southgate calls some "systemic repression." As she writes in *History: What and Why?*, "Some boundaries have to be agreed, some territory mapped out as potential subject-matter; and methodological parameters need to be established, in terms of which there are criteria for what are to count as admissible procedures and as 'valid' historical evidence." For Southgate, one of the boundaries that the discipline of history should clearly uphold relates to the period under study. She argues that works that focus on more contemporary events cannot fulfill what she considers the most important role of historical writing: its potential to "unshackle minds from the constraints of the present." Southgate criticizes scholarship and classes on contemporary history for never confronting the real nature of the past. Contemporary history is popular because it is familiar, but its very popularity sends the unhappy message that the "further removed" past is irrelevant and dispensable.[38] Histories focused on recent events, she insists, are fundamentally antihistorical because they imply that the "real" past has no relevance to our modern age.

Yet looked at another way, histories of the recent past promise to fulfill another key role that history has often sought to achieve: to shed light and historical understanding on the world we live in today. My work may well not be able to "unshackle minds from the constraints of the present," but it always aims to show how the present came to be, to make clear how the past shaped our contemporary practices and understandings.

Those of us who study recent history *are* historians, and we are, in fact, grappling with some of the most vexed and long-standing theoretical issues in our field. We should not allow ourselves to be "disciplined" out of the discipline. Indeed, we have a great deal to contribute to history and to historical theory by centering compelling questions about sources, historiography, narrative, and perspective. Theorist John Tosh—one of the only scholars consulted for this chapter who explicitly discusses the project of writing recent history—argues that the study of the recent past is a vital project. It is this past that people draw on for historical analogies, and it is this past that proves "a fertile breeding ground for crude myths," which can gain power only when scholarly work doesn't exist to test their credibility. Academic neglect of contemporary history, Tosh insists, "has dangerous consequences."[39] Even if we cannot write the histories as well as we might like, and even if our versions of the recent past are sure to be revised as time passes, it is important that we try.

Notes

1. I don't believe that I am alone in devoting little in-depth consideration to issues of methodology. Although historians clearly have a method, we aren't always taught to recognize it as such. John Lewis Gaddis notes that most historians prefer to keep their "ductwork," or their methods, hidden so their narratives will flow more smoothly. In part as a result, historians tend to be far less adept than practitioners from other disciplines in articulating and defending their methods. Historical methods, he argues, are "more sophisticated than our own awareness of them." See *The Landscape of History: How Historians Map the Past* (New York: Oxford University Press, 2002), 92.

2. Works consulted for this essay include John Tosh, *The Pursuit of History*, 3rd ed. Silver Library (Harlow, England: Longman, 2000); David Cannadine, ed., *What Is History Now?* (New York: Palgrave Macmillan, 2002); Michael Oakeshott, *On History and Other Essays* (Totowa, N.J.: Barnes and Noble Books, 1983); E. H. Carr, *What Is History?* (New York: St. Martin's Press, 1961); Beverly Southgate, *History: What and Why?*

Ancient, Modern, and Postmodern Perspectives, 2nd ed. (London: Routledge, 2001); Hayden White, *The Content of the Form: Narrative Discourse and Historical Representation* (Baltimore: Johns Hopkins University Press, 1990); Peter Charles Hoffer, *The Historian's Paradox: The Study of History in Our Own Time* (New York: New York University Press, 2008); Keith Jenkins, *Re-Thinking History* (London: Routledge, 2003); Gaddis, *Landscape of History.*

3. Gabrielle Spiegel, "The Task of the Historian," *American Historical Review* 114, no. 1 (2009): 3, 4.

4. Carr, *What Is History?*

5. Southgate, *History*, 13.

6. Michel de Certeau, *Writing of History*, trans. Tom Conley (New York: Columbia University Press, 1988), quoted in Spiegel, "Task of the Historian," 3, 4; Oakeshott, *History and Other Essays*, 33; Tosh, *Pursuit of History*, 5; Hoffer, *Historian's Paradox*, 1.

7. *Monty Python and the Holy Grail*, directed by Terry Gilliam et al. (2001; Culver City, Calif.: Sony Pictures, 1975), DVD.

8. Tosh, *Pursuit of History*, 22; James Joll, *Europe since 1870: An International History* (Harmondsworth, UK: Penguin, 1976), quoted in Tosh, *Pursuit of History*, 22; David Lowenthal, *The Past Is a Foreign Country* (Cambridge: Cambridge University Press, 1999).

9. Tosh, *Pursuit of History*, 37.

10. See, for example, Lawrence Levine's *Black Culture and Black Consciousness: Afro-American Folk Thought from Slavery to Freedom*, 30th anniversary edition (Oxford: Oxford University Press, 2007).

11. Tosh, *Pursuit of History*, 57; Carr, *What Is History?*, 13–14.

12. Gaddis, *Landscape of History*, 34.

13. I'm grateful to the insights of Robert Self for helping me to think through these issues.

14. Southgate, *History*, 28–29. Historian Gertrude Himmelfarb has been a staunch defender of the idea of historical truth. See, for example, "Some Reflections on the New History," *American Historical Review* 94, no. 3 (1989): 661–670.

15. Hoffer, *Historian's Paradox*, 2.

16. Ranke's original phrase was "*wie es eigentlich gewesen.*"

17. David Hackett Fischer, *Historians' Fallacies: Towards a Logic of Historical Thought* (New York: Harper and Row, 1970), 66; Gaddis, *Landscape of History*, 32, 45; Jenkins, *Re-Thinking History*, 13–14.

18. Paraphrased from Jenkins, *Re-Thinking History*, 18.

19. Jenkins, *Re-Thinking History*, 31; Hoffer, *Historian's Paradox*, 6.

20. Jenkins, *Re-Thinking History*, 82.

21. White, *The Content of the Form*, 4, 10.

22. For a summary of this debate, see Jacqueline Dowd Hall, "The Long Civil Rights Movement and the Political Uses of History," *Journal of American History* 91, no. 4 (2005): 1233–1263.

23. Good examples of this new scholarship are J. Todd Moye, *Let the People Decide: Black Freedom and White Resistance Movements in Sunflower County, Mississippi, 1945–1986* (Chapel Hill: University of North Carolina Press, 2004) and Emilye Crosby, *A Little Taste of Freedom: The Black Freedom Struggle in Claiborne County, Mississippi* (Chapel Hill: University of North Carolina Press, 2005).

24. See White, *Content of the Form*, esp. chapters 1 and 2.

25. Ibid., 5.

26. The entry for "historian" in the *Oxford English Dictionary* suggests how powerful the association between narrative and legitimate history has become. A historian, the OED offers, is "one who produces a work of history in the higher sense, as distinguished from the simple annalist or chronicler of events, from the mere compiler of a historical narrative." The second entry for historian defines it as "one who relates a narrative or tale, a story-teller." *Oxford English Dictionary Online*, s.v. "historian," Oxford University Press, 2010, http://dictionary.oed.com.

27. Bolingbroke, quoted in Southgate, *History*, 143.

28. Southgate, *History*, 10, 122.

29. Tosh, *Pursuit of History*, 32.

30. Hoffer, *Historian's Paradox*, 126.

31. Tosh notes that "it can be argued that scholars today are too close to the events of this period to achieve sufficient detachment," although Tosh himself criticizes that view. *Pursuit of History*, 33.

32. This phrasing borrows from Hoffer, *Historian's Paradox*, 111.

33. Gaddis, *Landscape of History*, 4, 3.

34. *New Oxford American Dictionary*, s.v. "hindsight," accessed August 15, 2011, available through Apple Dictionary, version 2.0.3.

35. Tosh, *Pursuit of History*, 121–122.

36. Jenkins, *Re-Thinking History*, 15–16.

37. Gaddis, *Landscape of History*, 34.

38. Southgate, *History*, 143, 131, 11.

39. Tosh, *Pursuit of History*, 33.

SHELLEY SANG-HEE LEE

Working without a Script

Reflections on Teaching Recent American History

"I REMEMBER AT THE TIME it was a big deal but I didn't quite understand why. It was only after I read about it in the textbook that I understood how huge it was." This captures one student's contribution to a discussion about the very recent past, made during the final section meeting of History 104: The United States since 1877, a course I taught at Oberlin College in spring 2010.[1] The student was referring to the contested presidential election of 2000 between Al Gore and George W. Bush. This topic was among the last we read about, and it was one of the few historical events of which students had personal memories. Although they were in elementary or junior high school at the time, they recalled the controversy over the election and subsequent Supreme Court case in much detail and with emotion. Students reminisced about the prolonged drama over the results, the entry of such terms as "hanging chads" into the popular vocabulary, and how they felt as they witnessed it all. The conversation also piqued students' curiosities about the history of U.S. elections and sparked questions about how to place 2000 against a larger backdrop, as they inquired about the origins of the Electoral College system and whether there had been other similarly contested presidential elections.

After this walk down memory lane, I tried to build on their questions and push the discussion in a more analytical direction. I asked the students to think about how such an election stands out as a harbinger or watershed and to imagine how it might be assessed in history courses forty or fifty years from now. To what extent was this event unprecedented or a culmination of patterns that were years, perhaps decades, in the making? I had pushed students to think along these lines before, but when it came to analyzing a very recent event, they struggled more than they had at earlier moments in the course. Reflecting more generally on how we study recent events, we agreed that the difficulty stemmed in part from the fact that the legacy of these critical moments is still taking shape and subject to active debate. Some students also acknowledged that because the election stood out in their living memories—and brought up some emotion—it was difficult for them to exercise the same critical distance that they brought to discussing the election of 1876, for example. Finally, we also realized that, because historians had only begun giving close attention to and writing about the recent past (I would characterize the 1970s on as recent), teachers and students alike face significant methodological and interpretive challenges, a "crisis of confidence," if you will, when they wade into this territory. In this regard, my students and I often feel like actors working without a script, daunted by the lack of guiding materials but excited by the possibilities of what the journey may uncover.

This class meeting highlighted some of the delights and downsides of teaching recent U.S. history, one of my major tasks in my courses at Oberlin. For this essay, I discuss examples from three classes: the United States since 1877, American History and Culture in the 1970s, and Asian American History. The high level of interest that students tend to bring to studying the recent past certainly makes teaching it very enjoyable. Socially and culturally, the United States in the 1970s and 1980s more resembles the world they know than, say, the United States in the 1860s or 1930s. And teaching the very recent past, when students have lived through it, as opposed to just studied it, seems to further elevate the subject matter's relevance. This familiarity with and proximity to recent events also elicits emotional and personalized responses to history in ways that I have seen less frequently when teaching about the more distant past. Such moments bring a welcome element of dynamism to a classroom, but they can take away from the critical analysis of issues and change over time. Such challenges are further compounded by the shortcomings of available teaching materials: textbooks and monographs give at best limited historical, thematic, and interpretive overviews of recent history.

Nonetheless, the difficulties of teaching recent history are, I think, outweighed by the rewards and opportunities to teach students about the discipline and methodologies in a way that captures their imaginations. In terms of the knowledge they gain, students have remarked to me that studying the second half of the twentieth century and beyond fills a gap in their understanding, since the U.S. history classes they had taken in high school would cut off anywhere between the end of World War II and the 1960s. For those who wondered about what happened in that forty- to sixty-five-year period between the mid-twentieth century and the present, learning about those decades answers many of their questions while illuminating important links between contemporary conditions and the recent events that have had the greatest impact on how we live now. Above all, I find that the relatively uncharted territory of the history of the past forty years is a liberating space in which students can develop their own interpretive skills without being weighed down by historiography. I frame the relative lack of scholarship and "master narratives" as a call to them to undertake the work of examining evidence, constructing narratives, and formulating historical interpretations. Through this intellectual process, the heart and soul of what historians do, students can discover firsthand the ways in which history, far from being a static chronicle of events or a single, objective truth, is dynamic, contested, and continually changing.

One of the most enjoyable aspects of teaching recent history is that students' engagement tends to start out high, as they may already have some acquaintance with the subject matter or a clear set of reference points. The proliferation of both traditional and nontraditional media has made history from the past twenty to forty years more salient in today's culture, compared to how recent history might have appeared in earlier eras. In turn, this wider accessibility has the potential to shape students' decisions when choosing history classes, which became apparent in a seminar I taught in fall 2009 called Crisis of Confidence: American History and Culture in the 1970s. Television shows such as VH-1's *I Love the 70s* (which has other iterations but tellingly goes no earlier than the 1960s) and the cable channels *Nickelodeon* and *TV Land* have done much to fuel the decade's revival and maintain its cultural relevance, even among those born years later. Additionally, many students are introduced to the cultural history of this decade by their parents. On the first day of class I asked the students, who were born in the late 1980s or early 1990s, why they were interested in this period. Several answered that they were fans of seventies popular culture, having been exposed to it through television and movies, but also at home by their parents. Already possessing an impressive knowledge (backed up by the T-shirts they wore to class) of everything from the music of the Ramones to the early films of Woody Allen, students' affinity for popular culture tended to animate and fuel their desire to learn about the social, political, and economic aspects of the United States in the 1970s.

Although not a new phenomenon, generational relationships shaped students' interest in and unique emotional connections to recent history. Students in their late teens and early twenties have active conduits to the decades after the 1960s in their parents, high school teachers, and other older adults with whom they interact extensively. Whereas these years were formative to the lives of people who have a direct and major influence on them, earlier eras do not seem to loom as large because of a lack of direct, personal connections. Sometimes even older generations can have a similar impact. In my Asian American history class during discussions about Japanese American internment, students of Japanese ancestry remarked that studying this episode gave them better understandings of their grandparents' lives. In my course on the 1970s, this impulse to study history to better understand a close family member was common. Many students said that they came to the class hoping to learn about the world in which their parents came of age. Some would talk with their families about the course and then share with the class what their parents recalled about events such as the trial of Patty Hearst, the Watergate scandal, and the controversy over busing and desegregating public schools in Boston. One student, whose father was in Boston during those events, excitedly recounted a conversation about the ways in which the turmoil changed his life, while another student expressed disappointment that his parents barely remembered the events and lamented that "they must have been pretty out of it at the time." Such remarks, which might in another context seem indulgent and irrelevant, were actually productive. We could use them as illustrations of the varied distances between major historical events and the everyday lives of ordinary people.

Heightened student interest and the greater accessibility of cultural artifacts and primary materials from recent years present many pedagogical advantages. For one, students who bring their extensive knowledge of popular culture or personal curiosity to a class tend to be more active and amenable participants in exercises that ask them to closely analyze the sights, sounds, and moods of a historical era. In my seminar on the 1970s, the class even managed to recreate the tastes of a decade, as one evening makeup session turned into a potluck featuring cheese fondue, Jell-O, and Waldorf salad. Researching recipes, listening to music, and watching video clips were not the point of the class, but such activities could help to create a backdrop against which to investigate more conventional historical questions and events. We began this class by reading Christopher Lasch's

1979 bestseller, *The Culture of Narcissism*, which discusses the heightened cynicism and alienation that was purportedly a hallmark of U.S. culture at the time.[2] Not only is this text a fascinating primary source as a window into the era's interest in explaining social patterns in terms of psychiatric diagnoses, but it also established a framework that we could return to and debate as we explored other primary materials, which included scenes from the movie *Taxi Driver* and the book *All the President's Men*.[3] In addition to marveling at the frightening intensity of Travis Bickle—and, thus, indulging some of their curiosity about popular culture—we used the scenes as a springboard into a discussion about cynicism, urban struggle, and moral crisis in the seventies. When students engaged in a spirited discussion of the surprising twists and turns of *All the President's Men*, we used this book about celebrity journalism to frame a discussion of the admittedly confusing events of the Watergate investigation and the crisis of political leadership launched by the Nixon administration. Recognizing that these kinds of materials were the "hooks" drawing students to the class, I sought to use them to expand students' acquaintance with primary sources while also bringing depth and context to their critical understanding of history and culture in the 1970s. One student who was a Cinema Studies major even acknowledged that although he had studied *Taxi Driver* in other courses, considering it as an historical document broadened his understanding of this film that he had seen nearly one hundred times.

Although the digitization of documents and the proliferation of electronic databases have exponentially enriched teachers' options regardless of the period they teach, those who teach recent history still have marked advantages in terms of the array and number of archives and sources. An additional nonscholarly interest likely helps to further ensure the preservation and dissemination of primary materials from more recent periods. I have especially noticed these differences in the U.S. survey and in Asian American history classes as we move from the distant to recent past. When focusing on the nineteenth or early twentieth centuries, I am limited to sources available through databases such as Proquest Historical Newspapers, document readers, and materials I have saved over the years. As we move into the recent past, while continuing to draw on traditional sources, my students have access to public newspaper archives, YouTube, and Netflix. Not only do these sources illustrate a period, they give us a text to analyze together. A simple Internet search, for example, turned up a video of Jimmy Carter's famous "Crisis of Confidence" speech from 1979.[4] Watching the video transported us back to that time, while allowing for a rich conversation about the substance, optics, and tone of the speech. Students talked about its contents but also pondered aspects such as Carter's somber expression, debating whether these were intentional and effective.

The benefits of readily accessible primary sources extend to student research projects, which generally do not rely on access to traditional archival manuscript collections. For example, one student in the 1970s seminar who wished to write about the family in U.S. culture during this decade assembled a rich set of sources that included books by James Dobson and Benjamin Spock as well as episodes of the television show *American Family*, obtaining all her materials from the Oberlin library stacks, interlibrary loans, or Amazon.com. A student undertaking a similar project focusing on the 1870s or even 1920s would likely encounter considerable obstacles to identifying and accessing a set of original sources and completing the work in one semester. Another research advantage, which ties back to the reason for many students' interest in recent history, is the presence of living sources; even if students are not conducting interviews, they can consult with people who lived through events they are studying and get helpful ideas about primary materials.

There are some potential hazards to teaching recent history that I have become increasingly aware of, however. Because there are a greater variety and number of databases and search engines that students can consult to generate leads on potential sources, it can be that much more of a challenge to discern what materials are worthwhile and how to sift through them. In addition, while I have turned to the Internet for supplementary teaching materials, doing so has also thrown light on why it is so important for students who use the Internet for research to approach it with clear parameters and an understanding of what kind of information they are looking for. For instance, while I think it is fine to go online to access certain primary sources (e.g., Jimmy Carter's speech), I generally discourage students from relying on online secondary materials (e.g., using an unvetted essay found on a history website), unless it comes from an academic database, and I urge them to take great care to verify the reliability of what they find.

Despite these hazards, the advantages of sources and accessibility substantially impact the quality and richness of students' learning. For instance, in early Asian American history, because of historical patterns of discrimination as well as class and language barriers, documented perspectives from people of Asian ancestry are rare, and much of what we know about Asian American experience is filtered through whites who often held deeply Orientalist views. Asian-language sources such as newspapers, speeches, and other records provide valuable firsthand insights, but translations are not always available. As a result, for Asian perspectives, we tend to become overly reliant on the voices of multilingual Asian elites, such as the nineteenth-century immigrant journalist and critic of anti-Chinese racism Wong Chin Foo. Owing to factors such as heightened immigration, changes in race relations, and the Asian American movement of the 1960s and 1970s, the past few decades have seen a dramatic proliferation of writings and other forms of self-representation by Asian Americans, including novels, memoirs, poetry, transcribed oral histories, ethnic newspapers, mainstream journalism, photographs, and films.

These developments have greatly expanded the quantity and quality of materials available to teach from and have in turn widened the range of perspectives from which to study Asian American history, making it more inclusive of women, homosexuals, children, the poor, and smaller Asian ethnic groups. Students benefit tremendously if they can learn about the gender debates accompanying the rise of Asian American literature in the 1970s and 1980s through reading works by the iconic writers Maxine Hong Kingston and Frank Chin.[5] The same can be said for supplementing the study of post-Vietnam Asian refugee experiences with written oral histories by Vietnamese refugees and the documentary *A.K.A. Don Bonus* (which gives a firsthand view on being an eighteen-year-old Cambodian immigrant in San Francisco in the early 1990s).[6] In end of the semester evaluations for Asian American history, for example, students have consistently singled out books such as Maxine Hong Kingston's *The Woman Warrior*, Monica Sone's *Nisei Daughter*, John Okada's *No-No Boy*, and Yoshiko Uchida's *Desert Exile*—all of which are novels or memoirs—as their favorites.[7] Such materials, with their emphases on point of view and lived experiences, humanize history much more powerfully for them than a scholarly monograph typically can.

Because tackling recent history can feel like stepping onto uncharted ground compared to covering earlier eras, this grants teachers space to be original and interpretive in selecting materials and writing lectures. When it comes to teaching an event such as the Great Depression in a survey course, I feel compelled to stick to the "script"—that is, the narrative laid out in textbooks and monographs. Although the existence of a tried and tested set of materials and interpretations is helpful and convenient, becoming wholly reliant on them can also feed the impression that there is a definitive approach or a "right way" to doing and understanding history, a rule that we know much of the best scholarship breaks. With respect to history from the 1970s on, recent scholarship and synthetic works have brought into view the beginnings of a discernible narrative, which is helpful for structuring units in recent history.[8] Yet the relative lack of established pedagogies, authoritative interpretations, and set reading lists for teaching this period can also be freeing, calling for a degree of innovation and experimentation that I feel less at liberty to exercise when teaching earlier periods. For instance, when it came to assigning a popular book for my 1970s seminar—something I do in most of my classes—I narrowed down a list of contenders that were quite literally all over the place. After considering books that included *Fear of Flying*; *I'm OK, You're OK*; *Jonathan Livingston Seagull*; and *Carrie*, I settled on *All the President's Men* for its cultural and political value as well as the fact that it is a riveting read.[9] The liberating aspects of entering the terrain of recent history and learning without a defined set of interpretations and authoritative works extends to students as well, as they must also bring their critical skills to understanding and explaining historical events without merely regurgitating what historians have already written or argued.

Although I mostly regard teaching recent history as a positive challenge for teachers and students, I do not wish to underemphasize the difficulties and dangers. It is like working without a safety net—the safety net being authoritative interpretations and established scholarship. The more extensively studied a period is, the more defined the "master narrative" tends to be, with its touchstone events, significant individuals, and key readings. Teachers wishing to enrich or complicate the conventional narrative might emphasize different interpretive models or stress the importance of less well-known figures or events, but the established narrative remains useful as a baseline for understanding events. But some fields benefit from the lack of this narrative: in Asian American history, for example, the latter decades of the twentieth century are now highly important, but the historical scholarship has not kept up. One of the later sessions in that class focused on the revival of the "yellow peril" in U.S. life in the 1980s, which refers to the racial backlash against Asian Americans fueled by Japan's global economic rise. Because this topic has not received the full scholarly treatment by historians, I cobbled together a lecture and lesson plan using newspaper articles, Hollywood movies, documentaries, and scholarship from disciplines other than history. In doing this work, I was not just making my own arguments about the past but also crafting a narrative and fitting it within a broader history. Questions about the similarities and differences between the anti-Asian racism of the 1980s and that of earlier periods were very new ones. Although exploring these questions without the benefit of other scholars' takes or research could make some students timid, ultimately, these conversations were rewarding because they afforded them the chance to see up close the evaluative and interpretive work that goes into doing history.

That said, a drawback of teaching recent history is the limited room to investigate historiography and historical debates, a skill that is crucial to mastering the craft. Historiography is integral to learning history, especially in advanced courses, but because the scholarly literature on recent events is always going to be new and relatively thin, this leaves little to work with. To draw on an example from Asian American history, the anti-Chinese movement of the late 1800s is a much-studied subject, and there are several book-length studies that explain why the movement emerged and prevailed.[10] This rich literature, the result of decades of research, can be culled to provide students with a detailed understanding of the history of anti-Chinese politics and allows them to evaluate different arguments about whether it was principally motivated by race or class concerns or whether it was a national initiative from the start or a regional movement that succeeded in gaining a national audience. Achieving such a multifaceted engagement with recent history is far more difficult. When the first wave of scholarship on an era or topic is just emerging, those fields are far from having a discrete set of interpretations and debates. In the seminar on the 1970s, we recognized this as a limitation for our discussions. Similarly, a session devoted to learning about the Iran hostage crisis, for which the book *Taken Hostage* by David Farber served as the main text, was lively and engaging.[11] Students did a fine job of critiquing and evaluating Farber's work, but because the history of the United States' encounters with Middle East terrorism is a new field, at least among U.S. historians, we were unable to compare his take with other historians' or otherwise bring any historiographical analysis to bear on the discussion.

Finally, the closeness of recent events to the present can pose significant challenges of perspective, particularly when asking students to bring their enthusiasms to the materials in the first place. This is precisely what makes recent history interesting for some students, but it can be a barrier to thinking historically about the not-so-distant past. Because the past three or four decades occupies a middle ground between the present and what we more traditionally regard as "history" (i.e., the distant past), it can be tempting to approach these years only in terms of how they illuminate, or are a part of, the contemporary world. I have dealt with this in the unit on the revival of the "yellow peril" in the late twentieth century in Asian American history. In addition to assigning primary and secondary readings, I screen the 1988 documentary *Who Killed Vincent Chin?*, a chilling piece about the violent death of a Chinese American in Detroit at the hands of two unemployed white autoworkers who mistook him for a Japanese, and the fight for justice in the wake of a judge's lenient sentence.[12] As the killing took place in 1982, by situating the crime against the backdrop of deindustrialization, unemployment, racial tension, and anti-Japan economic nationalism in the 1980s, the film shows that anti-Asian violence is not merely a vestige of the nineteenth century. The film highlights how these historical developments gave rise to a renewal of anti-Japanese propaganda and violence, which in turn took a toll on many Asian Americans who were not Japanese. Historicizing the killing was, paradoxically, difficult, because students were more aware of this event's proximity than of its status as history. One student remarked that it highlighted the need for stronger hate crimes laws, without thinking to ask whether hate crimes laws have changed in recent years (they have). Others commented on how it showed the prevalence of anti-Asian racism in contemporary life and was a window into the struggles of the white working class. While those parallels and continuities were valid to a degree, they were also ahistorical, a problem that had not emerged when we discussed events that had occurred much earlier. Whether because there are more glimmers of the present in the recent past or students were born not long after it occurred, they reacted much more emotionally to this crime than they did to earlier instances of anti-Asian violence that were just as horrific.

But what was initially an impediment to discussion also generated some of the most insightful observations about the intersections of class and race all semester. Because Chin's killing occurred not too long ago and the students did not learn about it from a textbook, they seemed to establish a quicker grasp of how the legacy and meanings of events can be contested. When I asked the class to step back from the event itself and consider why Vincent Chin had become such a prominent figure in Asian American history in the late twentieth century, they handled this with more skill and confidence than they had brought to discussions of earlier, more thoroughly studied events. One student argued that Chin's inclusion seemed arbitrary in light of the fact that he was probably one of many victims of anti-Asian violence during this time. Another proposed that the event's power lay in its demolishing the view that Asian Americans, as "model minorities," were immune to racial violence. Yet another wondered if Chin's martyrdom was meaningful because it gave Asian Americans a recognizable name to rally around. While the students agreed that Chin's death and the ensuing fight for justice were important and belong in Asian American history, if for no reason other than their galvanizing and politicizing effect on many Asian Americans, they also understood that how the incidents were analyzed and the degree to which they were emphasized in a larger narrative came down to interpretive decisions made by historians. When a student pointed out that the same could be said of all history, as a teacher I could not have been prouder.

While initially what appealed to me most about teaching recent history was the way that the subject matter seemed to bring students alive, I have come to appreciate it more broadly for all its challenges and opportunities. Intellectually, methodologically, and pedagogically, the history of the United States since the 1970s is a unique animal. On the one hand, it is closely connected to the present, which makes it inherently and immediately interesting. On the other hand, as a field it is perpetually in an undeveloped state, which can make its historical relevance elusive. While these qualities might make teachers reluctant to engage the recent past as an area of study, the rewards for students and instructors alike, in terms of the distinctive knowledge, intellectual demands, and disciplinary insights, make the journey very worthwhile.

Notes

1. I team-taught this class with Clayton Koppes and Pablo Mitchell of the Oberlin History Department. We each held weekly discussion sections with a third of the class, and it was in one of these meetings that this conversation occurred. The textbook we used, and in which students read about the election, was Eric Foner, *Give Me Liberty! An American History*, 2nd Seagull ed. (New York: Norton, 2008).

2. Christopher Lasch, *The Culture of Narcissism: American Life in an Age of Diminishing Expectations* (New York: Norton, 1979).

3. *Taxi Driver*, directed by Martin Scorsese (1976; Culver City, Calif.: Columbia Pictures, 2007), DVD; *All the President's Men*, directed by Alan J. Pakula (1976; Burbank, Calif.: Warner Brothers, 2006), DVD.

4. Jimmy Carter, "'Crisis of Confidence' Speech," video, 33:04, July 15, 1979, Miller Center of Public Affairs, University of Virginia, Washington, D.C., http://millercenter.org/president/speeches/detail/3402.

5. Maxine Hong Kingston, *Woman Warrior: Memoir of a Girlhood among Ghosts* (New York: Knopf, 1976); Frank Chin, *The Chickencoop Chinaman/The Year of the Dragon: Two Plays* (Seattle: University of Washington Press, 1981).

6. *A.K.A Don Bonus*, directed by Spencer Nakasako and Sokly "Don Bonus" Ny (San Francisco: National Asian American Telecommunications Association, 1995), VHS; Sucheng Chan, ed., *The Vietnamese 1.5 Generation: Stories of War, Revolution, Flight, and New Beginnings* (Philadelphia: Temple University Press, 2006).

7. Maxine Hong Kingston, *The Woman Warrior: Memoirs of a Girlhood among Ghosts* (New York: Knopf, 1976); Monica Itoi Sone, *Nisei Daughter* (Boston: Little Brown, 1953); John Okada, *No-No Boy* (Seattle: University of Washington Press, 1978); Yoshiko Uchida, *Desert Exile: The Uprooting of a Japanese American Family* (Seattle: University of Washington Press, 1982).

8. James T. Patterson, *Restless Giant: The United States from Watergate to Bush v. Gore* (New York: Oxford University Press, 2005); Bruce Schulman, *The Seventies: The Great Shift in American Culture, Society, and Politics* (New York: Free Press, 2001); Edward D. Berkowitz, *Something Happened: A Political and Cultural Overview of the Seventies* (New York: Columbia University Press, 2006).

9. Erica Jong, *Fear of Flying: A Novel* (New York: Holt, Rinehart, and Winston, 1973); Thomas Anthony Harris, *I'm OK, You're OK: A Practical Guide to Transactional Analysis* (New York: Harper and Row, 1969); Richard Bach, *Jonathan Livingston Seagull: A Story* (New York: Macmillan, 1970); Stephen King, *Carrie* (Garden City, N.Y.: Doubleday, 1974).

10. Alexander Saxton, *The Indispensable Enemy: Labor and the Anti-Chinese Movement in America* (Berkeley: University of California Press, 1971); Andrew Gyory, *Closing the Gate: Race, Politics, and the Chinese Exclusion Act* (Chapel Hill: University of North Carolina Press, 1998); Erika Lee, *At America's Gates: Chinese Immigration during the Exclusion Era* (Chapel Hill: University of North Carolina Press, 2003).

11. David Farber, *Taken Hostage: The Iran Hostage Crisis and America's First Encounter with Radical Islam* (Princeton, N.J.: Princeton University Press, 2005).

12. *Who Killed Vincent Chin?*, directed by Christine Choy (Detroit: Film News Now Foundation and WTVS, 1988), VHS.

PART TWO

Access to the Archives

LAURA CLARK BROWN AND NANCY KAISER

Opening Archives on the Recent American Past

Reconciling the Ethics of Access and the Ethics of Privacy

IN 1968 FIVE MEDICAL STUDENTS from universities in the Northeast spent the summer in the Mississippi Delta serving as interns in a public health clinic. Over the course of the summer, the students conducted medical assessments of impoverished African American families and compiled narrative case histories for each family. The case histories illuminate familial structures and relations, social networks, economic and living conditions, public health and social programs, and education in the Delta community. They also provide personal details about individuals' medical conditions and anomalies, hygiene, sexual habits and pregnancies, religious convictions, and social mores. The case histories, as well as the evaluations of the medical students' progress and administrative records of the clinic, form an archival collection held in the Southern Historical Collection (SHC) at the University of North Carolina (UNC) at Chapel Hill.

A collection of this sort has immense research value, offering historians of the recent American past a wealth of source material on African American families in 1968 Mississippi. Yet the collection's recentness presents particular problems for both historians and archivists. Many of the second or third parties represented in these records are likely still living, and the privacy of their health or student information is compromised if the collection is open to research.[1] Removing the names of individuals from the records offers some privacy protection but also erases the social relationships and webs of meaning that these records can otherwise reveal. Archivists at the SHC have therefore closed the portions of the clinic collection containing the medical case histories and the student evaluations for seventy years from the date of creation.[2] Closing the records for a set time that reaches decades into the future is an unhappy compromise for all parties—donors of archival collections, archivists, and historians. While the benefits to the second and third parties and to the archivists' consciences are obvious, the injury to the archives' mission of open access and to historical scholarship is equally apparent. These records will not be available for research by historians until 2038, unless donors of archival collections, archivists, and historians of the recent American past can find a way to share the responsibility of protecting privacy.

The obstacles to gaining access to the Mississippi health clinic records are representative of the complications faced by those who wish to study the more recent past. The SHC has collected materials that document the twentieth and twenty-first centuries, many of which contain private information in personnel files, health records, student records, and even personal correspondence and diaries that pertain to people who are still alive. When living persons are represented, the archivists wrestle with the ethical dilemma of open access to valuable historical records versus protection of private information that could potentially damage lives. The code of ethics developed by the Society of American Archivists (SAA)—North America's leading organization for the profession—provides broad guidance, but no clear directives in these cases, as it recognizes promoting "open and equitable access" to records *and* protecting "the privacy rights of donors and individuals or groups who are the subject of records" as key responsibilities for archivists.[3] Best practices for addressing the thin white space between these two sections of the ethical code do not exist for the profession as a whole. The variety of institutions and of institutional missions, cultures, resources, and constituencies means that one size will not fit all. Likewise, the important contextual information of each privacy concern makes it difficult to generalize institutional responses into a set of best practices even at the local level. Published case studies by professional archivists dispense sound advice for ethical dilemmas, but they are typically conservative, counseling repositories to privilege privacy over access through lengthy, but time-limited restrictions.[4] Archivists who seek to turn the dial and make records of the not-too-distant past accessible for research now are left to reconcile the two competing ethics each time a new privacy concern arises.

This essay offers a case study of how one manuscript archive is responding to the challenges posed by collections that include materials from the recent past. These challenges include identifying manuscript materials of a sensitive personal nature and determining their disposition and use; interpreting privacy laws in the context of archival research; and providing access through digital technology that makes archival information far more widely available than it has been traditionally. It is vital for historians who study the recent past to understand these challenges and to engage with the underlying privacy concerns. Unless historians familiarize themselves with the policies and concerns of the archival collections they seek to use, they may not recognize the ways in which their access to information is being limited or understand their ethical obligations to respect the privacy rights of the individuals they discuss. This essay thus addresses the breadth of the SHC's challenges with privacy and frames the conversations that must begin among archivists, historians of the recent past, and donors of archival collections.

The Southern Historical Collection and the Ethos of Access

The University of North Carolina at Chapel Hill's Board of Trustees officially established the Southern Historical Collection in 1930 and named historian J. G. (Joseph Grégoire) de Roulhac Hamilton the first director (curator of the collection). Prior to 1930, Hamilton had already begun to establish "a great collection of Southern human records" in Chapel Hill, and he spent the better part of three decades traveling the Southeast to amass more than 800 collections by the time he eased into retirement in the late forties.[5] In 2009 the SHC held more than 4,600 collections, and dozens of collections are added each year. Hamilton's successors have continued his work, building on early strengths, including antebellum plantation culture, the U.S. Civil War, and southern family life. Each curator has added a new and often contemporary dimension to the collecting scope to account for changes in southern history as a field and societal change itself. The "long civil rights movement," social justice activism since the 1960s, and the African American southern experience are recent examples of reoriented collecting.

Collections are sought and acquired based on the curator's assessment of research value for current and future users, and the majority of the SHC collections do not carry access and use restrictions. Recent SHC curators have made a conscious effort to minimize the number of restrictions placed on newly acquired collections. The curator encourages donors to forgo adding restrictions on usage, such as requiring the donor's permission prior to publication. Restricting access to the donor's hand-selected friends or to people who hold specific political viewpoints is unacceptable. For example, a donor who has extensive records about civil rights activities cannot prevent researchers with right-wing agendas from using the collection. Requests to close a collection indefinitely are not entertained.

Restrictions that sanction or result in inequitable access threaten both the integrity of historical research and the public's trust in the institution. The innate value of a public archive lies in the capacity for historians to return over and over to the same documents to check peers' work and to reinterpret the historical records in light of new methodologies and shifts in historiography. Historians' professional ethics demand access to the sources cited by members of their ranks, and privately held documents are suspect in that they cannot easily be examined by others for different interpretations. Before the SHC was established, most records of the U.S. South remained in private hands or were the property of private historical societies, not bound to provide access to anyone, much less equitable access.[6] The SHC has been and is a public research archive, and the use and reuse of the documents by historians and others remain at the core of its mission.[7] Its 2005 "Research and Instruction Ethos" articulates the archive's commitment to "provid[ing] the highest level of service to all users based on those needs, offering equitable access to holdings and equitable research services without regard to a patron's background, affiliation, credentials, or subject of research." While "respecting donors' restrictions, intellectual property rights, privacy, and preservation concerns," the archive has set the ideal of trying whenever possible "to connect the patrons with the materials they wish to use."[8] Historically the SHC has been open to anyone interested in exploring its holdings without concern for credentials and background or for purposes of research being conducted. The SHC search room has hosted individuals from all over the world, and anyone may examine unrestricted materials regardless of their qualifications. Restrictions on collections apply to all researchers regardless of status or affiliation, and open collections may be used by anyone who completes and signs a reader agreement. Since 2010, the SHC has sought to expand access to new groups of researchers and increase accessibility for the SHC's traditional audiences through the online presentation of manuscript collections.[9] The SHC's ongoing large-scale digitization will make many of its collections accessible to people all over the world.

The Challenges of Sensitive Materials in Collections

Open and equitable access is an ideal, but it is a difficult standard to sustain in the face of challenges posed by collections that document the recent past. What are these challenges and how might they affect those who seek to do research in late twentieth- and twenty-first-century collections? Archivists face a sometimes overwhelming task in trying to identify sensitive materials from large, modern collections and determine their disposition based on personal and professional ethics and on interpretation of privacy laws. As a result, they might restrict access to the collection, replace sensitive items with redacted copies, close the collection entirely, or decide that a compelling case can be made to open access to sensitive materials. Or, archivists could miss sensitive materials altogether and mistakenly provide researchers access to documents that should be restricted.

To date, researchers have not alerted SHC archivists to this type of inappropriate access. For example, several researchers examined the family medical histories and student evaluations in the decade after the Mississippi health clinic records collection was accessioned in 1992. None raised alarms with the archivists about the private health information and student records that they were allowed to see. The sensitive nature of the collection materials was discovered only when it was reprocessed in a 2008 initiative to enhance this and other collections' descriptions. At the time of reprocessing, the SHC staff made the collective and reluctant decision to close these materials from use because of the invasion of privacy as well as the legal and ethical peril to archivists, donors, and historians alike.

The reprocessing of the Mississippi health clinic records collection illustrates the larger challenge facing archivists who seek to maximize access to collections. Processing a collection involves many laborious tasks. Placing materials into chronological order and annotating dates takes considerable time. Preservation measures to ensure the long-term life of the materials— removing rusty paperclips and staples, enclosing photographs in special envelopes, and rehousing entire collections into acid-free archival-quality folders, to name just a few of the routine preservation tasks—is painstakingly slow. Identifying and removing restricted materials, which is still the norm in many repositories where the archivist is beholden to protection of the donor's privacy at all costs, requires an item-by-item approach. Given the nature of these processing tasks, it is no wonder that many repositories have a backlog of unprocessed collections that are, in most cases, "hidden" from researchers. But archivists at the SHC and many at other large repositories believe that they cannot stand by an ethic of access while allowing backlogs of unprocessed collections to accumulate. In the groundbreaking article "More Product, Less Process: Revamping Traditional Archival

Processing," archivists Mark A. Greene and Dennis Meissner argue that it is far more important to get the material out to the researchers than to remove every staple and put all items in chronological order.[10] What good are archival collections to the study of history if they remain unknown to researchers because there are not enough archivists to get them to an ideal state of readiness for use?

Identifying sensitive material and then imposing restrictions to protect privacy are anathema to a processing paradigm that emphasizes faster access to the collection. Late twentieth- and twenty-first century collections are typically large, with thousands of individual items achieving value to researchers only in the aggregate.[11] These collections also come in more varied formats that require specific technology, much of it obsolete even before the materials arrive in the repository. Digital materials—such as e-mail, blogs, digital photographs, and databases—are the coming storm. Strong gusts are already shaking the archives' foundation. Early in 2010, the daughter of a recently deceased social activist emptied her father's hard drives and delivered the gigabytes for accessioning. The activist's "papers" are doubtless filled with valuable research materials for historians of the very recent American past examining de facto segregation in housing, struggles of organized labor, and contested memory and monument building. Beyond the challenges of technical obsolescence and digital storage, how will the processing archivist locate the digital content that threatens second- and third-party privacy in the millions of bytes? Some archivists project that identifying sensitive materials in digital records will be a more efficient, simple, and comprehensive process than it is with paper. By running algorithms, the processing archivist will be able to identify all uses of specific terms likely to be found in sensitive materials, but such a method of identifying sensitive materials presupposes systematic use of terms, feasible in organizational records such as forms, but unlikely in personal writings.

In the meantime, paper collections continue to present their own problems of scale. Sensitive documents can be buried in mounds of undifferentiated paper, hidden in attachments, and spread throughout a collection in duplicate and triplicate. In 2007 a nonprofit organization that strove to empower the working poor and the unemployed from the 1970s through the 1990s, donated an enormous collection of an estimated eighty-seven thousand items. By chance, rather than through a comprehensive review, the processing archivist discovered photocopies of a negative employee evaluation in several different and unrelated files. The evaluation was scathing; in it, the author speculated that the employee had a serious personality disorder. Short of reading every document in the massive collection, the archivist had no chance of discovering every instance of this and other similarly sensitive documents. If archivists seek to make these collections available to historians in a timely manner, they will certainly miss some of these sensitive documents, which places the onus on the researcher to determine how and whether to use them.

Historians need to be aware that these challenges and the ways that archivists meet them affect what information is available to them in very concrete ways. As just one example, archivists' concerns about both copyright and privacy will prevent the online presentation of most collections with date spans in the mid-twentieth century and later. If archival repositories digitize only those collections utterly free of privacy concerns the equity of access is skewed. More catastrophic than inequitable access is no access — physical or virtual — which effectively closes entire lines of inquiry to two or three generations of historians.

Closing SHC collections entirely is rare because the SHC archivists err on the side of leaving collections open and unrestricted. But historians must recognize that the price of that access is increased ethical and legal responsibility on their part. They cannot assume that if the archive made the materials "available" to them — intentionally or accidentally — then the materials must be okay for them to see, to use, and to publish. That assumption has two fallacies. The first is that archivists know or have seen everything in a collection. The second is that by opening a collection archivists have sanctioned any and all uses of the information found within. Historians still have an active role to play in identifying what information is sensitive and in determining responsible uses of that information based on professional and private ethics and the law.

Legal Implications

At the same time that a lighter, more efficient processing strategy is becoming an accepted standard to promote access to the archives, legal protections and expectations for different kinds of privacy are expanding or gaining new bite. In 1992 the Southern Historical Collection received the first accession of the Mississippi health clinic records, and in a decision prefiguring Meissner and Greene's "Less Process" approach, chose to open the records unprocessed and with only a donor-created box list serving as the contents description. Archivists reviewed the box list prior to posting the skeletal archival description online, but they clearly failed to anticipate the presence of private health and student information in the collection. In fairness to the archivists who opened the unprocessed collection, "privacy" and "health" were not legally intertwined until the 1996 Health Insurance Portability and Accountability Act (HIPAA) privacy regulations took effect in April 2003.[12] The archivists probably overlooked the student evaluations because they did not expect to find them in a collection of health clinic records.

Federal privacy laws like HIPAA and the 1974 Family Educational Rights and Privacy Act (FERPA), and state laws such as the North Carolina State Personnel Act are complicated and difficult to interpret in the archival context.[13] In almost all cases, legal loopholes make the SHC exempt from letter-of-the-law compliance. HIPAA requires covered entities—health-care providers that conduct transactions in electronic form, health-care clear-inghouses, and health plans—to protect health information in perpetuity no matter whether it is transmitted orally, on paper, or electronically. Man-uscript repositories, such as the SHC, frequently contain "protected" private health information but are not bound by this law to protect that informa-tion because they are not covered entities. Some repositories such as a hos-pital's archives are covered entities, and under HIPAA they would be bound to protect even a nineteenth-century physician's account ledger with patient names and treatments.[14] When the ledger is owned by the SHC, it is not pro-tected by HIPAA. Although the SHC is exempt, some of the SHC's donors are not. The SHC can stay on the right side of HIPAA law if it makes the Missis-sippi health clinic records available, but the clinic's founders, who donated the records, could be prosecuted in civil and criminal court for violations of HIPAA or sued by a complainant for violation of privacy. Historians who publish private health information could also be liable for violating privacy.

Likewise, manuscript repositories often contain information about or created by students—transcripts, evaluations, recommendations, papers— that is usually protected by FERPA. Faculty members should not retain graded student work without explicit permission from the students or leave an institution with student records. But they often do, and those records sometimes make their way to a manuscript collection, with or without explicit or implicit permission from these second parties to include their records in the collection. The SHC owns numerous collections of faculty pa-pers and more than likely most, if not all, of them contain student papers—

student records as defined by FERPA—that were retained without permission of the students. If the faculty member taught at the University of North Carolina at Chapel Hill or in the seventeen-campus UNC system, the SHC is legally bound to comply with FERPA by restricting, redacting, or removing those records. If the faculty member taught elsewhere, then the SHC does not need to comply with FERPA; the SHC is not legally responsible for a faculty member's mistaken retention and subsequent donation of student papers from another institution. These student records can sometimes be of great research interest, as in the case of a prominent documentary filmmaker whose pedagogical work with several generations of documentarians was at least as influential as his own filmmaking. His evaluations of students, some of whom are in the film industry today, reveal details about personal life that exceed name, address, and grade or critical comments on an essay. The SHC is not bound to protect the student records in this collection, but the processing archivist let FERPA guide her decision to close these materials for seventy-five years from the date of the document.

Personnel records can be even murkier ground for a manuscript repository. The North Carolina State Personnel Act restricts access to the personnel records of state employees for ten years following separation from employment with the state. Other states do not permit public access to state employees' personnel files, and still others, including California, will provide public access following redaction of personal identifiers. However, these state laws govern only the personnel records of employees of the respective state. An easy argument could be made that all other employee records are therefore fair game for public research, but a room full of archivists at a 2009 symposium hosted by the SHC tensed at the prospect of turning personnel files loose for public consumption.[15] In the case of the nonprofit social justice organization records, the processing archivist opted to close the clearly labeled personnel records for ten years after the apparent dissolution of the organization. This restriction, although not required by law, was modeled after the North Carolina State Personnel Act.

The SHC's minimal legal risks are further mitigated by the low chance of discovery and misuse of materials containing private information. The vast majority of these documents live in practical obscurity, such as the nonprofit personnel records found in project files and granting agency correspondence, and the painstaking effort required in archival research would discourage most researchers from using this avenue to acquire private information for exploitive purposes. SHC archivists take it on faith that researchers will not intentionally violate the privacy of a second or third party represented in SHC collections. And finally, should a complaint of violated privacy arise from a second or third party represented in an SHC collection, the burden is on the complainant to prove that damages resulted from the SHC's making its collections available for research.

Although the legal risks for the SHC are low, the donors who give the SHC sensitive materials and the historian who publishes individually identifiable private information without permission of those whose privacy may be violated could be liable for lawsuits. The SHC might be a party to such a lawsuit, but judicial opinions of privacy cases involving libraries as defendants suggest that it likely would emerge legally unscathed.[16] Regardless, legal fees would probably be substantial even with a favorable ruling, and, more alarming, the unflattering publicity of a lawsuit may have a chilling effect on future collecting by the curator.

Ethical Dilemmas and Difficult Questions

Many questions about handling sensitive materials persist beyond the cold comfort of low legal risks and the practical impossibility of locating all sensitive documents. What types of documents and information should be considered sensitive? Should the SHC follow FERPA, HIPAA, and state personnel records laws even when they do not apply or when legal risk is low? What are archivists' obligations to second and third parties represented in collections? Should ethical considerations change when the person is a well-known personality or is from a historically marginalized or disadvantaged group? And how should archivists handle sensitive information for which the laws offer no guidance other than the mandate to protect information that would be deemed highly offensive to a reasonable person?

These ethical questions are compounded by the Internet, the rising demand for digital versions of manuscript materials, and the growth of records available only in electronic form, born-digital materials. Some archivists will argue that the Internet changes nothing. If a collection is available for researchers in the search room, it can and should be made available online. But others suggest that some sensitive materials that might be opened in the relative obscurity of the reading room should not be placed on the web because the Internet makes documents so easily accessible and greatly expands their audience. Of course, with the introduction of digital cameras in the search room, a researcher could photograph and upload documents that the SHC staff had deemed too sensitive for its own website. Other potential compromises, such as the SHC posting images of the documents without full-text search capabilities, are also limited, because anyone could easily grab the image and transcribe the words into searchable text and then post it in a different forum. And born-digital records are inherently full-text searchable and easily transportable to other sites. Once the image or electronic record is exposed on the Internet, the cat is out of the bag.

The complicating factors of the Internet only heighten long-standing questions about the obligations of archivists to historians and the obligations of historians to the people they write about. There may well be a context in which access is more important than privacy, especially if closing a portion of a collection limits its usefulness to historians or if archival records might have the potential to inform not only scholarship but also policy and legislation.[17] But in such cases, will historians recognize sensitive information as needing special consideration, or assume its presence in a reputable repository makes it fair game? The historians' professional organizations could consider addressing the use of sensitive materials in their own codes of ethics and professional conduct, but even if professional historians align with the archivists in an ethical stance that protects privacy and keeps access as open as it can be, where does that leave the thousands of nonprofessional researchers who examine archival material every day and who have no professional code of conduct or context for the use of sensitive information?

The Pitfalls of Policy

In an effort to address some of these questions, the Southern Historical Collection has attempted to develop policies for sensitive materials, a task that has proven difficult and unending. Written policy requires constant revision because each influx of material from recent historical periods provokes new challenges. Social mores and concepts of privacy have fluctuated rapidly in the digital age and with the national security vigilance of the post-9/11 era, and past decisions to close materials can appear naive and ill informed after only a brief lapse of time. Baseline community standards for the SHC have proven impossible to establish. The balance of opinion shifts with personnel changes or even with a single problematic acquisition whose particulars negate prior feelings and decisions on similar cases. Consensus can disintegrate easily with each new case.

SHC archivists hold widely different views of what constitutes sensitive material and of what length of lapsed time is sufficient to consider even the most sensitive information unlikely to harm. We can agree that a person's rights to privacy are those suggested by the liberties afforded and protected in constitutional amendments and that those rights end with death.[18] In death, an individual is no longer a legal persona with constitutional rights and therefore cannot be deprived of rights within the constitutional or statutory framework. Privacy is a living individual's right that cannot be legally transferred to others or claimed by survivors following death. Survivors do have their own rights to privacy, and although it is difficult to do, they can seek remedy for damages that stem from the tarnishing of a deceased family member's reputation. The maxim that privacy ends with death offers a community standard for assessing the sensitivity of information held in an archival collection, but it is a guideline rife with problems, providing little ethical or methodological relief for archivists concerned with both privacy and access. Moreover, the death dates of the tens of thousands of mostly obscure individuals represented in the collections are rarely, if ever, known. Archivists can open even the most private records dating earlier than 1900 with absolute certitude that the persons represented in the collections are deceased, but this cut-off date, although ethically safe and methodologically possible, is too conservative for a repository with rich twentieth-century collections and a growing body of twenty-first-century holdings. The SHC has, thus, adopted the U.S. Census Bureau's standard and will not restrict or redact materials that are more than seventy-two years old in order to protect privacy.[19] Collections containing newer materials are then evaluated on a case-by-case basis.

A case-by-case methodology leaves individual archivists to wrestle with their own ethics and those of their colleagues. SHC archivists can collectively agree on an ethical perspective to err on the side of access, but may differ on when and for which individual collections this ethic should prevail. One SHC archivist recently drew the line at a post–World War II letter, which identified a soldier by his full name and stated that he had contracted a venereal disease. Most of her colleagues felt the distance in time was sufficient to warrant leaving the letter in place without restriction or redaction and cited the prevalence of venereal disease in the armed services at the time. Another archivist found a mid-1970s letter to a judge noting the rape of the letter writer's adolescent daughter, whom he named; he also named the city and the date on which the crime was committed. The research archivist who discovered the item wanted to redact a copy and close the un-redacted original document for a period sufficient to cover the woman's lifetime. Others were unalarmed despite the document's relatively recent date. They pointed to the high potential for a judge's collection being rife with many more such disclosures that the staff did not have the resources to track down.[20] These archivists did not see sufficient cause to worry over one found item—archivists cannot and do not find everything—and suggested that because the collection has been open, unrestricted, and heavily used for more than a decade, it was too late to worry about preventing this disclosure. Still others argued that the responsibility rests with researchers, who must exercise sound ethics and not use sensitive information carelessly or maliciously. Furthermore, archivists should not impose themselves or their biases on what constitutes sensitive information and should remain neutral and objective.

The counterargument is, of course, that the archivist's objectivity and neutrality are myths. Subjectivity and biases are built into the entire archival process, starting with the curator's decision to accession a collection, through the processing archivist's choices of topics to emphasize in finding aids, to the research archivist's assessment that a particular collection is or is not worthwhile for a researcher's project. Archivists cannot escape their individual ethics or their cultural, generational, and gender biases when choosing to restrict, redact, close, or turn away and do nothing. All are agonizing and deliberate choices.

The seemingly least agonizing choice to turn away and do nothing proves untenable when information is potentially dangerous, even life threatening. Few archivists will argue with the need to restrict or redact the names and addresses of former abortion clinic employees in a collection from the late twentieth century. But some do, seeing such measures as pushing in a wedge and leading to vetting of all information in collections of the recent past. Even if we can agree on restricting the abortion clinic employee list—which we cannot—then we still disagree on innumerable other situations, and we arrive back at square one again and again.

Neither the seek-and-restrict approach nor the turn-away-and-do-nothing approach appeases the archivist's ethics because the former threatens access, the latter privacy. It is difficult to make the decision to restrict or leave open documents and even more difficult to trust the wisdom of a decision. Restrictions imposed decades ago or even five years past often seem overly cautious, and redaction feels perilously close to censorship. Nearly all current SHC archivists regard a decision made fifteen years ago to restrict portions of an openly gay man's collection as prudish (the archivists at that time worried about outing identified second and third parties represented in the collection). The same archivists are currently more divided on a case that arose five years ago in which a document made clear that a letter writer was not out to his wife and children. The SHC wanted to close access to the document for the lifetime of the second party to protect the privacy of the individual as well as his family. The openly gay donor objected to any restrictions and withdrew the document from the collection. No archivist wants to be the prude or the censor of tomorrow, but neither does any archivist want to risk damaging someone's life today when sensitive information is revealed. We must trust ourselves to make the appropriate decisions, recognizing that the decision may suit the case today but be viewed as wrong by succeeding generations of archivists. No archivist-imposed restriction should ever be irreversible.

Preventative Solutions

Redaction is one possible solution to graying out the black-and-white difference between unfettered access and no access. To redact a document, an archivist first scans the original documents and prints paper copies. Next, the archivist marks out identifying information—personal names, social security numbers, and street addresses at a minimum—on the paper copies. The original documents are then stored separately and closed for a specified period of time. The redacted copies are made available for research.

Redaction, though, has many drawbacks both for archivists and for researchers. First, it is a time-consuming process. In one experiment, a research archivist spent three hours redacting a single folder of medical case studies in the records of the Mississippi health clinic records. Redacting identifying information from the dense narratives required a close reading of all 180 pages of the documents. Aside from the time it takes, the real struggle is answering the question of how much redaction is appropriate and how much is too much. The goal is to mark out enough to protect privacy, but not so much that valuable information and context are obscured and the documents rendered useless. HIPAA offers a standard; it requires the protection of all individually identifying information. However, SHC archivists are reluctant to suppress all of HIPAA's eighteen personal identifiers, including geographic units smaller than a state and "any other unique, identifying characteristic."[21] At a certain point in the removal of identifying information, the documents may become utterly useless to the researcher. For example, the medical case studies demonstrate the significant loss of context with even the most minimal of redaction. Staff decided to mark out only the personal names and street addresses (Social Security numbers do not appear in these records). The redaction of names resulted in the loss of the familial relationships and the crucial context for understanding the living conditions and sociological context.

> [redacted] is a very alert and curious boy. He goes to Head Start every day and likes it very much. . . . He sets a very good example for [redacted] and [redacted]. . . . He is particularly good with [redacted]. . . . There is no question that [redacted]'s behavior is the major problem in the [redacted] family. It is a problem which involves all of the children because [redacted] and [redacted] will play a critical role in helping [redacted].

The redaction also made the diagnoses and prognoses of individuals within a family impossible to follow.

> Mrs. [redacted] is the key person if [redacted] and [redacted] are going to improve their health. She recognized that both children were ill and took the responsibility for taking care of them. . . . Mrs. [redacted] is aware of [redacted]'s disease process. She feels that there was something born in [redacted] that has made her sick. . . . She also understands that [redacted]'s recovery process will be a very long one. . . . The prognosis in this case depends a great deal on Mrs. [redacted]. . . . But I do not think that Mrs. [redacted] realizes that [redacted] particularly needs a great deal of attention and love.[22]

Redaction may make the writing of some recent history impossible without restricting the scope of the inquiry or organizing the research in such a way as to avoid redacted material. Some research will require access to all the information. The SHC staff does not vet researchers or their research, and we do not want to decide whose research requires access to unredacted documents. Here, we want an all-or-nothing approach; either anyone or no one can examine a collection. Determining the exceptions to a "no one policy" is a responsibility we would eagerly shift to others, particularly a reputable, certified professional entity such as an Institutional Review Board (IRB) of an academic institution. With an IRB approval in hand, a researcher could have access to the unredacted documents. An IRB would carefully consider the intended uses of information gathered on human subjects, and the researcher who obtains an IRB approval would be bound to the strictures imposed by the IRB.

Yet like redaction, a policy requiring IRB approval raises more questions than it answers. With the notable exception of oral historians, most humanities scholars are unlikely to be familiar with the approval processes. An IRB policy would exclude independent researchers unaffiliated with an academic institution. Will those with access to an IRB bother to navigate the lengthy process? Will an IRB, which chiefly examines research requests for social or medical science studies that involve human subjects, even entertain a request for approval to conduct archival research? These unanswered questions and the disparity of access have ended the discussion of an IRB approval system at the SHC. As a result, the access and use restrictions on the Mississippi health clinic records stand as written until they expire or until an ambitious researcher finds another way into the collection.

A couple of years ago, one such researcher requested access to a collection documenting African American students placed in private college preparatory schools in the 1970s. The files, compiled by the charitable foundation that sponsored placement, contain information about each student's academic progress and socioeconomic background. The SHC is not required under FERPA to protect this student information that was not created at UNC. Nevertheless, the SHC decided to protect the privacy of these students, now middle-aged adults, and closed the records for seventy years from the date of creation. Undeterred by the restriction, the researcher identified the students from the foundation's published reports and independently located the individuals. She requested and obtained explicit written permission to view the individuals' files and gained access as allowed by FERPA. This researcher's efforts yielded access for her project, but provided no benefits to other researchers. The next researcher who wants to review the same sources either to reinterpret her work or to use them in a wholly different way will need to retrace the same steps unless the SHC revisits and then removes the restriction.

Redaction and permissions from second or third parties, although largely unsatisfying solutions, are the available options for restricted materials already held by the SHC. For newly acquired collections, the SHC must strike a balance between privacy and access that does not close avenues of research into the recent past. Collecting materials that cannot be made available for research within a reasonable amount of time is contrary to the ethic of access, but it is irresponsible to the annals of history to refuse collections of the recent past because they raise privacy concerns. In donor negotiations, the curator must emphasize the SHC's commitment to access while at the same time alerting donors to privacy issues and associated risks. Donors then need to play a role in identifying sensitive materials. At the request of donors, the SHC archivists have removed or restricted legal documents, such as client case files and materials containing information about children. When donors seek, intentionally or unintentionally, to sanitize the historical record, the SHC archivists negotiate alternatives. For example, the SHC recently processed a collection of family papers in which a discussion of divorce notably appears in the correspondence and as such is described in the finding aid. The donor, an octogenarian, requested that the description of divorce be suppressed so as not to embarrass anyone in the family, but the person whom she was presumably protecting, her son, a man in his sixties, was unconcerned and quipped that his mother was probably worried about his divorces. From one generation to the next, members of the same family disagree about what is private at a given point in time and what should remain private in perpetuity. It will be incumbent on the curator to have explicit conversations with donors, some of whom will perceive divorce, children born out of wedlock, homosexuality, and interracial relationships as taboo and thus private. The curator should be sensitive to these feelings while acting to limit donor-imposed restrictions on documents that reveal this type of "private" information.

At other times, donors may not see any need for a restriction when archivists do. A few years ago, the SHC acquired the papers of a Chapel Hill writer whose diary might modestly be described as erotica. The diarist wrote frequently of her professional relationship and extramarital sexual encounters with another well-known local writer and intellectual. The diary includes hand-drawn illustrations and photographs of his genitalia and letters to her. Per the donor agreement with the diarist's estate, the collection is open for research. But in the decision to let this collection "cool off" and to offer some measure of privacy protection to her still-living lover, the processor did not identify him in the collection's finding aid. This suppression of information diminishes the contextual details available to researchers, thus compromising intellectual access, but the diary is open for use by researchers. Despite its sanitized description, the ethic of access has prevailed. But now sensitive information is out there for use and misuse by researchers who may mistake the diary's availability for the endorsement of its use. Researchers must be aware of the risks of using sensitive information and the lack of vetting done by the archivists.

The obvious time to start raising awareness and educating the researchers is before they enter the reading room. The SHC's finding aids include a carefully crafted privacy notification statement approved by legal counsel.[23] The SHC's reader agreement carries the same statement, and researchers must sign the agreement prior to gaining access to materials. However, staff frequently observe researchers signing the agreement without reading it. Casual researchers simply want to view the manuscript materials as quickly as possible, and the more experienced users assume they already know the rules. The SHC staff considered putting the notification on call slips and on posters in the search room, but ultimately decided that the omnipresence of the notification diluted the message, much as the copyright notifications on photocopiers have become a part of the background we no longer notice. Signatures on the forms and ubiquitous notifications could protect the SHC if it became party to a legal suit, but they do not guarantee the researchers' recognition of the risks and legal implications.

Verbal notification is another means to raise awareness. SHC archivists alert researchers to privacy concerns in collections with known sensitive materials during research consultations. Of course, not all sensitive information is known to the SHC archivists, and the majority of professional historians do not consult with the archivists until permission letters are required by publishers.[24]

The SHC has considered adding the privacy notification statement to the permission letter provided to researchers, but at this stage, it is probably too late to raise awareness about the travails of privacy. The author has likely put the book or essay to rest, and the idea of revising potentially large portions of text or diluting illustrative examples by stripping all identifying information to protect privacy concerns will be unbearable. As a result, the researcher might choose to ignore admonitions about the uses of sensitive materials and the potential harm of publishing private information without the permission of a donor or second or third party. Although some privacy transgressions will be inconsequential, others could lead to lawsuits, and if not meeting the libelous threshold, could still cause irreparable damage to the reputations of second or third parties, donors, and ultimately the SHC.

Reactive Solutions

The Southern Historical Collection responds quickly to all invasion-of-privacy complaints, including those from donors and from second and third parties who played no role in the collection's placement in the SHC. Archivists will make every effort to resolve privacy concerns for living individuals who complain that their privacy was invaded by exposure in the reading room or online. Resolutions, however, are the results of a staff member's judgment on the particular set of circumstances, rather than the application of policies or the interpretation of precedents. For example, an individual who discovered letters he had written in a public figure's collection demanded that they be returned. Here, property rights provided cover for the tough, negative response the curator had to give. Letters are the physical property of the recipient, who can transfer ownership, and although the correspondent retains copyright to the documents he authored, he has no valid claim to the physical letters themselves. The curator denied the request to return the letters but chose to close the correspondence for the lifetime of the complainant plus ten years.

His privacy concerns may well have been compelling, but should every similar complaint result in the closure of a collection or portion thereof? What constitutes "compelling"? The solution—embargo for a lifetime plus ten years—placated this complaining individual, but is it always or ever necessary? It saddles the SHC staff with the responsibility of ascertaining death dates before opening portions of collections and robs researchers of complete collections.

The SHC has not yet had a complaint about invasion of privacy from a third party. One third party visited on multiple occasions to "read about myself" in the diaries of a recently deceased local politician who wrote extensively about his personal relationships. The researcher did not share any discoveries with archivists, nor did he request the removal or closure of the diaries. But someday the SHC will receive a compelling request because the person's private life is invaded in a life-altering or reputation-threatening way. How the SHC responds may depend on researchers' willingness to share the responsibility for identifying sensitive information and for protecting privacy.

Competing ethics of access and protection of privacy present daily challenges to the SHC staff and will continue to do so, especially as the recent past becomes a specific and defined field of interest for historians. Neither access nor privacy can trump all other considerations, and no one can shoulder all the responsibility for upholding both ethics. To meet these challenges, archivists, donors, and researchers must move to a new paradigm, one in which we share that responsibility.

Archivists must relinquish some control by resisting the urge to over-restrict, rejecting the role of gatekeeper, and trusting researchers to respect privacy when they discover sensitive information. Archivists must communicate with donors and researchers to teach them about sensitive information and privacy concerns and do so at the appropriate points in the donation or research processes. With guidance from the curators, donors must identify sensitive information in their collections and recommend appropriate disposition of documents with privacy concerns. Archivists must also recognize that notions of what constitutes private and sensitive are in a continuous state of flux, and they should be willing to revisit restrictions that are unnecessary or excessive in today's context—such as protecting an adult's sexual identity with a seventy-five-year closure.

Historians who study the recent past must reciprocate by using sensitive materials responsibly. At the outset of a project that will incorporate manu-scripts documenting individuals' lives, historians will want to familiarize themselves with privacy laws of the relevant states as well as the pertinent federal laws such as FERPA and HIPAA. Historians should be alert to privacy concerns during their archival research and remember that archivists have not vetted every piece of paper or every byte of electronic data. Examining private lives through the lens of what a reasonable person of today would want to protect from public view will help historians to recognize potentially sensitive information and to determine if and how to use it. In choosing to use sensitive information in a publication, historians need to consider the impact of public disclosure on an individual's life. With the full-text search capabilities of Google Books and electronic journals, scholarly works no longer have practical obscurity, and individuals could easily find their names and private information cited in a monograph with even a small press run. Given the amplified digital environment in which we live, eliminating or masking names to make private information anonymous is an option to be weighed. Of course, some individuals will be too central to the scholarly work to render them anonymous. In such cases, historians will need to strike some balance between protecting individuals' privacy and preserving the integrity of their scholarship.

Historians should also teach their students about ethical practices in archival research. All too often, history graduate students are left to their own devices to "figure out" the travails of archival research, an approach that might suffice for U.S. historians of the distant past who work with eighteenth- and nineteenth-century letters. Historians of the recent past, however, need guidance in both archival research methodologies and the use of sources with sensitive information. Archivists can provide some of this guidance. Academic historians and graduate advisors need to provide opportunities for archivists to teach historians in training, recognizing that archivists have more to offer than just access to content. Archivists could present in historical methodology courses to students in a variety of specialties and fields and provide illustrative examples that would be useful beyond the subject specialty of the repository.

If we are to open the archives on the recent American past, we need all parties, including donors, to acknowledge the critical value of the ethic of access and the ethic of privacy. Neither can supplant the other; we need both. We also need partners in the historian community who, with us, will develop, adopt, and disseminate responsible practices to sustain these ethics. Historians of the recent American past are natural allies for the endeavor, and we invite them to join this partnership sooner rather than later.

Notes

The authors wish to gratefully acknowledge their colleagues, particularly Jackie Dean and Matt Turi, in the Southern Historical Collection, who contributed time and energy to our many discussions on privacy and access.

1. A second party is a creator (e.g., a letter writer) who has had no agency in the disposition of the document (i.e., its inclusion in an archival collection) that he or she created. A third party is a person represented in the collection (e.g., the subject of a document), but who is not a donor or a creator.

2. The SHC applied a seventy-year restriction to all sensitive materials, including health and student records, which required closure for the lifetime of the individual affected. The seventy-year restriction on student records has since been expanded to seventy-five years for new collections in accordance with the policy used by UNC Chapel Hill's University Archives and recommended by University Counsel.

3. "Code of Ethics for Archivists," Society of American Archivists, 2005, http://www .archivists.org/governance/handbook/app_ethics.asp. See also "ACRL/SAA Joint Statement on Access to Research Materials in Archives and Special Collections Libraries," Association of College and Research Libraries, Society of American Archivists, 2009, http://www.ala.org/ala/mgrps/divs/acrl/standards/jointstatement.cfm.

4. See for example: Karen M. Benedict, *Ethics and the Archival Profession: Introduction and Case Studies* (Chicago: Society of American Archivists, 2003) and Menzi L. Behrnd-Klodt and Peter J. Wosh, eds., *Privacy and Confidentiality Perspectives: Archivists and Archival Records* (Chicago: Society of American Archivists, 2005).

5. Joseph Grégoire de Roulhac Hamilton, "The Significance and Value of a Great Southern Collection at the University of North Carolina" (unpublished essay, ca. 1920s), record group no. 40052, Manuscripts Department, University Archives, Louis Round Wilson Special Collections Library, University of North Carolina at Chapel Hill.

6. For a discussion of Hamilton's motivations and the SHC's impact on historiography, see Thavolia Glymph, "The Southern Historical Collection and Civil War and Reconstruction History: A Past and a Future" (presented at *Southern Sources: A Symposium Celebrating Seventy-Five Years of the Southern Historical Collection*, March 18–19, 2005), Louis Round Wilson Special Collections Library, http://www.lib.unc.edu/mss /shc/southern_sources_intro.html.

7. Not all archives are open to all researchers. Many valuable research collections are held by privately funded libraries, and access to those materials is at the discretion of the curatorial staff. Some repositories require users to hold a PhD, to be a published author, or to possess a letter of introduction from a notable scholar.

8. "Research and Instruction Ethos" (unpublished internal document, 2005–9), Southern Historical Collection, Louis Round Wilson Special Collections Library.

9. In 2007 the SHC launched a two-year grant project funded by the Andrew W. Mellon Foundation, titled "Extending the Reach of Southern Sources: Proceeding to Large-Scale Digitization of Manuscript Collections." The aims of the project were to explore mass digitization and online presentation of all items in entire collections—rather than boutique digitization of carefully chosen documents—and to develop and establish an SHC digitization program. A selection process proved crucial to building a sustainable digitization program. Following lengthy discussions with scholars of the U.S. South and input from leading archival professionals, including legal experts in intellectual property, project and SHC staff created a complex "decision matrix" to guide the selection of collections for digitization. Among the factors affecting a collection's placement in the digitization queue are the date spans of the collection materials, copyright, and the knowledge of or the potential for inclusion of sensitive materials that might invade the privacy of second or third parties or donors.

10. Mark A. Greene and Dennis Meissner, "More Product, Less Process: Revamping Traditional Archival Processing," *American Archivist* 68 (Fall/Winter 2005): 208–63.

11. An "average" large collection might occupy seventy linear feet of shelf space.

12. The Health Insurance Portability and Accountability Act (HIPAA) was passed by Congress on August 21, 1996, but the regulations were not finalized according to the time schedule set up by the act. Enforcement, with penalties for noncompliance, began on April 14, 2003. "Research Repositories, Databases, and the HIPAA Privacy Rule," National Institutes of Health, U.S. Department of Health and Human Services, 2004, http:// privacyruleandresearch.nih.gov/research_repositories.asp.

13. For information on the Family Educational Rights and Privacy Act of 1974 see Family Educational Rights and Privacy Act Regulations, U.S. Department of Education, 2009, http://www2.ed.gov/policy/gen/reg/ferpa/index.html; North Carolina State Personnel Act, Privacy of State Employee Personnel Records, N.C.G.S. § 126–22 et seq., North Carolina General Assembly, North Carolina General Statutes, 2010, http:// www.ncga.state.nc.us/EnactedLegislation/Statutes/PDF/ByArticle/Chapter_126/Article _7.pdf.

14. A covered entity must protect private health information in perpetuity, but researchers can gain access to private health information of decedents if certain conditions are met. See "Research Repositories."

15. "Legal and Ethical Implications of Large-Scale Digitization of Manuscript Collections: A Symposium Hosted by the Southern Historical Collection," February 12, 2009, Louis Round Wilson Special Collections Library, University of North Carolina at Chapel Hill.

16. In a June 2008 privacy case involving Cornell University Library, a U.S. district court judge of the Southern District of California dismissed a suit in which a complainant asserted that the university libeled him and disseminated private information about him online when it digitized past issues of the *Cornell Chronicle*. The March 1983 issue of the *Chronicle* contained information about the complainant's involvement in campus thefts. The complainant went to court when the library refused to remove information about him from the online version of the *Chronicle*. The court dismissed the suit on the grounds that the university's exercise of free speech and freedom of the press from punitive lawsuits was protected by the California anti-strategic lawsuit against public participation (anti-SLAPP) statute; furthermore, the complainant was defamed because the information in the *Chronicle* was substantially true and newsworthy. Bill Steele, "Libel Lawsuit over 1983 Chronicle News Item Is Dismissed," *Chronicle Online*, Cornell University, June 9, 2008, http://www.news.cornell.edu/stories/June08/VanGsuit.ws.html.

17. For a discussion of the impact of archival records on public policy and the need for access to ensure government accountability, see Tywanna Marie Whorley, *The Tuskegee Syphilis Study: Access and Control over Controversial Records* (PhD diss., University of Pittsburgh, 2006).

18. For example, the first amendment's protections suggest an individual's right to privacy of beliefs, and the protections of the fourth amendment indicate an individual's privacy for the body and for possessions. For a fuller discussion of privacy rights in the archival context, see Heather MacNeil, *Without Consent: The Ethics of Disclosing Personal Information in Public Archives* (Lanham, Md.: Scarecrow, 1992).

19. "In keeping with the Census Bureau's commitment to confidentiality, the Census Bureau information collected in the Decennial Census of Population and Housing on individuals does not become available to the public until after 72 years." "Genealogy," U.S. Census Bureau, 2009, http://www.census.gov/genealogy/www/.

20. Judicial collections frequently contain correspondence from prisoners and victims of crimes.

21. The eighteen identifiers are enumerated at section 164.514(b)(2) of the regulations: "The following identifiers of the individual or of relatives, employers, or household members of the individual must be removed: (1) Names; (2) all geographic subdivisions smaller than a state, except for the initial three digits of the ZIP code if the geographic unit formed by combining all ZIP codes with the same three initial digits contains more than 20,000 people; (3) all elements of dates except year, and all ages over 89 or elements indicative of such age; (4) telephone numbers; (5) fax numbers; (6) email addresses; (7) social security numbers; (8) medical record numbers; (9) health plan beneficiary numbers; (10) account numbers; (11) certificate or license numbers; (12) vehicle identifiers and license plate numbers; (13) device identifiers and serial numbers; (14) URLS; (15) IP addresses; (16) biometric identifiers; (17) full-face photographs and any comparable images; (18) any other unique, identifying characteristic or code, except as permitted for re-identification in the Privacy Rule." "Research Repositories."

22. Excerpt of family case study in the Delta Health Center Records, no. 4613, Southern Historical Collection, Louis Round Wilson Special Collections Library.

23. The privacy notification statement reads, "Manuscript collections and archival records may contain sensitive or confidential information that is protected under federal or state right to privacy laws and regulations, the North Carolina Public Records Act (N.C.G.S. § 132 1 et seq.), and Article 7 of the North Carolina State Personnel Act (Privacy of State Employee Personnel Records, N.C.G.S. § 126–22 et seq.). Researchers

are advised that the disclosure of certain information pertaining to identifiable living individuals without the consent of those individuals may have legal ramifications (e.g., a cause of action under common law for invasion of privacy may arise if facts concerning an individual's private life are published that would be deemed highly offensive to a reasonable person) for which the University of North Carolina at Chapel Hill assumes no responsibility."

24. With few exceptions, the SHC does not hold rights to its collections beyond those pertaining to the physical property. However, if a collection is unrestricted, staff will write a "permission" letter stating that the SHC has "no objection to the plans described." The letter also contains the preferred citation and copyright notification. The SHC will refuse "permission" only if the collection carries a donor restriction that prohibits the "plans described" in the researcher's or publisher's request. The letter with boilerplate text approved by University Counsel does not actually grant any permission because the SHC cannot provide permission for rights it neither owns nor holds.

GAIL DRAKES

Who Owns Your Archive?

Historians and the Challenge of Intellectual Property Law

I SHOULDN'T HAVE TO VIOLATE federal law to give a paper at a major history conference. The plan was to present my work on how copyright law had been used to prevent and allow use of civil rights movement images, and to what end, as part of a panel at the annual meeting of the American Historical Association. I ended with a mention of the 2001 television commercial for Alcatel Americas (the domestic arm of a French company that builds voice and data networks), in which the special effects team from Industrial Light and Magic—the wizards that brought us *Star Wars*—took footage from the 1963 March on Washington and digitally removed all the participants in the march from the National Mall. Everyone is gone except Martin Luther King, Jr., who is shown at a podium giving the "I Have a Dream" speech to a reflecting pool.[1] This controversial ad—which was made with the permission of the King estate—must be seen to be believed. But how could I get my hands on the commercial? I couldn't find it in any archive, and there was no clear means by which I could request access to it from the company. Furthermore, such a request might very well be refused, given the level of negative publicity the ad had received.

Despite all these challenges, I still managed to find a copy of the commercial—via YouTube. A grainy low-resolution version of the Alcatel advertisement is (as of this writing) available on YouTube, compliments of the AdClub of Boston—who uploaded a copy of it as an example of the quality advertising work coming out of Arnold Worldwide, the agency that created the spot for Alcatel.[2] Could I show the video via YouTube during the presentation? No. Although the panel members assumed that there would be wireless Internet access available in the conference center, the signal was spotty at best. I could *describe* the ad, as I've done here, but I couldn't help but feel that my description would never make my point as effectively as would evidence of the authorized erasure of the activists, organizers, and everyday people that made the civil rights movement possible. So in an act that was possibly a violation of U.S. copyright law and probably a violation of YouTube's "Terms of Use," I used a software program that allowed me to download the video from the site, and I screened it at the end of my presentation.[3] Several members of the audience gasped audibly as they saw the image of King standing at the front of the empty Mall.

This essay highlights just a few examples of the friction between historical scholarship and intellectual property (IP) law, drawing on my own research on the construction of contemporary African American historical memory. What is the connection between the two? It's a fair question. Of all the clauses in the U.S. Constitution that have been vigorously debated for their significance to the lives of black people in the United States, I recognize that the so-called copyright clause—tucked in the list of congressional powers just after the authority to create post offices and a little before the responsibility to punish piracy on the high seas—is rarely among them.[4] But it might be time for that to change. I would argue that for African Americans, among whom the ability to find and share information about their collective past has been an ongoing struggle, the fate of the "cultural commons" is an issue worthy of concentrated attention.

What are the connections between IP law and the work of historians more generally? They are more extensive than any of us might think and become even more relevant for scholars of contemporary history. Access to the surviving traces of the past is at the heart of historical research. Threats to that access in the United States have taken many forms, from poorly indexed collections in underfunded archives to government reluctance to grant access to documents related to controversial moments in the nation's history. But the last decades of the twentieth century saw the growth of a somewhat unexpected threat: the utilization of copyright and other IP laws to assert private ownership of historical materials to regulate (or refuse) use of materials. During this time, more and more of the sources that could enrich the work of historians of the recent past have been claimed as "intellectual property" by individuals and media corporations, making the work of quality historical scholarship that much more difficult, as scholars attempt to tie their arguments to the evidence they have actually used or wish to use.

While the significant expansion of copyright law since the mid-1970s is in many regards reason enough for concern, it is only one reflection of an even more widespread tendency to view information as private property and as a source of potential profit. This commodification of information (often by parties who had no role in creating it) can create significant challenges for historians in general, but the possible threats to the work of those of us studying the late twentieth and early twenty-first centuries are generally unexplored. Historians of the recent past are far more likely to encounter media corporations who charge exorbitant fees to those who wish to use the archive of news footage owned by the corporation. In other instances, those who study recently deceased individuals must deal with family members (and other interested individuals) who can now more easily use copyright and "right of publicity" laws to maintain, protect, or polish the image of a family member posthumously. For those of us whose work focuses on the recent past, issues of privacy, pride, and profit can loom large among the challenges we face in our work.

I admit that the vagaries of IP law were the furthest things from my mind as I began my dissertation on African American history and collective memory. But as I began to conduct my research, I soon realized that my project was as much about understanding my lack of access to sources as it was about the use of sources available to me. For those of us whose work focuses on the history of people of color in the United States (or on any group whose historical traces have not always been preserved and archived), this is a familiar story. But unlike those moments when I had found that the materials I needed no longer existed, I now found myself with a very different challenge. The materials I needed to move forward in my work existed—in some cases they had been carefully archived and catalogued—but were often inaccessible to me due to the cost of accessing the archive, the private ownership of the documentation I wanted to review, or legal concerns about the intellectual property rights of the historical subjects. I soon realized that this inaccessibility and the forces that had caused it were part of the story I wanted to tell. To understand what had influenced the shape of contemporary collective memories of the 1960s, I needed to better understand the evolution of United States copyright law since the 1970s.

Fortunately, as I made this realization, I also came to find out about the wide variety of provocative scholarship on the cultural effects of IP law. In the past decade, scholars such as Siva Vaidhyanathan, Kembrew McLeod, and Lawrence Lessig have documented critical issues in the field and the limits that copyright can put on creative and intellectual production.[5] In 2010 historian Adrian Johns offered a comprehensive history of intellectual property debates, which follows the concept of "piracy" from the birth of print culture in the fifteenth century to the reign of the Internet in the twenty-first.[6] Other work, both within and outside of the historical discipline, has made important contributions to this growing literature. Eva Hemmungs Wirtén's *Terms of Use: Negotiating the Jungle of the Intellectual Commons* (2008) and *No Trespassing: Authorship, Intellectual Property Rights, and the Boundaries of Globalization* (2004) put questions regarding copyrights and the cultural commons in both historical and global perspective, while Eduardo Peñalver and Sonia Katyal's *Property Outlaws: How Squatters, Pirates, and Protesters Improve the Law of Ownership* (2010) helpfully argues for the role of resistance in the forming and reforming of IP law. Martha Woodmansee's studies of authorship explore the shifting meaning of a concept fundamental to copyright, and Ann Bartow's work, including her important 2006 essay, "Fair Use and the Fairer Sex: Gender, Feminism and Copyright Law," provides an important feminist intervention into a field where questions of gender (or race, for that matter) generally go unmentioned.[7]

It is in part thanks to the work of these authors and scholars (as well as those writing in fields as varied as fan fiction, library science, and public health) that the conversation about the cultural significance of IP law has moved beyond discussion of peer-to-peer file-sharing networks and music sampling in rap music into a more complicated interdisciplinary scholarly conversation about the significance of the public domain and the cultural commons. Yet despite the diversity of the literature in the field, I have been struck by how little mention there is of what the transformation in the IP landscape means to historians, or the challenge that the commodification of information poses to the goals of teaching and research more generally.

Although the right of the U.S. Congress to grant copyright protection is mentioned in the Constitution, the notion of copyright has been with us far longer than that, with Western antecedents traced back to the Statute of Anne in 1710.[8] While the expansion of copyright law that began with the Copyright Act of 1976 and the growing popularity of the notion of intellectual property are at the heart of the challenges many of us who study the recent past will face, the idea that historical artifacts are private property has been an issue faced by historians for centuries. For years, private collectors have been able to purchase and display a wide variety of important documents and items of historical value. Current restrictions to access are not simply tied to the wishes of an individual collector (although the wishes of the individual collector are still very relevant); they are also supported by the increasingly restrictive set of laws that support regulation of access not only to a physical item but also to its image and the information it might contain. So although the notion of private ownership of historical documents, items, and buildings has long been a point of tension for historians, the contemporary period has seen an increase in both the scope and the variety of legal regulations related to access.

Paradoxically, as my conference presentation illustrates, we don't always have permission to use everything we can see. The growth of the Internet has meant not only better access to preexisting sources but an explosion in both the number and type of new sources available to a historian of the recent U.S. past. The Internet has profoundly shifted the "one-to-many" media model to something much closer to a "many-to-many" model that provides insights into the hearts and minds of people that are often not represented in traditional archives. Instead of a few published letters to the editor, there are millions of online reader commentaries on the issues of the day. Blogs, videos, social media networks, and message boards provide an overwhelming amount of information (both insightful and inane) and allow for the possibility of international conversations in a manner we might not have imagined even a decade ago.

The expansion of IP law is a reflection of the more fundamental shift that faces scholars whose sources have come into being during the so-called information age—a historical moment in which the information landscape is dominated by international corporations whose primary mission is to generate a profit by regulating access. In this context, not-for-profit attempts to extract information from that system have become increasingly difficult. The reduced access to information relevant to a historian's work as a result of legislation or corporate policy equals a shrinking of the public domain that can profoundly affect the future of historical scholarship. All of us who require access to evidence and texts—especially nonprint sources created since the 1970s—should consider what the notion of information as private property might mean to our work.

The Changing Face of Copyright Law: How Did We Get Here?

Generally speaking (and perhaps understandably), Supreme Court justices have not busied themselves with writing about historians and the challenges of our craft. It is this fact that made Justice Stephen Breyer's dissent in *Eldred v. Ashcroft*—the 2003 case that challenged the constitutionality of the Copyright Term Extension Act—noteworthy:

> [This Act] threatens to interfere with efforts to preserve our Nation's historical and cultural heritage and efforts to use that heritage, say, to educate our Nation's children. It is easy to understand how the statute might benefit the private financial interests of corporations or heirs who own existing copyrights. But I cannot find any constitutionally legitimate, copyright-related way in which the statute will benefit the public. Indeed, in respect to existing works, the serious public harm and the virtually nonexistent public benefit could not be more clear.[9]

To put this comment in context, we need to make a trip to the not-at-all-distant past: 1998, to be exact, the seventieth anniversary of Mickey Mouse and the year that also marked the passing of pop star–turned-politician Sonny Bono.

It was in that year that the Walt Disney Company took the lead on coordinating lobbying efforts in Washington—to the tune of $6.3 million—in support of extending copyright.[10] They found many a sympathetic ear, including that of representative Sonny Bono of Palm Springs, California. As a musician, Bono was personally invested in the extension of copyright terms that covered his own works and had proposed legislation to that end. According to his wife, Mary, his wish was for copyright to last forever.[11] Despite the unconstitutional nature of this wish, the folks at Disney certainly found common cause with Bono, as did the Hollywood studios, record labels, and publishing associations that joined the effort. Disney sought to have the copyright to the 1928 animated film *Steamboat Willie* extended for the third time.

Why all the fuss over a seventy-year-old cartoon? This cartoon was among the first to introduce the world to the now iconic Disney character of Mickey Mouse. Mickey was scheduled to enter the public domain in 2003, just prior to other notable characters such as Goofy, Donald Duck, and Pluto.

Disney's efforts were successful. With little fanfare or public note the Sonny Bono Copyright Term Extension Act—named after the now deceased representative—was passed by Congress and signed by President Clinton. The act extended the term of protection by twenty years for works copyrighted after January 1, 1923. Works copyrighted by individuals since 1978 received copyright protections for the life of the author, plus an additional seventy instead of fifty years. "Works for hire" (those created by or on behalf of a corporation) were granted copyright for ninety-five years, as were works copyrighted before 1978, regardless of how they were produced.[12] The year 1998 also saw the signing of the Digital Millennium Copyright Act that, among other key provisions, criminalized the production and sale of devices or services that aided in the circumvention of copyright protection measures, as well as the act of circumventing a copyright protection measure.

The implications of the Digital Millennium Copyright Act were far-ranging, prompting a coalition of library associations to express concern about the ways in which the new law prevented the public from accessing lawfully acquired information.[13] This led Congress to request that the Library of Congress review the act with the goal of determining what classes of works should be exempted from the law. In 2000 this office voiced comments about "potential damage to scholarship" and harm to "American creativity" that were unintended consequences of the new law. The report on the act (the first of such reports to be generated every three years) included a comment from the assistant secretary for communications and information in the Department of Commerce, who asserted that the law needed to be amended to

> promote inclusion of all parts of society in the digital economy and prevent
> a situation in which information crucial to supporting scholarship, research,
> comment, criticism, news reporting, life-long learning, and other related law-
> ful uses of copyrighted information is available only to those with the ability to
> pay or the expertise to negotiate advantageous licensing terms.[14]

The Copyright Term Extension Act and Digital Millennium Copyright Act played no small part in expanding the relevance of copyright law and informed the decisions of those who sought to assert more aggressively their intellectual property rights at the start of the twenty-first century.

But legislative changes in the late 1990s were only one step in what had been a decades-long expansion of copyright regulations and of the concept of intellectual property more generally. From the Berne Convention (1988), to the Uruguay Round Agreements Act (1996), to the secret negotiations regarding the Anti-Counterfeiting Trade Agreement (2010), the international forces influencing the expansions in IP law are perhaps even more powerful than Mickey Mouse. Meanwhile, verdicts in cases such as *New York Times v. Tasini* (2001) and *Bender v. West Publishing Company* (1999) have affected what sources are available to scholars.[15]

In any discussion about scholarly use of copyrighted materials there needs to be a mention of the concept of "fair use." The fair use provisions within U.S copyright law allow for the use of protected materials for purposes "such as criticism, comment, news reporting, teaching, scholarship, and research." There are no clear standards about what exactly constitutes fair use—but the law does set out "four factors to be considered in determining whether or not a particular use is fair: 1) The purpose and character of the use, including whether such use is of commercial nature or is for nonprofit educational purposes; 2) The nature of the copyrighted work; 3) The amount and substantiality of the portion used in relation to the copyrighted work as a whole [and]; 4) The effect of the use upon the potential market for, or value of, the copyrighted work."[16] Depending on one's perspective, these factors seem either usefully or frustratingly vague. Whereas the lack of clarity on what constitutes fair use once allowed for considerable leeway in the utilization of the provision, the more aggressive intellectual property climate of the 2000s has made claiming fair use feel far more perilous. Meanwhile, the freedom that the notion of fair use is meant to convey is very often surrounded by a new crop of restrictions on developing and using tools that allow us to access the materials we might hope to fairly use. The concept of fair use is meaningful only if the public knows what is *available* for use—and much of the sources that are born digital exist behind a corporate pay-per-view wall. Fair use is alive—if not in the most robust health—and should be staunchly defended.[17] Yet for a historian of the recent past, the dependence on fair use that has served other scholars is simply not enough.

The ways in which emerging technologies are shifting some of the basics of sharing information for the casual consumer are already becoming clear, but for scholars the implications of this fundamental clash between for-profit and not-for-profit models of access are only now emerging. If someone buys a paperback or hardcover book, that person is free to loan it, sell it, or give it away. However, if that same consumer purchases an e-book (often for the same price as a printed book) that person is often permitted to read the e-book only on hardware created or approved by the company that sold the book, and they do not have the right to resell or even give the book away. In fact, Barnes and Noble initially distinguished its e-book reader, the Nook, from the competition by making it possible for Nook owners to lend an e-book to a friend, presuming the friend also owns a Nook.[18] What might it mean to scholars that the ability to lend a book you "own" to a friend or colleague is perceived as an innovation? What about the attempt of an influential publisher in 2011 to create e-books for libraries that self-destruct after the book has been loaned a certain number of times?

Many of the phenomena I have described are focused on generating income from a consumer, whether that person is a scholar or a general reader. But, as I argued at the beginning of this essay, private ownership has affected access to the archive itself. From the series of auctions, thefts, and threatened lawsuits that have hindered the development of a comprehensive scholarly Malcolm X archive, to the sometimes aggressive claims on the intellectual property of Martin Luther King, Jr., by the King family since his death in 1968, this essay focuses on how intellectual property law and the larger notion of private ownership have affected access to historical artifacts associated with two of the most well-known figures in the modern U.S. civil rights movement. The essay concludes with a discussion of how IP laws affect the availability of audiovisual and digital sources, which are often the central "texts" of recent U.S. history, and some of the ways IP law affects our work as teachers and researchers.

Of Archives and Auction Blocks: Malcolm X

The Malcolm X Project, created by Manning Marable at Columbia University in 2001, sought to create an archive of materials related to the life and work of Malcolm X and to transform the famous *Autobiography of Malcolm X* into a multimedia package that would serve as the spine of an innovative civil rights movement/African American history high school curriculum for New York City public schools.[19] My own work on this exciting project made it increasingly clear that although Malcolm X certainly was one of the most beloved and controversial leaders of the civil rights movement, the amount of historical material about his life and work available to scholars was quite limited. There was no central repository for his papers and no location, digital or analog, where one could find transcripts or recordings of all his speeches. There were several Internet sites devoted to Malcolm X, but these sites were rarely the work of anyone with an academic background in history or African American studies. Those of us working on the Malcolm X project that year learned what Manning Marable—who was in the midst of writing the comprehensive, scholarly biography of the leader that would be published soon after the scholar's tragic death in 2011—already knew: despite the centrality of Malcolm X in both the history and mythology of the black freedom struggle in the 1960s, historians of the contemporary United States had very few accessible historical archives related to the life and work of the charismatic leader.[20]

In the midst of our collective efforts to assemble primary source materials about Malcolm X for the multimedia autobiography, news we received in February 2002 could not have been more of a shock. The Butterfields auction house announced the upcoming sale of a massive collection of personal and movement-related materials that had been the property of Malcolm X. Several phone calls and Internet searches later, many of us at the institute left our computer screens and telephones behind and gathered in the hallways to ask each other the questions that were buzzing in our heads. What Malcolm-related materials would be on the auction block? Were the materials authentic? Many of us involved in the project had been in touch with members of the Shabazz family, and there had been no mention of the sale. Was it possible that a sale of this significance could happen without their knowledge? Some of the researchers thought that there had been some mistake or misunderstanding, and that the rumors of the auction were untrue. But soon the facts became undeniable. Dr. Marable was able to obtain a photocopy of the auction catalog from Butterfields, which contained a vast array of historical artifacts related to Malcolm X. And the items were authentic: according to Malcolm's daughter Ilyasah Shabazz, the objects in the catalog matched the description of items that had been last seen in their (now deceased) mother's home.

That meant that this collection represented the largest and most historically significant group of materials on Malcolm X. According to David Garrow, a civil rights historian at Emory University, the size and scope of the collection was "simply mind-boggling." The historian, known for his groundbreaking biography of Martin Luther King, made the significance of the collection clear: "There are so few truly personal Malcolm documents in public archives that this apparent collection swamps the total corpus of all other materials several times over."[21] Hundreds of pages of handwritten drafts of speeches, personal letters, and photographs were included in the collection, as was the copy of the Koran Malcolm X took on the trip to Mecca that changed his life, as well as journals that detailed his thoughts about his life and his relationship to the Nation of Islam. Two decades of Malcolm X's life was going on sale, grouped in a dozen or so lots, each of which would be sold to the highest bidder. The auction was scheduled for March 20, just one month away, and would be held simultaneously at the San Francisco offices of Butterfields and on the Internet.

Butterfields was already familiar to some of us in the office. The auction house had found itself embroiled in controversy in 1999 when they attempted to auction the bloodstained, bullet-torn diary/address book that Malcolm X had in his coat pocket when he was assassinated in the Audubon Ballroom on February 21, 1965. The auction house claimed that they were able to acquire the book after the New York State Municipal Archives (where evidence from old cases is stored by the district attorney's office) had purged their older materials.[22] After both the Shabazz family and scholars discovered that no such "purge" had occurred and challenged the legitimacy of the sale, Butterfields canceled the auction. It was eventually discovered that the collector who was offering the item had purchased it from a Manhattan Supreme Court clerk who had stolen it in 1991 from a courthouse safe.[23]

So although it was possible to question the legitimacy of the sale based on Butterfields's prior conduct, it seemed unlikely that they would attempt another high profile, large-scale sale of Malcolm X artifacts if they were not fairly confident of their right to do so. Butterfields was initially unwilling to name the owner of the collection, stating only that the individual was not a member of the Shabazz family. But such details were hard to keep secret for very long. The collection was now considered the private property of James Calhoun, who was completely unknown to the Shabazz family. How could it be that the auction house had yet again acquired historical materials of such significance? The answer was a convoluted one, wrapped within a sad tale of family drama, bad decisions, and dumb luck, all of which had moved this significant collection further from access by scholars. And while the story of how these materials ended up on the auction block can hardly be viewed as typical, it still poses critically important questions about how the commodification of historical materials can serve as an impediment to historical research.

In May 1999, the same year Malcolm's stolen diary was discovered, more "unauthorized acquisitions" were occurring. Just two years after the tragic death of Betty Shabazz in a fire set by her grandson, Malcolm's youngest daughter, Malikah, removed many boxes of her father's papers and personal belongings from her mother's home and placed the materials in a rented storage bin at the Public Storage facility in Casselberry, Florida, near Orlando, where they remained until 2001. For reasons that are still unclear,

Malikah neglected to keep her payment for the storage unit current, and in September of that year the storage facility—as is their policy—sold the contents of the abandoned unit to recover the six hundred dollars they were owed. James Calhoun, a local junk dealer, initially had no idea that the items in the unit were important. It was only after the auction was completed that he was able to examine the contents more carefully and understand their potential value.[24] It was at this point that he contacted Butterfields, seeking bidders on his unexpected treasure.

With a date already set for the auction, and having learned that Butterfields planned to sell the items in twenty-one lots (meaning that the items could end up in the hands of multiple individual private buyers), the parties interested in halting the sale needed to work fast or else risk losing access to these items forever. While the Shabazz daughters issued statements to the press, family lawyer Joseph Fleming filed injunctions to verify the ownership of the materials and to stop the sale. Manning Marable, meanwhile, hastily arranged meetings with other scholars and archivists interested in the collection and, with Columbia's provost, attempted to raise the institutional funds that would allow the university to purchase the collection in case the sale could not be prevented.

In fact, the auction of the collection was prevented: there were questions as to whether the storage facility gave Malikah adequate prior knowledge of the sale, and the items were returned to the Shabazz family.[25] Although Columbia University was the home of the Malcolm X Project (which had been endorsed by several of the Shabazz daughters), it was the New York Public Library's Schomburg Center for Research in Black Culture—located on Malcolm X Boulevard in Harlem—that was selected to provide both safekeeping and wide access to the collection.[26] According to the terms of the arrangement, the collection is still owned by the family, but is on loan to the library for seventy-five years. Even if this outcome is better than one that would see these historically significant materials in the hands of private collectors and out of the reach of historians of the black freedom struggle, it is hard to ignore that it is only a legal technicality that prevented the dispersal of this important collection from moving forward.

In other words, the rights of the public were secured only by accident and by the effective action of a dedicated scholar backed by a private university and working with the family of the historical figure. This incident exposes an uncomfortable truth: there is no general right of the public to have access to the archives of a public figure who had a dramatic impact on history.

What rights, if any, should historians or the public have to access the type of historical materials and information represented by this collection? How might these rights be best represented or protected? How is the work of historians—especially historians of the recent American past—connected to the idea of the public domain? While these questions were raised by the Butterfields incident, they were not resolved.

Some in the private sector would argue that their private ownership of historical materials should not be a cause for concern among historians. Shortly before the auction, the *New York Times* reported that Catherine Williamson, director of fine books and manuscripts at Butterfields, claimed that concerns about the sale posing a challenge to historians' access to the materials were unfounded. "I deal every day with libraries and private collectors," she said. "I don't see a big gulf between the two. Every major institution in the country was founded on a collection put together by a private collector, and every responsible collector makes their material available to scholars."[27] But an earlier sale of historically significant Malcolm X materials in 1992, in which unpublished chapters from the *Autobiography of Malcolm X* were sold to a private collector, makes it obvious that private ownership of such documents has very real consequences for historians.

Keeper of the Word: Malcolm X's Autobiography as Private Property

After Alex Haley's death in 1992, many of his personal papers and belongings were sold at auction to settle claims made against his estate. Haley, most famous for his novel *Roots* (1976), which inspired the award-winning miniseries of the same name, had made his mark in the world of African American history and literature a decade earlier, as the coauthor of the best-selling *Autobiography of Malcolm X* (1965).[28] Prior to the Marable biography, the *Autobiography* was the central text on the life of Malcolm X. It has been continually in print since its initial publication, and in 1992 it served as a basis of an Academy Award–winning Spike Lee film that was the catalyst to a nationwide revival of interest in the slain leader of the Nation of Islam. Alex Haley's work as ghostwriter for the book has been a critical issue for those who study Malcolm X. Scholars have delved into the text and archival materials for insights on where the thoughts and insights of Malcolm X end and where the opinion and perspectives of the more conservative Alex Haley begin. The editing of this "autobiography" became even more controversial when it was discovered that Haley was freely providing information about Malcolm X to the FBI during his work on the book and because Malcolm X's death prior to completion of the manuscript meant that he never approved the final text. Correspondence between Haley and the executive editor at Doubleday makes it obvious that both the publisher and editor had goals for the autobiography that differed greatly from that of the civil rights leader.[29]

Given the complicated history of one of the most important autobiographies of the late twentieth century, the opportunity to learn more about the process by which the book was completed and the manuscript itself would be of obvious interest to historians. But when the manuscript and other materials related to the autobiography were auctioned, it was a lawyer, not a scholar or archive, who seized the opportunity to buy a piece of history.

Gregory Reed, a Detroit-based lawyer and founder of the Keeper of the Word Foundation, "with a long and controversial relationship to the purchase and use of materials related to African American history," purchased the manuscript of the *Autobiography of Malcolm X* for $100,000.[30] For $21,500 Reed also purchased the manuscripts and notes related to three chapters that were omitted from the original book.[31] What did Reed have in mind for the missing chapters? Would he donate them to a university archive or a museum of African American history? Would he make them available for scholars interested in the insights on both Haley and Malcolm X that the chapters surely provided? No. Instead, these materials went directly into Reed's personal safe, far from the prying eyes of the public or civil rights movement scholars, where they would sit, largely undisturbed, for almost twenty years.

In his book *Living Black History* (2006), Manning Marable describes the result of his efforts to access the manuscripts for the autobiography and the missing chapters.[32] Upon learning of Reed's purchase of the manuscript and chapters, Marable contacted Reed and after some negotiation, Reed agreed to allow Marable to review them. Marable flew from New York to Detroit and called Reed to let him know that he was on his way to Reed's office. The lawyer instead instructed the historian to meet him at a restaurant. The stated time for the meeting came and went: a half hour later, Reed arrived and announced that he had changed his mind. He was not willing to allow Marable the level of access to the manuscript that had been previously agreed on. Instead, he took selections from the manuscript and told Marable that he could look at the documents in the booth of the restaurant for fifteen minutes. Marable had little choice but to accept terms that violate conventional historical practice. Despite the significance of the chapters to his work and perhaps to African American history, they were Reed's private property and as such he had the right to grant or deny access to the materials as he chose.

Marable set upon the papers to glean what he could in the time available. As it turns out, the missing chapters focus on a key period of Malcolm's life—the period before his split with Nation of Islam, when he clearly questioned Elijah Muhammad's approaches to black liberation and his own role within it. The chapters promised critically important insights into a period of Malcolm's life that was not covered in detail within the published autobiography. That fact also begged the questions of why the chapters were removed from the original manuscript and whether they were removed before or after Malcolm's death. These questions would have to remain unanswered. After the fifteen minutes were up, Reed came back to the booth, picked up the chapters, placed them back in his briefcase, left the restaurant, and returned the manuscript to his safe.[33] More than a decade later, no historian, archivist, or museum curator has been granted access to the manuscript, as far as we know.[34]

That a self-storage facility, secret meetings, stolen merchandise, and Internet auctions figure so prominently in the history of the scattered Malcolm X archive is a sad and strange reality. But while Butterfields and Reed acquired their treasures in different ways, the results easily could have been the same: restricted access to the kinds of materials through which historians create their narratives and society reproduces and transforms its collective memories of the black freedom struggle. What are the implications for historical memory if these materials can be controlled by the highest bidder? While the thefts and purchases of the Malcolm X papers might suggest to some that historians would be better served if personal papers and other artifacts remain controlled by the family, the increasingly tight control of the intellectual and physical property of Martin Luther King, Jr., by his family makes it clear that the desire to profit from the past is not restricted to outsiders.

Protecting a Legacy, Protecting Profits: Martin Luther King, Inc.

Months had passed since I had been awarded a travel grant to visit the university archive that held a significant collection of materials directly related to my dissertation, but I still hadn't received confirmation that I would be able to access the collection. Everyone I was in contact with was very apologetic. The delays had come from an unexpected source: the university's legal counsel had to approve my work in the archive because of concerns about legal action by the estate of Martin Luther King as a result of my research. The King family's history of aggressively protecting the intellectual property rights to everything concerning King meant that the university wanted to ensure they did not make themselves vulnerable to lawsuits by allowing me to view the documents in their possession—documents not by or about Martin Luther King himself, but letters from representatives of the King family, included in the collected papers of the subject of my research. As I waited for word from the university counsel, I couldn't help but reflect on the expansive and chilling effect that the King estate's approach to intellectual property and privacy was having on research on the civil rights movement more generally.

Although the stated goal of the King family has been to protect Martin Luther King's legacy, their increased utilization of intellectual property law in the management of the estate has meant considerable private profits for the family at the expense of access by both historians and the public. Initially, Coretta Scott King sought to consolidate her husband's papers and physical artifacts at the King Center for Nonviolent Social Change in Atlanta, the organization she founded in 1968 after his death. In the years since, the family, and most notably the youngest sibling, Dexter, has expanded their use of intellectual property and right of publicity laws to regulate and profit from the use of King's words, voice, and likeness.

As I waited to use my travel grant, I had time to consider how this delay was an unexpected consequence of the systematic attempts on the part of the King family to consolidate and control materials that had been legally acquired and were open to researchers. A milestone of this decades-long effort came in 1987 when Coretta Scott King filed suit against Boston University, arguing that the estate was the rightful owner of the more than eighty-three thousand pages of King documents held in the university's Special Collections Library. The suit was filed after the university denied Coretta Scott King's repeated requests to remove the documents from their archive so that she could deposit them at the King Center. Although Martin Luther King had presented the documents to the university himself, Mrs. King argued that they had become the property of the estate upon King's death. Mrs. King also claimed that the university was not providing adequate care for the items, citing historians such as King biographer David Garrow, who claimed that the documents were jammed into folders and showing signs of overuse.[35]

Despite the potential embarrassment the lawsuit would bring, Boston University was not willing to give up the collection, even if that involved a fight with the widow of an assassinated civil rights icon. The lawsuit was ultimately unsuccessful, with the judge finding that the King documents were the property of the university.[36] At the heart of Boston University's case was a letter from Martin Luther King, Jr., that, according to the jury, indicated Martin Luther King's intention to offer the papers not just for safekeeping during a tumultuous time in the South but as an outright gift to his alma mater.[37] The ruling meant that the Dr. Martin Luther King, Jr., Archive in the Howard Gotlieb Archival Research Center at Boston University would remain one of the largest collections of King materials available to scholars.[38]

Why the family wanted the return of the papers was not clear, but consolidating the collection may have been only one of their goals. Valued at $30 million by Sotheby's auction house in New York, the King family agreed to give "a $10 million gift to the country" by offering to sell the collection in their possession to the Library of Congress for $20 million, which would be the largest sum ever paid by an institution, especially one that had acquired some of its most important collections through donation.[39] In 1999 a tentative agreement to purchase the collection was made with the family, but despite energetic fund-raising efforts, the money was not raised.[40]

Meanwhile, the papers continued to languish at the King Center, subject to restrictive policies regarding access by scholars and less-than-ideal archival conditions. Coretta Scott King died in January 2006, before she could find a new home for the papers, leaving her children to continue the work of "protecting" the King legacy. Despite the family's repeated claim that it wanted the collection to be housed at Morehouse, the Kings did not reduce their asking price to make the purchase more feasible for the cash-strapped historically black college, and instead decided to place the entire collection up for sale at Sotheby's auction house in 2006. Concerned that the purchase of the papers by a private collector would mean that the original materials would be even harder for scholars to access, historical institutions, libraries, and university archives nationwide attempted to find the money needed to preserve the collection's integrity. In Atlanta, this took the form of a massive fund-raising campaign, involving a wide range of academic and community leaders, politicians, philanthropists, and businesspeople. The group, led by Atlanta mayor Shirley Franklin, raised the money to remove the items from the auction block and donate them to Morehouse.[41]

Despite this happy ending, access problems persist. Because the sale granted Morehouse only the right to house the papers, the intellectual property rights are still held by the King estate. As Phillip Madison Jones, the King family lawyer who brokered the deal, explained in a interview on NPR, the real challenge in having the sale move forward was not the price, but having all parties involved understand what was and was not available for sale: "Some of the complexities involved were . . . making certain that the King family felt that they were going to the right place and that the intellectual property was preserved for all time." He praised Mayor Franklin for her ability to understand that this point was nonnegotiable.[42]

Jones's focus on controlling the intellectual property rights of the King estate represents the family's more general shift toward regulation of access through intellectual property laws rather than physical possession. While the family had spent years seeking the highest bidder on the more tangible remnants of Martin Luther King's life, King's youngest son had begun to shift his attention to the less tangible aspects of the King legacy. Where Martin Luther King had a "dream" for the nation, colleagues and critics of Dexter King have claimed that he has a "vision" for the King estate: a lucrative financial future for the King Center (and for his family), resulting from the expansion and rigorous protection of the King brand, based on the licensing of the King image and use of King quotations.[43]

Under Dexter King's leadership, the King Center has emphasized the potential for profits over the importance of scholarly work and cultural memory. Soon after becoming chair of the center, Dexter traveled to Graceland to meet with the team that manages the intellectual property of Elvis Presley.[44] Subsequently, Dexter helped friends and relatives who shared his interest in building the King brand by moving them into powerful positions within the King organization. He invited his college friend, the aforementioned Phillip Madison Jones, to lead Intellectual Properties Management, the company that manages all intellectual property licensing for the King estate. Dexter's cousin, Issac Newton Farris Jr. assumed the position of president and chief operating officer for the King Center. Soon enough, Dexter King and Phillip Jones announced plans for an interactive museum "attraction" called the "King Dream Center," sponsored by major corporations such as Pepsi and Microsoft.[45] Although that idea was ridiculed in the press as "I Have a Dreamland," Jones and Dexter King were undaunted.[46] "In this new media paradigm," said Jones, "the only way to get [King's message] out there is to do a business deal, where people in the publishing community can package it, put millions of dollars in to market it and make money off it. That's how it works now."[47]

The King Center and Intellectual Properties Management have spent more than a decade crafting multimillion-dollar deals that have determined who is allowed to represent the words or likeness of Dr. King. However, exerting near complete control of the uses of the King name, words, and images is a difficult task. A quick search of the Internet yields hundreds of unlicensed uses of Martin Luther King's intellectual property. However, a recent deal with UK music giant EMI might mean changes on this front. In March 2009, Dexter King announced that having "examined the ever-evolving, global, digital landscape," the King Center had entered an agreement with EMI "to monitor and bring under compliance the unauthorized usages of Dr King's words and intellectual property on the Internet and digital media" to "increase the King Estate's ability to preserve, perpetuate, and protect the great legacy of Martin Luther King, Jr."[48] EMI chairman and chief executive Roger Faxon said in a statement, "Assuring that Dr. King's words are accorded the same protection and same right for compensation as other copyrights works is a profound responsibility, and we are proud of the confidence that the Estate has placed in us to fulfill that responsibility."[49]

There is little doubt that EMI has a great deal of work ahead, as it attempts to prevent unauthorized invocations of Dr. King on the Internet—or that the King estate has high expectations in terms of the aggressive defense of its "right for compensation." Most recently, the estate drew criticism from many when it became known that it was considering lawsuits against street vendors who were selling shirts, buttons, and posters that featured the images of both Dr. King and President Obama.[50] The estate was also requesting licensing fees from the coalition of citizens who were lobbying and fund-raising for a monument to Dr. King on the National Mall. As of this writing, that group has paid the King Center approximately eight hundred thousand dollars in licensing fees for the use of Dr. King's words and likeness in their fund-raising materials.[51]

Uncharted Territory: Teaching and Research
in the Shadows of Intellectual Property Law

Although these stories of auctions, courthouse thieves, and powerful families might seem distant from the issues that most historians face, the policies and laws designed to regulate the use of intellectual property potentially affect all historians of the recent past. These cautionary tales may have an increasing impact on all of us who depend on access to documents, images, and sounds to do our work.

Among the circumstances in which history faculty find themselves dealing directly with questions of copyright is the process of assembling readings for their courses. Those who follow the regulations regarding copyright clearances for course packs may find themselves making tough decisions based on the varied royalty costs for each article. Although some faculty are not aware of (or choose to disregard) the rules regarding reprint permissions for book chapters and journal articles, publishers have become more forceful in their requests for campus compliance with copyright regulations.[52] Cases that involved commercial entities, such as *Princeton University Press v. Michigan Document Services* in 1996, have been an important part of the case law in this area, but more recently faculty and universities have been pulled into the fray. In 2008 Georgia State University was sued by a coalition of university presses claiming that the university provided unlicensed copies of copyrighted material to students through "electronic course packs" and other online services.[53]

And as we find ourselves looking for articles to include in those course packs, historians are now less likely to roam up and down the library stacks looking for a volume of a journal and much more likely to consult one of the online databases to which their campus library subscribes. Yet how many of us stop to consider the ownership structures that are making digital access to these journals possible? Access to the digitized versions of the primary and secondary sources many historians depend on is increasingly centralized, and although databases such as JSTOR are created and maintained by academic institutions, many more are owned by private companies who specialize in providing information to academic institutions and businesses for a fee. The company that maintains the popular ProQuest databases was acquired by the Cambridge Information Group in 2007, with the goal of further expanding the company's dominance in the academic arena. "Serving over 30,000 institutions worldwide," the group boasts on its website that "virtually every college and university located in North America has at least one product or service from a CIG company."[54]

While the convenience and popularity of digitized, searchable collections cannot be denied, this consolidation means that the decision by university libraries whether to subscribe to an individual journal that costs hundreds of dollars has been eclipsed by the need to subscribe to electronic databases that cost tens of thousands of dollars, which exacerbates the already significant access gap between scholars affiliated with colleges and universities with larger library budgets and those who are not. These companies also customize databases based on the school's ability to pay. The name of the database remains the same, but the content included varies. This means that a scholar might find that the results of identical searches of a database owned by a for-profit company could be significantly different when the search is undertaken at a regional state university campus versus a better-funded private research university.

The vast databases of companies such as the Cambridge Information Group are impressive and valuable to the historian, but they are generally restricted to print formats. What of the rich sources made possible by the rise of network television in the mid-twentieth century or the dominance of cable television in the twenty-first? The lack of affordable, comprehensive, accessible not-for-profit audiovisual archives poses a problem to historians of the recent past. Thanks to the Cambridge Information Group, my university-sponsored access to the ProQuest databases means that I can review the full text of the *New York Times* coverage of the stock market crash of 1929; however, obtaining video footage of more contemporary events can be much more difficult and expensive.

Scholars of the recent past draw on a wide variety of sources to do their work, and although those sources may indeed be digitized, not all are accessible. Many of the rich televisual sources that have emerged since the 1970s can be found only behind the pay-per-view walls of the large media corporations that sponsored their creation (or bought the companies that did). The licensing of photographs, news coverage, and film clips has become a multimillion-dollar industry, and the restrictions on these materials for historians is an unintended consequence. Limited access to audiovisual materials is nothing new, but whereas a researcher once had to lament the absence of substantial archives (in the case of much radio and early television broadcasts) or had to negotiate with a local media outlet, historians now often contend with corporate archives that charge by the second for any use of the footage they own.

In the classroom, a professor who wanted students to see the George Holliday footage of Rodney King's encounter with the police might plan to reserve a copy of a documentary on the Rodney King trial from the university library to screen in class. Unfortunately, an increasing number of historical documentary films are out of circulation due to copyright licensing restrictions, and others will never be made due to the chilling effect that media company conglomeration and expansions in copyright law are having on the genre. A notable example of this problem is the classic documentary series, *Eyes on the Prize: America in the Civil Rights Years* (1987), which was largely out of circulation from 1995 until 2005.[55] The filmmaker could afford only the most limited licensing agreement on the hundreds of photographs, news footage, and sound recordings used in the film. Once any one of those agreements lapsed, the entire series was out of compliance with copyright law and could not be broadcast on television, released on DVD, or purchased (with the possible exception of VHS copies being sold for a thousand dollars on eBay or Amazon) until massive fund-raising and activist campaigns led to the rerelease of the film in 2006.[56] Many of the critically acclaimed historical documentaries from the film's production house, Blackside, remain out of circulation for the same reason.

Although access to news footage can be prohibitively expensive, the fact that archives of some television news and entertainment programs even exist, and that others are in development, is a promising development for historians of the recent past. The idea that messages on Twitter are archived by the Library of Congress might seem strange to some, but archived tweets are an affirmation that online sources are important to academic scholarship and that access to them ought not to be privatized.[57] Most rich material available on the Internet is not archived or indexed. With the exception of valuable sites such as the Internet Archive (with its useful Internet Wayback Machine, which archives a wide variety of web pages from 1996 to the present), the Internet lacks a long-term memory.[58] The perpetual present tense of the Internet adds yet another level of complexity to the efforts to use it in serious historical research. The current strength of the Internet is in its ability to facilitate the flow of information, but the means by which that information is stored and organized on the web leaves much to be desired by the historian. Sites such as YouTube—much like Pandora, Hulu, the reformed Napster, or many other popular online music and television sites—allow for streaming of content, but attempts to preserve that flow for scholarly use are often difficult, illegal, or both.

Current copyright restrictions also hamper or constrain innovation in the ways we share our work with others, as well as in the way we teach and learn. In a course I taught on the cultural implications of IP law, the students learned about the history of national and international copyright law, the fundamental concepts of authorship and ownership underlying the notion of intellectual property law, and the limits of the fair use protections in education. With all they had learned, my students came to me with a critical question about their group midterm project: "If the midterm project we create is illegal, is that going to be ... a problem?" As it turned out, one of the projects in the class did push the limits of fair use. The online element of that project managed to receive some positive attention from national and international blogs (including the *New Yorker*). All the students in the course, and their instructor, were excited, proud ... and concerned. Choosing not to tempt fate, the students stopped directing traffic to their site.

It could be argued that historians are not only users of copyrighted materials but also holders of copyright as well. But this privilege is granted due to historians' distance from—not investment in—the current IP regime. As Corynne McSherry argues in "Who Owns Academic Work?," this exception from the current regulations regarding IP is critically important to the maintenance of the privileges college faculty currently enjoy.[59] Historians typically retain authorship and ownership rights to their work due to court rulings based on the idea that much of the academic world exists largely outside the market economy and is sui generis—in a class of its own. If faculty lectures and other writings are understood as the property of the institutions at which we work—as is also the case for the writing and research of college and university staff and administrators—the implications for everything from academic freedom to the increased use of casual faculty labor are wide ranging. With ongoing attempts to make humanities education more "efficient" and the increasing focus on distance learning as a way to increase enrollment and profit, full integration into the current IP law regime would make it easier for lectures, syllabi, and other course materials created by university faculty to be used, reused, and repackaged in a variety of formats without the consent of the faculty member. While the role of author/owner is an important one for historians and other scholars, protection of our authorial identities might be best served by resisting the legal definitions of those terms that are in many ways out of touch with the goals of the scholarly community.

It was through my teaching and research on the recent past in the United States that it became clear to me that an unchecked expansion of intellectual property law is not only bad for scholars but for the public more generally. As the social media revolution seeks to provide constant updates on the shape of the ever-shifting present, it becomes more important than ever that we maintain our collective access to the past. The work of the historian is to explore and celebrate the past and to shape the surviving traces— information that has now been reimagined as intellectual property—into historical narratives. There are few groups with as much at stake, and as much to gain, in the fight to protect the past from the encroachment of intellectual property law as those of us who have committed our professional lives to its study.

The Founding Fathers understood copyright to be a significant enough right to be worthy of mention in the Constitution—and perhaps it is worth returning to the language of that clause. The U.S. Congress has the power "to promote the Progress of Science and useful Arts, by securing for limited Times to Authors and Inventors the exclusive Right to their respective Writings and Discoveries."[60] Like so much of the Constitution, the clause is both succinct and rich with meaning. While subsequent debates and legislation have encouraged many of us to now think of copyright exclusively as a means of providing remuneration for individual authors, the clause makes it clear that the primary goal of copyright in the United States is to "promote the progress of science and useful arts," and it is to that standard that the current IP legislation is usefully held. While both U.S. and international IP law provide an important service by creating and maintaining protections for individual authors, the goal of benefiting society must remain the central focus.

Notes

1. Paul Farhi, "King's 'Dream' Becomes Commercial: Civil Rights Leader's Heirs Approved Use of Image by Alcatel," *Washington Post*, March 28, 2001, http://www.washingtonpost.com/ac2/wp-dyn?pagename=article&node=&contentId=A2981-2001Mar27&notFound=true.
2. "Alcatel Commercial Spot," YouTube video, March 30, 2001, http://www.youtube.com/watch?v=GQ5I_0M2HWY.

3. "Terms of Use: Community Guidelines," YouTube, accessed February 24, 2010, http://www.youtube.com/t/terms.

4. U.S. Const. art. I, § 8, cl. 8.

5. These three scholars alone have made a sizable contribution to the literature on culture and IP law. Kembrew McLeod, *Freedom of Expression: Resistance and Repression in the Age of Intellectual Property* (Minneapolis: University of Minnesota Press, 2007); Siva Vaidhyanathan, *Copyrights and Copywrongs: The Rise of Intellectual Property and How It Threatens Creativity* (New York: New York University Press, 2003); Siva Vaidhyanathan, *The Anarchist in the Library: How the Clash between Freedom and Control Is Hacking the Real World and Crashing the System* (New York: Basic Books, 2005); Lawrence Lessig, *The Future of Ideas: The Fate of the Commons in a Connected World* (New York: Vintage, 2002); Lawrence Lessig, *Free Culture: The Nature and Future of Creativity* (New York: Penguin, 2005); Lawrence Lessig, *Code: And Other Laws of Cyberspace, Version 2.0* (New York: Basic Books, 2006); Lawrence Lessig, *Remix: Making Art and Commerce Thrive in the Hybrid Economy* (New York: Penguin, 2008).

6. Adrian Johns, *Piracy: The Intellectual Property Wars from Gutenberg to Gates* (Chicago: University of Chicago Press, 2010).

7. Eva Hemmungs Wirtén, *Terms of Use: Negotiating the Jungle of the Intellectual Commons* (Toronto: University of Toronto Press, 2008); Eva Hemmungs Wirtén, *No Trespassing: Authorship, Intellectual Property Rights, and the Boundaries of Globalization* (Toronto: University of Toronto Press, 2004); Eduardo Peñalver and Sonia Katyal, *Property Outlaws: How Squatters, Pirates, and Protesters Improve the Law of Ownership* (New Haven, Conn.: Yale University Press, 2010); Martha Woodmansee and Peter Jaszi, eds., *The Construction of Authorship: Textual Appropriation in Law and Literature* (Durham, N.C.: Duke University Press, 1994); and Ann Bartow, "Fair Use and the Fairer Sex: Gender, Feminism and Copyright Law," *American University Journal of Gender, Social Policy and the Law* 14, no. 3 (2006): 551–584.

8. "Statute of Anne (1710)," in *Primary Sources on Copyright (1450–1900)*, ed. Lionel Bently and Martin Kretschmer, UK Arts and Humanities Council, March 19, 2008, http://www.copyrighthistory.org/cgi-bin/kleioc/0010/exec/showTranscription /"uk_1710"/start/"yes.

9. *Eldred v. Ashcroft*, 537 U.S. 186 (2003).

10. Chris Sprigman, "The Mouse That Ate the Public Domain: Disney, the Copyright Term Extension Act, and *Eldred v. Ashcroft*," *FindLaw's Writ*, Findlaw.com, March 5, 2002, http://writ.findlaw.com/commentary/20020305_sprigman.html.

11. Mary Bono, Sonny Bono's wife and congressional successor, spoke on the floor of the U.S. House of Representatives in support of the Copyright Term Extension Act: "Actually, Sonny wanted the term of copyright protection to last forever. I am informed by staff that such a change would violate the Constitution. . . . As you know, there is also [then MPAA president] Jack Valenti's proposal for term to last forever less one day. Perhaps the Committee may look at that next Congress." 144 *Cong. Rec.* H9952 (1998).

12. Sprigman, "Mouse."

13. Prue Adler and ARL staff, eds., "Copyright Timeline: A History of Copyright in the United States," Association of Research Libraries, accessed June 24, 2011, http://www.arl .org/pp/ppcopyright/copyresources/copytimeline.shtml.

14. "Exemption to Prohibition on Circumvention of Copyright Protection Systems for Access Control Technologies, Final Rule," *Federal Register* 65, no. 209 (2000), 64561.

15. *New York Times Co. v. Tasini*, 533 U.S. 483 (2001) and *Bender v. West Publishing Co.*, 158 F.3d 674 (2nd Cir. 1998).

16. "U.S. Copyright Office—Fair Use," United States Copyright Office, November 2009, http://www.copyright.gov/fls/fl102.html.

17. The Center for Social Media at the School of Communications at American University is among the leaders in fair use advocacy for scholars, students, and media professionals. *Fair Use: Center for Social Media*, accessed February 24, 2011, http://www.centerforsocialmedia.org/fair-use.

18. "NOOK Friends, Social Reading, Share eReading—Barnes and Noble," Barnes and Noble, accessed June 30, 2011, http://www.barnesandnoble.com/u/nookcolor-feature-nookfriends/379002482.

19. "Project Portfolio, the Autobiography of Malcolm X," Columbia Center for New Media Teaching and Learning, Columbia University, accessed February 24, 2011, http://ccnmtl.columbia.edu/portfolio/culture_and_society/the_autobiography_of.html.

20. Manning Marable, *Malcolm X: A Life of Reinvention* (New York: Viking Adult, 2011).

21. David Garrow, quoted in Emily Eakin, "Malcolm X Family Fights Auction of Papers," *New York Times*, March 7, 2002, http://www.nytimes.com/2002/03/07/arts/malcolm-x-family-fights-auction-of-papers.html.

22. Kevin Flynn, "Malcolm X's Diary for Sale, but Ownership Is in Doubt," *New York Times*, May 15, 1999, http://www.nytimes.com/1999/05/15/nyregion/malcolm-x-s-diary-for-sale-but-ownership-is-in-doubt.html.

23. "Bullet-Riddled Malcolm X Diary off Block," *New York Beacon*, June 2, 1999, http://ezproxy.library.nyu.edu:34344/docview/368066497/131E51646CA249CA849/1?accountid=12768.

24. Emily Eakin, "Auction House Withdraws Items Attributed to Malcolm X," *New York Times*, March 13, 2002, http://www.nytimes.com/2002/03/13/us/auction-house-withdraws-items-attributed-to-malcolm-x.html.

25. Eakin, "Auction House."

26. Lynne Duke, "Malcolm X's Papers Come Home: Documents, Effects Will Be Archived at Harlem Library," *Washington Post*, January 8, 2003, http://pqasb.pqarchiver.com/washingtonpost/access/275089631.html?FMT=ABS&FMTS=ABS:FT&date=Jan+8%2C+2003&author=Lynne+Duke&pub=The+Washington+Post&edition=&startpage=C.01&desc=Malcolm+X%27s+Papers+Come+Home%3B+Documents%2C+Effects+Will+Be+Archived+at+Harlem+Library.

27. Eakin, "Family Fights."

28. Malcolm X and Alex Haley, *The Autobiography of Malcolm X* (New York: Grove, 1966).

29. Manning Marable, "Rediscovering Malcolm's Life: A Historian's Adventures in Living History," *Souls* 7, no. 1 (2005): 20–35.

30. Linda Jones, "Detroit Lawyer Pays $100,000 for Haley's Original 'Malcolm X,'" *Detroit News*, October 2, 1992, http://ezproxy.library.nyu.edu:34344/docview/404809487/131E51C993E32F61A76/1?accountid=12768.

31. Les Payne, "An Author's Life on Sale," *Newsday*, October 4, 1992, http://ezproxy.library.nyu.edu:34344/docview/278546039/131E51DC03549C02DD5/1?accountid=12768.

32. Manning Marable, *Living Black History: How Reimagining the African-American Past Can Remake America's Racial Future* (New York: Basic Civitas, 2006).

33. Marable, *Living Black History*, 156–157.

34. In the spring of 2010, Reed made a surprising announcement. He was going to read from the missing chapters during a public event at the Schomburg on Malcolm X's birthday. So on May 19, 2010, Reed not only read from the chapters but announced a plan to publish the missing chapters with a foreword by Malcolm's X's daughter, Ilyasah Shabazz. Further details have yet to be released, but historians eagerly anticipate the release of the chapters and the insights they will bring on the life of an icon. "Malcolm X's Daughter to Add to Father's Autobiography," *New York Post*, April 10, 2010, http://www.nypost.com/p/pagesix/restoring_lost_malcolm_5Z5l1GHO3m4BMrucBPMG2N.

35. Richard Bernstein, "Dr. King's Widow Sues Boston U. for Return of His Documents," *New York Times*, December 10, 1987, http://www.nytimes.com/1987/12/10/us/dr-king-s-widow-sues-boston-u-for-return-of-his-documents.html.

36. Doris Sue Wong, "Jury Rules BU Rightful Owner of King Papers," *Boston Globe*, May 7, 1993, https://secure.pqarchiver.com/boston/access/2580319.html?FMT=ABS&FMTS=ABS&type=current&date=May+7%2C+1993&author=Wong%2C+Doris+Sue&pub=Boston+Globe&edition=&startpage=1&desc=Jury+rules+BU+rightful+owner+of+King+papers.

37. *Coretta Scott King v. Trustees of Boston University*, 420 Mass. 52 (1987).

38. In the years since the lawsuit, the collection has brought a considerable amount of positive attention and grant funding to the university. But there are signs the university still feels the need to counter the negative publicity the lawsuit generated: on the homepage of the King archive website, there is a prominently featured audio clip of Martin Luther King at a press conference at BU explaining his decision to donate his papers to the university. "Dr. Martin Luther King Jr. Cataloguing and Electronic Finding Aid Project," Dr. Martin Luther King, Jr., Archive, Howard Gotlieb Archival Research Center, Boston University, accessed February 24, 2011, http://www.bu.edu/dbin/mlkjr/.

39. "Library of Congress Offers to Buy M. L. King Papers for $20 Million," *Los Angeles Times*, October 29, 1999, http://articles.latimes.com/1999/oct/29/news/mn-27596.

40. The agreement remained tentative as the $20 million price tag sent the Library of Congress scrambling for a way to come up with the money. In 2001 the library worked with Congress (specifically Senator Mary Landrieu of Louisiana and Representative James Leach of Iowa) to introduce the "Commemorative Coin Act," which would allow the design and production of up to five hundred thousand silver coins "with the proceeds going to the Library of Congress for the purpose of purchasing and maintaining historical documents and other materials associated with the life and legacy of Dr. King." Dr. Martin Luther King, Jr., Commemorative Coin Act of 2004, 108th Cong., S. 2146. (2004).

41. Ernie Suggs, "The King Papers: King Collection Celebrated, Franklin Hails Unique Archive," *Atlanta Journal-Constitution*, October 10, 2006, http://nl.newsbank.com/nl-search/we/Archives?p_product=AT&p_theme=at&p_action=search&p_maxdocs=200&s_hidethis=no&s_dispstring=King%20Collection%20Celebrated,%20Franklin%20Hails%20Unique%20Archive&p_field_advanced-0=&p_text_advanced-0=%28King%20Collection%20Celebrated,%20Franklin%20Hails%20Unique%20Archive%29&xcal_numdocs=20&p_perpage=10&p_sort=YMD_date:D&xcal_useweights=no.

42. National Public Radio, "Morehouse College to Get MLK Collection," *News and Notes*, June 26, 2006, http://www.npr.org/templates/story/story.php?storyId=5511141.

43. Kevin Sack, "King Legacy Takes New Turn under Son's Leadership," *Houston Chronicle*, August 24, 1997, http://ezproxy.library.nyu.edu:34344/docview/395644027/13 1E52CE5D16315C03D/1?accountid=12768.

44. Hollis R. Towns, "'Tasteful' Marketing of MLK: Heirs Agree to License the Words, Image of Martin Luther King Jr.," *Atlanta Journal-Constitution*, February 4, 1996, http://nl.newsbank.com/nl-search/we/Archives?p_product=AT&p_theme=at&p _action=search&p_maxdocs=200&s_hidethis=no&s_dispstring=Tasteful%20 marketing%20of%20MLK:%20Heirs%20Agree%20to%20License%20the%20Words,%20 Image%20of%20Martin%20Luther%20King%20Jr.&p_field_advanced-0=&p_text _advanced-0=%28Tasteful%20marketing%20of%20MLK:%20Heirs%20Agree%20 to%20License%20the%20Words,%20Image%20of%20Martin%20Luther%20King%20 Jr.%29&xcal_numdocs=20&p_perpage=10&p_sort=YMD_date:D&xcal_useweights=no.

45. Ronald Smothers, "Son Envisions a Multimedia Martin Luther King," *New York Times*, October 3, 1994, http://www.nytimes.com/1994/10/03/us/son-envisions-a -multimedia-martin-luther-king.htm.

46. Cynthia Tucker, "King Heirs Seek to Turn U.S. Icon into Dollar Sign," *Atlanta Journal-Constitution*, April 1, 2001, http://nl.newsbank.com/nl-search/we/Archives?p _product=AT&p_theme=at&p_action=search&p_maxdocs=200&s_hidethis=no&p _field_label-0=Author&p_text_label-0=Tucker&p_field_label-1=title&p_bool _label-1=AND&s_dispstring=King%20Heirs%20Seek%20to%20Turn%20U.S.%20 Icon%20AND%20byline%28Tucker%29%20AND%20date%28all%29&p_field _advanced-0=&p_text_advanced-0=%28King%20Heirs%20Seek%20to%20Turn%20 U.S.%20Icon%29&xcal_numdocs=20&p_perpage=10&p_sort=YMD_date:D&xcal _useweights=no.

47. Vern E Smith and John Leland, "The Children Who Would Be King," *Newsweek*, April 6, 1998, 48–52, http://www.washingtonpost.com/wp-srv/national/longterm/mlk /children/children.htm.

48. Dan Sabbagh, "The Dream Ticket: Dr Martin Luther King and EMI," *Times*, March 18, 2009, http://business.timesonline.co.uk/tol/business/industry_sectors/media /article5927856.ece.

49. "EMI Music Publishing Signs Groundbreaking Deal to Represent the Works of Dr. Martin Luther King, Jr.," *Business Wire*, March 17, 2009, http://www.bloomberg.com /apps/news?pid=conewsstory&refer=conews&tkr=EMI:LN&sid=aDwy2hI9iVRc.

50. Robbie Brown, "King Estate Considering Suit over Unlicensed Obama Items," *New York Times*, November 15, 2008, http://www.nytimes.com/2008/11/15/us/politics/15king .html.

51. Zack Burgess, "King Family Puts Price on Legacy," *Philadelphia Tribune*, July 19, 2009, http://michigancitizen.com/king-family-puts-price-on-legacy-p7605-75.htm.

52. *Princeton University Press v. Michigan Document Services, Inc.*, 99 F.3d 1381 (6th Cir. 1996).

53. *Cambridge University Press et al. v. Becker et al.* (N.D. Ga. 2010).

54. Cambridge Information Group, accessed February 24, 2011, http://www.cig.com/.

55. Thom Powers, "'Eyes on the Prize' off the Shelf Due to Copyright Issues," *Boston Globe*, January 16, 2005, http://www.boston.com/news/globe/ideas/articles/2005/01/16 /eyes_on_the_prize_off_the_shelf/.

56. DeNeen L. Brown and Hamil R. Harris, "A Struggle for Rights: 'Eyes on the Prize' Mired in Money Battle," *Washington Post*, January 17, 2005, http://www.washingtonpost .com/wp-dyn/articles/A14801-2005Jan16.html.

57. Cecilia Kang, "Big, Permanent Retweet by Library of Congress: Scholars Will Comb through Messages to Gain Cultural Insight," *Washington Post*, April 16, 2010, http:// www.washingtonpost.com/wp-dyn/content/article/2010/04/15/AR2010041505752.html.

58. "Internet Archive: Digital Library of Free Books, Movies, Music and Wayback Machine," Internet Archive, accessed February 24, 2011, http://www.archive.org/.

59. Corynne McSherry, *Who Owns Academic Work? Battling for Control of Intellectual Property* (Cambridge, Mass.: Harvard University Press, 2001).

60. U.S. Const. art. I, § 8, cl. 8.

PART THREE

Working with Living Subjects

MARTIN MEEKER

The Berkeley Compromise

*Oral History, Human Subjects, and
the Meaning of "Research"*

THE STUDY OF RECENT HISTORY almost demands that schol-
ars augment their archival research with oral history interviews—if, in fact,
interviewing is not already the central methodology being employed. This
expectation, however, runs up against the fact that historians are rarely
trained in oral history methodology, and universities that offer such training are few and far between. This gap between expectation and training
opens scholars and their research to many potential pitfalls, from study
design through analysis of the interviews themselves. Given that oral history is by its nature an interactive methodology that requires interface with
living witnesses to historical events, one of the key areas in which scholars
may confront the limitations of their training is in the area described as
"interviewing ethics," which broadly covers interpersonal relationships, informed consent, publication of interviews and findings, and engagement
with university Institutional Review Boards (IRBs) established to protect
human research subjects. This essay explores the intersection of ethical and
epistemological issues of oral history methodology for those conducting
research on topics in recent decades. Historians of the recent past, many of
whom use interviews as a source, need to be more systematic about doing
oral histories as a form of research. I contend that cooperation with IRBs
offers one way to do that.

By all accounts, August 2003 should have marked a turning point, if not
also an occasion for expressions of relief and even celebration, among practitioners of oral history interviewing. After all, following years of meetings
and negotiations, leaders of the Oral History Association (OHA) and the
American Historical Association (AHA), with the apparent blessing of the

U.S. Office for Human Research Protection (OHRP) of the Department of Health and Human Services (DHHS), issued a statement that clarified, and perhaps shifted, the way in which federal human subjects research regulations were to be applied to oral history interviewing. In essence, the statement asserted that because oral history interviewing did not contribute to "generalizable knowledge," oral history projects did not constitute "research" as defined by DHHS regulations; the reasoning followed that because oral history projects did not cross the definitive threshold of "research," those projects should be excluded from oversight by campus IRBs established to protect human research subjects.

The main engineers of this apparent policy change, Linda Shopes of the Pennsylvania Historical and Museum Commission and Donald Ritchie of the U.S. Senate Historical Office, were understandably optimistic that oral history would henceforth become exempt from bureaucratic hassles *and* that practitioners of oral history would be delighted by the outcome. However, initial cries of jubilation gave way to dismay. What has since transpired has instead engendered much confusion. Many years later, with individual university IRBs responding to the statements of the OHA, AHA, and OHRP in thoroughly inconsistent ways, if they have engaged with the statements at all, who and what governs oral history practices is virtually indecipherable, and the future remains unclear at many institutions.

Confusion and questions, however, can often be good for a field of study. This is particularly true for one as interdisciplinary, yet methodologically unified, as oral history interviewing. In this case, not only are new, dynamic approaches to the regulation of human-subjects research emerging, but the very concept of what constitutes research itself vis-à-vis oral history is undergoing a close examination. In this essay I offer a quick history of IRBs and the oral history "problem." Through an examination of how the Regional Oral History Office at the University of California (UC), Berkeley—one of the oldest and most respected oral history programs in the nation—has navigated the contemporary environment and developed a negotiated solution to human-subject research regulation and review, I attempt to help guide scholars through one of the densest methodological thickets confronting those who study recent history today. In the course of this review, I offer a critical perspective on the evolving definition of research in the context of oral history interviewing.

The Early History of Human-Subjects Protection

Historians date the beginning of modern human-subject protection ethics and protocols to the code developed by the Nuremberg Military Tribunal to evaluate the nature of Nazi atrocities following World War II. The tribunal hoped to establish an ethical standard by which future human research might be conducted. The first sentences of the Nuremberg Code are worth printing in their entirety, for they frame the stakes of human research, whether medical, psychological, or ethnographic:

> The voluntary consent of the human subject is absolutely essential. This means that the person involved should have legal capacity to give consent; should be so situated as to be able to exercise free power of choice, without the intervention of any element of force, fraud, deceit, duress, over-reaching, or other ulterior form of constraint or coercion; and should have sufficient knowledge and comprehension of the elements of the subject matter involved as to enable him to make an understanding and enlightened decision.[1]

A unified, federal policy on human-subjects research first appeared in the United States in 1953 from the Clinical Center at the National Institutes of Health (NIH). A brief history of the origins of NIH policies notes that it provided for ethical review of research projects; thus, it arguably generated the first IRBs.[2] Ethics and procedures for protecting human subjects were further refined and institutionalized throughout the 1960s and 1970s. Central to this process was the establishment of the National Commission for the Protection of Human Subjects of Biomedical and Behavioral Research, which was included in the Department of Health, Education, and Welfare (now the Department of Health and Human Services, or DHHS) and established by the passage of the National Research Act in 1974. After meeting for four years, the commission published its final recommendations for three ethical principles to guide human-subject research: that there must be informed consent; that research should maximize possible benefits and minimize possible harms; and that all subjects must be treated fairly and equally. The DHHS regulations went into effect in January 1981 and were revised in 1991 to mandate that the policy applies to all federally funded research, not just that conducted under the auspices of DHHS.

While many readers of this essay may have had at least some experience working with IRBs, it is useful to review their basic structure and procedures. The power of the typical campus IRB is generally derived from a federal policy that research institutions must comply with federal regulations if that institution wishes to receive federal funding for research. These regulations further mandate that the entire scope of human-subjects research within an institution be reviewed by the IRB, not just the specific research that seeks or has received federal funding at any given time.[3] With the regulatory onus placed on the research institution itself, campus IRB administrators and committee members are given the responsibility of interpreting what research involving human subjects needs oversight. This interpretation varies considerably from one research institution to the next; moreover, due to any number of contextual factors, research eligible for review has shifted considerably over the past twenty years. Along with determining what kind of research is subject to oversight, and thus "not exempt" or "exempt" from review, IRBs often divide nonexempt research projects into two categories.[4] In the case of UC Berkeley's IRB, the Committee for Protection of Human Subjects (CPHS), this means that projects are either eligible for expedited review or subject to full committee review. In both cases, projects are first reviewed by the Office for the Protection of Human Subjects (OPHS) staff, which consults with DHHS guidelines to determine if projects are eligible for expedited review or, if risk is potentially substantial, should go to the full committee for review. As is the case with most campus IRBs, many projects, especially those situated in the social sciences, are eligible for expedited review and thus are handled by office staff. At Berkeley, no oral history project in recent memory has been subjected to full committee review. Although the line between methodology and intellectual content of research is a thin one indeed, to avoid infringing on intellectual freedom, OPHS staff and CPHS members are directed to focus on methodological questions rather than content questions.

Oral History, Ethics, and Human-Subjects Protection

While storytelling and listening is probably our oldest historical methodology, the invention of a distinct oral history methodology and practice parallels the professionalization of historical scholarship in general. Almost certainly the first U.S. historian to conduct interviews with any regularity and also preside over an extensive interview project was Hubert Howe Bancroft, who was not trained as a historian or employed by a university, but was a bookstore owner and expert amateur. Bancroft's "dictations," as they

have come to be known, were written documentation of conversations conducted in the 1870s with a wide variety of individuals who had contributed
to or witnessed the expansion of the United States into the American West.
The first major academic oral historian, however, was Allen Nevins, who
founded the Columbia University Oral History Research Office in 1948.
Other universities followed suit and established oral history programs over
the next several decades, one of which was the Regional Oral History Office (ROHO) at the University of California, Berkeley in 1954. But it was not
until the 1960s and 1970s, with the rising tide of social history research, that
oral history interviewing was widely pursued by academic historians. An
indication of this change can be seen with the founding of the Oral History
Association in 1966 and the introduction of a professional journal, the *Oral
History Review*, in 1973.

It is likely that there was very little interaction between historians and
IRBs until after the DHHS regulations went into effect in 1981. Coinciden-
tally, perhaps, this also was the period in which many oral historians, and
oral history programs, stepped up the process of professionalization by
exploring the question of methodology more rigorously and by seeking
greater funding for larger interview projects. Still, with very few oral history projects receiving substantial funding and many of the projects being
directed independently by faculty, not to mention the independent community history projects normally not subject to IRB review, the interactions
between university IRBs and oral historians remained rare. UC Berkeley's
ROHO had for many years a two-pronged approach to human-subjects oversight, characterized partly by engagement and partly by avoidance, due to
an ambiguous 1984 policy that granted what was subsequently interpreted
by ROHO as a blanket exemption from IRB review. From the mid-1980s until
2005, then, ROHO operated under a partial "hear no evil, see no evil, speak
no evil" arrangement with UC Berkeley's Office for the Protection of Human
Subjects. I suspect that there are many similarly ambiguous relationships
between oral historians and IRBs at other institutions.

Because of this lack of resolution, oral historians have been justifiably
concerned about the ethical implications of their work since at least the late
1960s, when OHA issued its first set of "goals and guidelines."[5] It was not until 1979, however, that the first clear list of "evaluation guidelines" was proposed and adopted by a vote of OHA members.[6] A variety of factors, including the increased use of oral histories in the classroom, the subpoenaing
of sealed interviews, and technological innovations, inspired a substantial

revision of these guidelines between 1988 and 1989 and again in 1998. The evaluation guidelines established in 1979 and then revised in 1989, however, are curiously passive; although extensive and certainly helpful to oral historians and other researchers, the guidelines come in the form of interrogatories, such as "What is the research design? How clear and realistic is it?" For declarative statements from OHA, oral historians had to wait until 1990, when OHA adopted official principles that articulated clear guidelines such as, "Interviewees should be informed of the purposes and procedures of oral history in general."[7]

Although the "evaluation guidelines" and the "principles and standards" offered a clear and nearly exhaustive discussion of the interviewer's responsibility to interviewees, the public, and the profession, in neither of these documents was there a discussion of how the interviewer might interact with campus IRBs—and, indeed, there was no suggestion that interviewers should consult an IRB before commencing an interview project. I suspect this was an oversight: IRBs may have scarcely been on the radar of the committee members who wrote the guidelines. Similarly, the AHA Council approved a "Statement on Interviewing for Historical Documentation" at its May 1989 meeting. The document, which was in large part based on OHA evaluation guidelines, also made no mention of IRBs (a brief discussion of IRBs was added when the document was revised in 1998).[8] Still, in the late 1980s and early 1990s, there was an emerging recognition of the importance of IRBs by oral historians, even if that recognition did not translate into engagement and failed to influence the OHA evaluation guidelines immediately.

An article from the OHA Newsletter in 1989 by Richard Cándida Smith, then OHA executive secretary, offers a glimpse at the situation on the verge of change. Cándida Smith wrote, "I was asked by a professor to comment on guidelines his university had developed which subjected oral history research projects to institutional review for the protection of human subjects." Although he declined to offer counsel on IRBs overall, Cándida Smith's comments deserve attention because his perspective on the role of these oversight committees is different from what came from the OHA in the late 1990s in one respect: he found that, rather than burdening the researcher, the IRB guidelines under discussion contained "several important omissions. The most glaring was the absence of any discussion of legal contracts between the academic researcher and the oral history interviewee." Cándida Smith believed that universities might soon take on a more proactive role in imposing human-subject protection requirements on oral history projects, given the increasing litigiousness of U.S. society and universities' desire to avert culpability. Cándida Smith raised the question of whether this development might impede oral history research and concluded by asking for input on the matter from OHA members.[9]

Perhaps due to these concerns, what might be described as a policy of mutual avoidance was abandoned sometime in the mid-1990s. By spring 1997 Cándida Smith, then OHA president, reported that the AHA professional division was working on a policy that would address the issue of human-subjects review. This latter group proposed disseminating a rather modest statement which, in effect, recommended that oral historians educate themselves about federal and campus policies for protecting human subjects and that they should "comply with all laws, regulations, and institutional policies applicable to their research activities." Cándida Smith did not offer explicit endorsement of the AHA statement. Instead, he noted that leading oral historians would be in contact with federal officials to determine whether voluntary adherence to OHA's "evaluation guidelines would constitute a reasonable and adequate effort by researchers to protect human subjects."[10] In September 1997, Linda Shopes, then OHA president-elect, OHA vice president Howard Green, and Cándida Smith met with leaders of the National Institutes of Health's Office for Protection from Research Risks (OPRR, which later became the OHRP). The meeting, which Shopes described as "cordial and informational," provided the opportunity to discuss researchers' complaints about their difficulties with their universities' IRBs.

At the meeting, federal officials stated that the ethical guidelines adopted by AHA and OHA were "not incompatible" with federal regulations. But they also told Shopes and Cándida Smith that "before beginning any research that may include oral history interviewing, historians should contact their IRBs for policies and regulations governing the use of human subjects in research projects."[11] In other words, while OPRR officials supported the ethical guidelines of the professional organizations, they also indicated that those guidelines were no substitute for a campus IRB review.

In November 1997 OPRR requested comments on the proposal that projects eligible for expedited review be expanded. Most of the more than one hundred written comments that were submitted pertained to the proposed changes regarding medical and pharmaceutical research.[12] However, a number of comments addressed proposals related to social science, ethnographic, and oral history research. Those comments resulted in the policy clarification issued in November 1998 that related specifically to oral history methodology. The new policy read that research categories eligible for *expedited* review included "collection of data from voice, video, digital, or image recordings made for research purposes" and "research on individual or group characteristics or behavior (including, but not limited to, research on perception, cognition, motivation, identity, language, communication, cultural beliefs and practices, and social behavior) or research employing survey, interview, oral history, focus group, program evaluation, human factors evaluation, or quality assurance methodologies."[13] This 1998 policy notice was the first explicit engagement with oral history by the federal IRB.

If the policy of mutual avoidance ended in the mid-1990s, within a few years an increasingly vocal critique of the 1998 OPRR policy clarification emerged. Apparently, the opening salvo in this emerging critique came with an opinion piece delivered by Linda Shopes before the National Bioethics Advisory Commission in April 2000. Shopes outlined her critique of IRBS succinctly:

The current regulations were designed to protect people from unwittingly subjecting themselves to harmful scientific research and medical experiments. Applied to oral history interviews and other forms of nonscientific research, they present numerous, serious difficulties. Many IRBS are constituted entirely of medical and behavioral scientists, who have little understanding of the principles and protocols of humanistic inquiry. Shopes provided examples of how IRB members, uninformed about oral history practice, had placed unreasonable and irrelevant demands on scholars. Historians, she wrote, "report that they have been told by IRBS to submit detailed questionnaires prior to conducting any interviews, to maintain narrator anonymity both on tape and in their published work, and to either destroy their tapes or retain them in their private possession after their research is completed." Although Shopes acknowledged the 1998 revision approving inclusion of oral history as a research category eligible for expedited review, she hinted at a much more radical revision. Oral history should not be subject to IRB review but, rather, "review of research protocols for oral history should take place among peers at the departmental level, according to the professional standards articulated in the Oral History Association's 'Principles and Standards and Evaluation Guidelines' and the AHA's 'Statement on Interviewing for Historical Documentation.'"[14]

Historians responded with gusto to Shopes's dissent. In a letter to the editor of *Perspectives*, fifteen members of the history department at Illinois

State University praised Shopes. Moreover, the letter's signatories offered support for the move to obtain blanket exemption for oral history interviewing, despite acknowledging that their university's "IRB has made clear its intention of cooperating with our department to develop viable procedures." The signatories argued further that "in discussions with federal officials and congressional staffs, the AHA and its partner organizations in the social sciences and humanities should emphasize the academic freedom and even the constitutional concerns raised by the expansion of human subjects review beyond its original purpose of preventing recurrence of well-documented abuses in medical and psychological research."[15]

Shortly after the developments of 1998, the American Association of University Professors issued the report *Protecting Human Beings: Institutional Review Boards and Social Science Research*.[16] This thorough and well-reasoned report created a forum for those who critiqued IRBs. However, the report advocated only modest revisions to the way in which IRBs approached social science research and fell far short of arguing for a wholesale rejection of or exemption from human-subjects review for oral history projects. In particular, the report cited the 1998 OPRR policy clarification as a sign that IRBs were open to thinking about social science research in new ways and that they could be made to accommodate the particular needs of social scientists while also fulfilling their mandate to protect human research subjects. However, the report also noted that some individual campus IRBs were not following the lead of the national office and instead continuing to give social science projects intense and perhaps unwarranted scrutiny. It recommended, therefore, that IRBs increase the representation of social scientists on the committees so that the review process would be fair as well as less cumbersome. Still, the official findings published in the report did not encapsulate the full range of opinions communicated during the fact-finding phase that preceded its publication. Alan Lessoff, a history professor at Illinois State University, expressed dismay that IRBs should exert *any* authority of review over historical research, even going as far as saying that any such review "amounts to censorship."[17]

The moderate path of IRB reform ended with the bombshell of fall 2003 that began this essay. According to a statement issued jointly by OHA and AHA, oral history interviewing was to be considered *excluded* from IRB review.[18] At the next OHA annual meeting in late August 2003, OHRP announced that it concurred with this conclusion.[19] The joint statement reads,

Most oral history interviewing projects are not subject to the requirements of the DHHS regulations for the protection of human subjects . . . and can be excluded from IRB oversight because they do not involve research as defined by the HHS regulations. HHS regulations at 45 CFR 46.102(D) define research as "a systematic investigation, including research development, testing and evaluation, designed to develop or contribute to generalizable knowledge." The Oral History Association defines oral history as "a method of gathering and preserving historical information through recorded interviews with participants in past events and ways of life."[20]

In essence the statement prepared by OHA and AHA asserted that oral history interviewing was an archival practice rather than a research methodology and thus did "*not meet the regulatory definition of research.*"[21]

As might be expected from oral historians who distrusted bureaucratic interference or were already mired in IRB review, the initial response to the concurrence was extremely positive. "Historians applauded the decision," wrote Bruce Craig in the AHA's *Perspectives*, adding that Linda Shopes, who represented the AHA before the OHRP, said, the office "heard our concern and has responded appropriately."[22] In the weeks and months that followed the press release, oral historians responded in varying, sometimes contradictory ways. Some were dismayed about the approach made by OHA's representatives. Upon learning of the OHA-AHA concurrence, E. Taylor Atkins of Northern Illinois University wrote, "I am stunned by the recent federal decision removing oral history projects from institutional review. I am even more appalled by the arguments made by the American Historical Association and the Oral History Association . . . that oral history is not research as defined in federal regulations. . . . it seems to me that the AHA and OHA have misrepresented the oral historian's work simply to avoid the inconvenience of having to submit proposals for review."[23]

Augmenting the confusion was the news from several sources that despite, or perhaps due to, the OHRP concurrence, campus IRBs around the country continued to demand review of oral history projects. Ritchie and Shopes reported in March 2004, "We are aware . . . of several memos in circulation in which IRB representatives have raised questions about the standing of the policy statement or suggested hypothetical cases in which oral history projects might still be subject to review."[24] Although IRB responses to the OHRP concurrence were idiosyncratic, at this point it makes sense to focus on the situation of one university-based oral history program and its successful attempt to negotiate its relationship with the campus IRB.

The Berkeley Dilemma

How did one of the oldest university-based oral history projects in the country navigate the process I have just described? And how do the policies developed in a specific place help historians, whether they are specialists or nonspecialists in oral history methodology, think about the use of interviews? The Regional Oral History Office (ROHO) of the Bancroft Library at the University of California, Berkeley, was founded in 1954 to preserve the histories of the American West, the state of California, and the San Francisco Bay Area. By the early 1980s, the UC Berkeley Office for the Protection of Human Subjects (OPHS) was asked to review ROHO projects. The office quickly determined that the collection of oral histories was beyond the scope of their charge and granted what was interpreted by ROHO as a blanket exemption.[25]

This understanding, such that either party remembered it, remained in effect until, roughly, the mid-1990s. At that point several changes shifted the context in which oral histories were conducted at ROHO—and the university's awareness of the interviewing being conducted. Perhaps the most important change came with innovations in communications technologies, such as the Internet, and the increasing ease with which oral history transcripts could be made publicly accessible. But more particular to ROHO was a less dramatic shift, one that was more related to a steady evolution of the program itself.

Always funded largely on soft money, ROHO had received most of its support through a small endowment and by the donations of individuals or companies who wanted specific interviews conducted. In the 1990s, however, an increasingly ambitious and academically oriented group of oral history scholars sought to put project formulation *before* the money, and they started applying for grants to support project-based interviews. Among the first of these ventures was what became known as the Disability Rights and Independent Living Movement oral history project. Initiated in 1996, project managers applied for funds through the U.S. Department of Education's National Institute on Disability and Rehabilitation Research. Institutionally, the gifts that funded much of ROHO's work had previously come in through the university library; the funds and the projects those funds supported had never cycled through the university's grant-administering and human-subjects bureaucracy (the grants-administering program generally does not release project funds until it receives confirmation that the project has been approved). In applying for a major competitive grant, however, ROHO project managers were obliged to navigate the university's grants-seeking and grants-administering bureaucracy and thus were compelled to complete a review with OPHS, UC Berkeley's IRB. The review was relatively easy and even though the interviewees constituted what is known as a potentially vulnerable population (in other words, people with disabilities), the OPHS did not force a full committee review and instead approved the project through expedited review. This situation—in which interview projects were vetted by OPHS only if the funding path required review—persisted until well after 2000.

Then, in 2003 the concurrence statement by the OHA, AHA, and OHRP became public. Many at ROHO believed that the oral history office would be freed from the restrictions of what then seemed like a pro forma bureaucratic review. Alas, such was not the case. The first test of the new situation came with a major five-year oral history project on Kaiser Permanente medical care. The project, proposed by ROHO and then funded by Kaiser through a grant, was scheduled to begin in 2004. After a few delays, the university grants-administrating office received the funds for the first grant year in mid-2005. However, when it was discovered that no human-subjects review had been conducted for this project, the funds were withheld and project planning stalled. Meetings between ROHO director Cándida Smith and new OPHS director Rebecca Armstrong ensued. After initial conversations, it became clear that Armstrong and her office found the 2003 OHA-AHA statement, as well as the rather flimsy "blanket exemption" most ROHO interviewers had operated under since 1984, unacceptable. Although employees of the OHRP publicly "concurred" with the OHA-AHA statement, it was in fact written by representatives of the two professional organizations and thus was not an official policy change by the OHRP itself, or the DHHS in general.[26]

Moreover, Armstrong took issue with the notion that oral history interviewing did not constitute "research." While differences existed in research methodologies, oral history, particularly large project-based interviewing, was capable of producing "generalizable knowledge," bearing strong similarity to interview-based sociological research. Assured that Armstrong's critiques were valid and that the OPHS would not unnecessarily delay the review or, if appropriate, approval of the Kaiser Permanente project human-subjects review, Cándida Smith moved ahead with submitting an application for approval. In the meantime, Armstrong, Cándida Smith, and

I entered into a conversation about how oral history projects should be reviewed in the future, what constitutes research, and if we could draft a compromise that would serve as a framework governing oral history and OPHS relations from this point forward.

Oral History Scholarship and the Meaning of Research

Many of those who still believe that oral history should receive a blanket exclusion from IRB review base their arguments on the notions that the nonbinding OHRP concurrence should be understood as definitive policy: this would lead to a second conclusion that oral history interviewing should not be considered research. Exploring both of these ideas in greater depth sheds light on how research-related policy is made and implemented and how oral history research fits within the larger frame of academic scholarship.

The policy question is the more straightforward of the two. Upon receiving news that campus IRBs remained unswayed even when presented with the OHRP concurrence, Shopes and Ritchie sought additional affirmation from the federal office. In March 2004 they reported in *Perspectives* that the OHRP had confirmed "its concurrence with the existing policy statement" and reaffirmed its concurrence "with *your* policy statement that oral history interviewing activities, in general, are not designed to contribute to generalizable knowledge and therefore do not involve research as defined by Department of Health and Human Services regulations . . . and do not need to be reviewed by an institutional review board."[27] This apparent affirmation was followed in June 2004 with the AHA's own reaffirmation of the joint OHA-AHA policy statement and OHRP concurrence.

Yet, as Robert Townsend and Mériam Belli reported in a subsequent issue of *Perspectives*, "despite this effort, a preliminary review of current institutional review policies in several universities . . . reveals that oversight of oral history projects remains a confusing patchwork of widely disparate policies and procedures."[28] As recently as February 2006, Townsend reported in *Perspectives* that since the 2003 OHRP concurrence, "an AHA staff survey of review board policies at 252 colleges and universities found the policies are largely unchanged."[29] Possessing no authority to change the policies of campus IRBs (and without the help of a bona-fide policy statement authored by the OHRP), it is clear that the backers of the concurrence (and thus oral history exclusion) found themselves in a difficult situation. Acknowledging this issue, Townsend warned oral history practitioners "to weigh their responsibilities at the institutional level and individual level." In other words, oral historians were left on their own, with neither a solid foundation on which to challenge institutional oversight nor with a careful recommendation for how to interact with IRBs in the process of human-subjects review.

Although the impasse regarding policy-writing authority largely precludes a wholesale acceptance of oral history exclusion by campus IRBs, it is still worth considering the intellectual point on which the exclusion was sought to begin with. That point is, according to the OHA-AHA statement, that oral history projects should be excluded from oversight because they do not constitute research, which the HHS regulations define as "a systematic investigation, including research development, testing and evaluation, designed to develop or contribute to generalizable knowledge." In response to initial critiques of this logic, exclusion advocates such as Ritchie and Shopes issued a series of clarifications on the point. For example, in late 2003, they argued, "federal regulations were designed for scientific and social scientific research projects that use standard questionnaires with generally anonymous sources to produce quantitative information for 'generalizable knowledge.' Since that is not the way most oral historians operate, the type of research they do is generally excluded from IRB review."[30] The issue persisted and a few months later Shopes and Ritchie explained further:

> While oral history clearly involves historical research and interviews can lend themselves to generalizations, oral historians' standard operating procedures do not fit the type of research defined by federal regulations: "a systematic investigation, including research development, testing and evaluation, designed to develop or contribute to generalizable knowledge." Individually tailored interviews with the narrator's informed consent do not meet this definition of "research." Nor do they contribute to "generalizable knowledge," even if conducted with people identified with a common group, theme, or event, and whether or not the interviewer or other researchers might draw some historical generalizations from multiple interviews. The interviews must be designed specifically to produce generalizable knowledge in the scientific sense.[31]

Not only did Rebecca Armstrong of the UC Berkeley OPHS (and many of her IRB colleagues around the country) disagree with this opinion, but many oral history practitioners, myself included, disagree as well. Take, for example, the argument that federally mandated human-subject protections were "designed for scientific and social scientific research projects that use standard questionnaires with generally anonymous sources to produce quantitative information." Factually, this statement is untrue; logically, it is peculiar. Federal oversight was instituted to protect individual subjects who might suffer physically or emotionally because of research; uncontroversial standardized questionnaires have long been covered by expedited review. Moreover, the statement that protections are appropriate only for anonymous individuals completing questionnaires used to produce quantitative information is curious logic. If anonymous survey respondents were in need of protection, wouldn't named participants in a revealing life history interview need to be doubly protected?

Embedded within the OHRP concurrence was the notion that IRBS previously uninterested in oral history oversight, or perhaps unaware of the extent of oral history interviewing, have in recent years been tempted by "mission creep," or the notion that IRBS have begun to exceed the boundaries of their original charters. Over the 1980s and 1990s, IRBS started interpreting the meaning of research more broadly, eventually including oral history and other interviewing methodologies within IRB purview. This critique of IRB policy found its clearest articulation in the Illinois White Paper "Improving the System for Protecting Human Subjects: Counteracting IRB 'Mission Creep.'"[32]

Although the White Paper makes a cogent argument for continuing to exempt journalism from IRB oversight, it profoundly mischaracterizes oral history methodology by suggesting that journalism and historical research are analogous. The authors of the White Paper fail to distinguish between the two and describe both, inaccurately, as little more than "two people talking." Such a description of oral history methodology is akin to describing archival research as "browsing an old newspaper" or "rustling through an attic." It accounts for none of the serious study design and intellectual work that goes into such work. It also ignores the fact that many oral historians are serious scholars who have ideas about how institutions behave and change occurs and who seek out qualified interlocutors with whom to test those hypotheses. Although the White Paper may stand, and although some IRBS may be engaging in mission creep in select quarters, the perspective offered by the authors of the White Paper obfuscates rather than clarifies the unique institutional position of oral history vis-à-vis IRB oversight.

Moreover, real historical contextual changes have given IRBS very good reason to expand their area of oversight, particularly in the arena of oral history interviewing. We live in an increasingly litigious society; the White

Paper asserts that the question of legal risk is a "weak argument for IRB expansionism" because, for example, "there is almost no experience of litigation in social science or humanities research involving human subjects." Yet a recent lawsuit directed at UC Berkeley and an experience with one of our interviewees offers a telling exception.[33] In this case, one interviewee made negative remarks about a private citizen in 1992, in an interview which was deposited in libraries in the 1990s. When ROHO posted the transcript on the Internet in 2002, enabling a far wider circulation of the transcript, the apparently maligned individual learned of how he was characterized by the interviewee and sued for defamation of character.

If the meaning of harm has remained the same, the world has changed because of the Internet, and oral historians need to recognize that. In the 1980s and 1990s, access to ROHO transcripts required traveling to libraries in Berkeley or Los Angeles, or purchasing interviews and having them shipped. Now these same documents are available instantly, to everyone and for free. Researchers need to be more aware of the potential harm to human subjects based on the information that circulates about them, and thus oral historians need to do more to protect their human subjects. They should not avoid conducting research, but, rather, they need to better provide for the sealing of transcripts until possible dangers have passed or the interviewee has died. This may mean that certain sources could remain unavailable to historians for a decade or two, but it seems to me that the alternatives are considerably less attractive. What I am suggesting might well be much less restrictive than what the White Paper recommends or even what the OHA guidelines propose. If, as the White Paper suggests, universities issue a blanket rule against public disclosure of all harmful, personally identifiable information, it would represent a much more draconian chilling of intellectual inquiry than a reasonable IRB review that ensures informed consent.[34]

The issue of protecting subjects aside, the question of whether oral history interviewing is research that contributes to generalizable knowledge deserves further examination. First, the point has been raised that because journalism has thus far remained immune (in most instances) from human-subjects review, so should oral history interviewing. Although I tend to agree that journalism should remain exempt from review, I do so because I see journalism as inherently dissimilar from oral history interviewing—a difference that is rooted in my belief that journalism is a public enterprise, while oral history interviewing is (or should be) a scholarly one. Whereas journalism seeks to inform or influence public opinion, scholarship seeks to create or influence knowledge. While most readers approach journalistic writing with a critical eye, aware of blatant bias and even hyperbole, people tend to approach peer-reviewed research with a critical eye but also with a belief that what they read is based to some degree on serious research and applies some version of the scientific method to the answering of a question, whether quantitative or qualitative.

Oral history practitioners have much to gain from placing their methodology much more clearly in a scholarly context in which ideas are introduced and tested in the situation of an interview or, even better, a series of interviews. Aside from shoring up the status of oral history within the academy, there is much to be gained from increasing the rigor of oral history research and interviewing. At Berkeley, larger grants and better projects have been the result of renewed attention to methodology and to increasing the quality of interviews and project planning. This is not to say that simply by submitting to the authority of IRBs that oral history projects will be seen on par with survey research in the minds of foundations and other granting bodies. However, by agreeing that oral history cannot be defined as research in the terms used by such granting bodies, oral historians acquiesce to a subordinate position in the hierarchy of scholarship. Although insisting on its status as research does not guarantee that oral history will be viewed that way, admitting lack of rigor and scholarly impact is the surest path to continued marginalization in the eyes of university administrations and granting organizations. The historical and continued marginalization of oral history interviewing within the university poses a far greater risk to the current development and future health of this field than a few overreaching IRBs.

The Berkeley Compromise

When setting out to negotiate a set of guidelines governing the review of oral history projects at UC Berkeley, we established a number of goals. First and foremost, the OPHS wanted to ensure that it fulfilled its obligation to abide by DHHS regulations and thus protect UC Berkeley's eligibility to receive federal funds for research. Yet UC Berkeley oral historians hoped to gain much out of the compromise as well. First, like our colleagues in the OPHS, we wanted to protect our interviewees from a variety of factors, including, potentially, lawsuits and possible repercussions from having their personal opinions widely broadcast through a clear process of informed consent. Second, considering the potential legal issues, we wished to protect the interviewers and the office they represented, to the extent possible, from lawsuits. Third, we wanted to ensure that the review process was fair insofar that it did not unnecessarily burden the interviewer and that it did not impede the intellectual and academic freedom of anyone involved in the design or execution of the project. Finally, although we remain critical of the notion that oral history should receive blanket exemption, we agree with the sentiment expressed in the Illinois White Paper that we should "discard the current 'one-size-fits-all' approach that relies so heavily on criteria and procedures developed for biomedical research." Instead, we developed guidelines in accordance with best practices in oral history.[35]

The solution achieved outlines clear guidelines for oral history projects. New projects must be submitted for review to the OPHS, which will then determine if a project can proceed under expedited review or, if regulations or serious risks posed to human subjects require it, a full committee review.[36] Continuing projects can proceed for a period of at least three years without additional review, even if new funding is secured. While the OPHS will review proposals, themes, and interview topics, interviewers are not expected to submit predetermined lists of interviewees (provided interviewees are not in high-risk categories) or explicit protocols (lists of questions). And new proposals should be granted expedited review, provided that those proposals abide by the agreed-on procedures, which include signed-and-returned invitation letters that provide informed consent by explaining the rights and responsibilities of all parties, including the right to resign from the project at any point prior to its completion; opportunity for the interviewee to read or listen to the interview, make edits, and seal portions of the interview if so desired; signed legal releases transferring ownership of the interview to the university; and, when the final transcript is produced, a transmittal letter along with a copy of the transcript sent to the interviewee, notifying that person that the interview will soon be considered complete and resignation from the project no longer a possibility.[37]

This agreement necessitated a few changes in the way in which ROHO conducted business. It meant that interviewers and project managers had to pay closer attention to the management of the project. As a result, orphan tapes and transcripts have become much less common. The agreement allows interviewees to "opt out" of the project at any point prior to the publication of the final transcript; a few interviewees have selected this option, which means that some work we do will never see the light of day. Although this can be costly and extremely frustrating, we recognize that it is necessary. We also strive to no longer solicit and circulate potentially invasive information (e.g., a mother's maiden name). Finally, although the specter of litigation was, and is, one key element driving greater scrutiny of oral history programs, it became evident that undergoing IRB review alone would not be enough to ward off lawsuits. However, working closely with our IRB and abiding by its recommendations does, we think, provide a measure of protection in at least two ways: first, the OPHS is expert in litigation that emerges from research and thus can contribute their experience in this field to our projects; and, second, in the event that we are sued, the buck need not stop at the desk of the program's director, which is key when thinking about the long-term viability of an oral history program on an intensely political campus such as Berkeley.

Not all oral historians work in a university, nor are all oral history projects subject to review by an IRB. This might well be a cause for relief among already busy community-based scholars or those whose institutions choose to exempt (or ignore) oral history projects. Still, something can be gained from interactions with IRBs regardless of the research setting and its goals. Oral historians outside the academy might also find to be useful some of what we have learned. For example, different from ROHO, where all of our interviews are transcribed, community-based historians often do not have the time or budget for transcription. This means that interviewees generally do not get to review their transcripts (or tapes) for accuracy before they are deposited in archives or used in scholarly work. More importantly, this lack of review results in a failure of closure: interviewees often do not know when the project is complete. They also do not know when or if their interview will be deposited in an archive, excerpted in an academic publication, or otherwise made public. Short of suggesting that community-based oral history programs or departments at colleges without IRB oversight set up ad-hoc review committees, oral historians in this case may wish to send a digital copy of the interview itself (easily burned on a compact disc) to each interviewee. The interviewee might be invited to review and submit suggestions for revision within a reasonable period of time.[38] The historian might stipulate that the interview will be considered complete if no edits or restrictions are requested by the interviewee within six weeks. The overarching goal here, then, is to achieve informed consent, not only at the beginning of the project, but also at the end, providing closure and letting interviewees know when they can no longer withdraw from the project. By adhering to this standard principle, oral historians who do not have the *benefit* of IRB review can still ensure that their projects meet the same ethical standards as projects that have been vetted.

In recent years, likely in response to the failure of the 2003 resolution, the OHA and its representatives have begun to acknowledge that long-standing opposition to IRB oversight might be futile. In a recent article posted to the OHA web page, Shopes admitted, "After more than a decade of largely ineffective advocacy vis-à-vis OHRP and its predecessor, oral historians are not likely to gain many concessions from federal regulators."[39] And although the new "Principles and Best Practices for Oral History" adopted by OHA in 2009 still makes no explicit mention of IRBs, the new list of best practices matches rather closely the standards established by IRBS across the country, including at Berkeley.[40]

The Berkeley compromise may not work at every institution. But by engaging with our campus IRB rather than trying to deny that it has authority, and with that authority might come useful expertise, ROHO has established a workable solution. Moreover, and equally important, this solution further integrates ROHO into the teaching and research mission of one of the nation's great research universities, rather than seeking exemption or, worse, marginalization from it. This solution alone will not make ROHO a well-respected engine of important scholarship on the Berkeley campus, but it is one step, a necessary one I think, that will help practicing oral historians move in that direction.

Notes

1. Nuremberg Code, as reprinted on the National Institutes of Health website, April 19, 2006, http://www.nihtraining.com/ohsrsite/guidelines/nuremberg.html. In subsequent decades, other international bodies convened with the goal of articulating ethical guidelines for conducting human research, particularly research in the medical field. Most notable among these was the 1964 World Medical Association meeting that produced the "Declaration of Helsinki on Ethical Principles for Medical Research Involving Human Subjects." See *Guidelines for the Conduct of Research Involving Human Subjects at the National Institutes of Health*, 5th ed., 2004, 15, available at http://www.nihtraining .com/ohsrsite/guidelines/guidelines.html.

2. See National Institutes of Health, *Guidelines*.

3. The policy states: "(1) Research that is conducted or supported by a federal department or agency, whether or not it is regulated as defined in §46.102(e), must comply with all sections of this policy. (2) Research that is neither conducted nor supported by

a federal department or agency but is subject to regulation as defined in §46.102(e) must be reviewed and approved, in compliance with §46.101, §46.102, and §46.107 through §46.117 of this policy, by an institutional review board (IRB) that operates in accordance with the pertinent requirements of this policy."

4. Exempt research, as defined by 45 CFR 46, reads as follows: "(1) Research conducted in established or commonly accepted educational settings, involving normal educational practices, such as (i) research on regular and special education instructional strategies, or (ii) research on the effectiveness of or the comparison among instructional techniques, curricula, or classroom management methods. (2) Research involving the use of educational tests (cognitive, diagnostic, aptitude, achievement), survey procedures, interview procedures or observation of public behavior, unless: (i) information obtained is recorded in such a manner that human subjects can be identified, directly or through identifiers linked to the subjects; and (ii) any disclosure of the human subjects' responses outside the research could reasonably place the subjects at risk of criminal or civil liability or be damaging to the subjects' financial standing, employability, or reputation. (3) Research involving the use of educational tests (cognitive, diagnostic, aptitude, achievement), survey procedures, interview procedures, or observation of public behavior that is not exempt under paragraph (b)(2) of this section, if: (i) the human subjects are elected or appointed public officials or candidates for public office; or (ii) federal statute(s) require(s) without exception that the confidentiality of the personally identifiable information will be maintained throughout the research and thereafter. (4) Research involving the collection or study of existing data, documents, records, pathological specimens, or diagnostic specimens, if these sources are publicly available or if the information is recorded by the investigator in such a manner that subjects cannot be identified, directly or through identifiers linked to the subjects. (5) Research and demonstration projects which are conducted by or subject to the approval of department or agency heads, and which are designed to study, evaluate, or otherwise examine: (i) Public benefit or service programs; (ii) procedures for obtaining benefits or services under those programs; (iii) possible changes in or alternatives to those programs or procedures; or (iv) possible changes in methods or levels of payment for benefits or services under those programs. (6) Taste and food quality evaluation and consumer acceptance studies, (i) if wholesome foods without additives are consumed or (ii) if a food is consumed that contains a food ingredient at or below the level and for a use found to be safe, or agricultural chemical or environmental contaminant at or below the level found to be safe, by the Food and Drug Administration or approved by the Environmental Protection Agency or the Food Safety and Inspection Service of the U.S. Department of Agriculture." CFR Part. Code of Federal Regulations, title 45, Public Welfare Department of Health and Human Services, art. 46, Protection of Human Subjects, June 23, 2005, http://ohsr.od.nih.gov/guidelines/45cfr46.html#46.102.

5. Donald Ritchie, foreword to "2000 Oral History Evaluation Guidelines," *Oral History Association*, pamphlet 3, last modified September 2000, http://www.oralhistory.org /do-oral-history/principles-and-practices/oral-history-evaluation-guidelines-revised -in-2000/.

6. Ritchie, "Evaluation Guidelines." See also "Evaluators Draft Standards at Wingspread," OHA *Newsletter*, Summer 1979, 1; and "Evaluation Guidelines Adopted by Membership," OHA *Newsletter*, Fall 1979, 1, 6.

7. See Donald Ritchie, "From the President," OHA *Newsletter*, Spring 1987, 4; Ron

Marcello, "New Committee Will Begin Updating the Evaluation Guidelines," OHA *Newsletter*, Spring 1988, 5; and "Evaluation Guidelines Revised," OHA *Newsletter*, Winter 1989.

8. "AHA Adopts Statement on Interviewing for Historical Documentation," OHA *Newsletter*, Fall 1989, 3.

9. Richard Cándida Smith, "From the Executive Secretary," OHA *Newsletter*, Winter 1989, 5.

10. Richard Cándida Smith, "Council Considers Proposed Human Subjects Guidelines," OHA *Newsletter*, Spring 1997.

11. Linda Shopes, "Institutional Review Boards Have a Chilling Effect on Oral History," *Perspectives*, September 2000, http://www.historians.org/perspectives/issues/2000/0009/0009vie1.cfm. See also, "Revised Rules Could Affect Oral Historians," OHA *Newsletter*, Winter 1998, 6.

12. Department of Health and Human Services, National Institutes of Health, "Protection of Human Subjects: Categories of Research That May Be Reviewed by the Institutional Review Board through an Expedited Review Procedure," *Federal Register* 63, no. 216 (1998): 60364–67. See also "OHA Involved in New Rules Affecting Academic Oral Historians," OHA *Newsletter*, Winter 1999, 3.

13. Department of Health and Human Services, "Protection of Human Subjects."

14. Shopes, "Chilling Effect." I find the call for methodological review at the department level to be disingenuous; in most cases, decentralized review would mean no review at all.

15. Lucina McCray Beier et al., letter to the editor, *Perspectives*, January 2001, http://www.historians.org/perspectives/issues/2001/0101/0101let1.cfm.

16. Donald Ritchie served as the OHA representative, and Linda Shopes represented the AHA on the AAUP panel. The panel produced a brief survey on the activities of campus IRBs that was disseminated through the newsletters of the AHA, OAH, and OHA; the report was based in part on the survey and was initially published in the May–June 2001 issue of *Academe* and is currently available at http://www.aaup.org/statements/Redbook/repirb.htm. The preface states, "This report was prepared by the staff of the Association following meetings in November 1999 and May 2000 with representatives of the American Anthropological Association, the American Historical Association, the American Political Science Association, the American Sociological Association, the Oral History Association, and the Organization of American Historians to consider the experiences of social scientists and scholars in other academic disciplines whose research is subject to the government's rules for protecting human being." Linda Shopes subsequently reported that it was authored by AAUP staff member Jonathan Knight; see Shopes, "Historians and Institutional Review Boards: An Update," *Perspectives*, October 2001, http://www.historians.org/perspectives/issues/2001/0110/0110not2.cfm. See also "Oral Historians Asked about Institutional Review Boards," OHA *Newsletter*, Winter 2000, 5.

17. Alan Lessoff, quoted in "Panelists Defend, Criticize Campus IRB Process," OHA *Newsletter*, Winter 2001, 6.

18. The preface to the statement acknowledged that those projects which "conform to the regulatory definition of research" still will need to undergo IRB review.

19. Donald Ritchie and Linda Shopes, "An Update: Excluding Oral History from IRB Review," OHA *Newsletter*, Spring 2004, 1; also published in *Perspectives*, March 2004.

20. Oral History Association, "Application of the Department of Health and Human Services Regulations for the Protection of Human Subjects at 45 CFR Part 46, Subpart

A to Oral History Interviewing," Internet Archive, Wayback Machine, accessed October 10, 2011, http://web.archive.org/web/20060709071405/http://omega.dickinson.edu/organizations/oha/org_irb.html. The first word in this statement deserves closer scrutiny: "most." If only "most" but not "all" oral history projects should be immune from IRB review, who is to determine which projects need to be reviewed? This might well be interpreted by administering bodies as sending all oral history projects to IRBS at least for an initial review. On a recent implementation of policy that includes another "most" statement, similarly unexplained, see "Columbia University articulates IRB policy," *OHA Newsletter*, Spring 2008, 7.

21. "Application" (emphasis added).

22. Bruce Craig, "Oral History Excluded from IRB Review," *Perspectives*, December 2003, http://www.historians.org/perspectives/issues/2003/0312/0312news5.cfm.

23. E. Taylor Atkins, letter to the editor, *Perspectives*, December 2003, http://www.historians.org/perspectives/issues/2003/0312/0312let3.cfm; Atkins learned of the decision from an article published in the *Journal of Higher Education*: Jeffrey Brainard, "Federal Agency Says Oral-History Research Is Not Covered by Human-Subject Rules," *Journal of Higher Education*, October 31, 2003, A25. As a scholar working in one of the country's more visible oral history programs, I received e-mails and telephone calls from a number of colleagues seeking clarification on the OHRP concurrence. While some of the correspondents asked how the situation had changed at my institution, others, previously unaware of university IRBs and the history of oral history interaction with them, requested general background information to end the confounding of their confusion.

24. Linda Shopes and Donald Ritchie, "Exclusion of Oral History from IRB Reviews: An Update," *Perspectives*, March 2004, http://www.historians.org/perspectives/issues/2004/0403/0403new1.cfm.

25. This story is poorly documented in paper records; my account comes from conversations with Ann Lage and Richard Cándida Smith, Berkeley, California, 2007–8.

26. In a correspondence, Linda Shopes indicated to me that an official policy change was not sought because of the lengthy process and because, in her words, "OHRP has made it clear that this is not an option"; Shopes, e-mail message to author, April 22, 2006.

27. Shopes and Ritchie, "Exclusion of Oral History."

28. Robert Townsend and Mériam Belli, "Oral History and IRBS: Caution Urged as Rule Interpretations Vary Widely," *Perspectives*, December 2004, http://www.historians.org/perspectives/issues/2004/0412/0412new4.cfm.

29. Robert Townsend, "Oral History and Review Boards: Little Gain and More Pain," with Carl Ashley, Mériam Belli, Richard Bond, and Elizabeth Fairhead, *Perspectives*, February 2006, http://www.historians.org/perspectives/issues/2006/0602/0602new1.cfm.

30. Shopes and Ritchie, letter to the editor, *Perspectives*, December 2003, http://www.historians.org/perspectives/issues/2003/0312/0312let6.cfm. If a 2008 statement by the AHA executive director is an indication of the current situation, "impasse" is still the reigning paradigm; see Arnita Jones, "AHA Statement on IRBs and Oral History Research," *Perspectives*, February 2008, 14–15.

31. Shopes and Ritchie, "Exclusion of Oral History."

32. C. Kristina Gunsalus et al., "Improving the System for Protecting Human Subjects: Counteracting IRB 'Mission Creep,'" *The Illinois White Paper—Improving the System for Protecting Human Subjects: Counteracting IRB Mission Creep*, research paper

no. LE06-016, Center for Advanced Study, University of Illinois, Law and Economics, 2005, http://ssrn.com/abstract=902995.

33. John Neuenschwander, "ROHO Prevails in Defamation Lawsuit," OHA *Newsletter*, Fall 2005, 1, 3; alas, Neuenschwander paints a very rosy picture of the outcome of the lawsuit, which was not so definitive.

34. Similarly, I think that the extensive oral history evaluation guidelines first adopted in 1989 are, while well-meaning, far too extensive and overreaching to be a reasonable point of departure for many oral historians. IRB's narrower concerns with informed consent, first and foremost, should be the sole concern of research oversight. OHA's evaluation guidelines can be found at "Evaluation Guide," OHA, last modified on December 9, 2008, http://www.oralhistory.org/wiki/index.php/Evaluation_Guide.

35. Center for Advanced Study, "Improving the System," 3.

36. The understanding is that under normal conditions, oral history projects should be granted expedited review.

37. This list is not exhaustive, and contains few of the details included in the written collateral sent to interviewees.

38. My suggestion here that community-based projects establish their own oral history project review committees is meant to be serious, even if I realize the chances of this happening are slim. Given the complexity of oral history projects and the fact that so many are run so poorly (lacking informed consent, lacking closure, etc.), I believe that some established mechanism for review of project methodology is warranted and, in fact, beneficial to interviewee, interviewer, and sponsoring organization.

39. Linda Shopes, "Human Subjects and IRB Review," OHA, June 21, 2010, http://www .oralhistory.org/do-oral-history/oral-history-and-irb-review/.

40. "Principles and Best Practices," OHA, June 21, 2010, http://www.oralhistory.org /do-oral-history/principles-and-practices. This document replaces the "Oral History Evaluation Guidelines."

WILLOUGHBY ANDERSON

The Presence of the Past

Iconic Moments and the Politics of
Interviewing in Birmingham

THE CIVIL RIGHTS DEMONSTRATIONS and keen resistance to
desegregation in Birmingham, Alabama, loom large in the national imagination. Police dogs and fire hoses turned on black schoolchildren made
international headlines in the spring of 1963, putting the city into the center
of a civil rights media storm. The power of those days has not ebbed in local
minds. Interviewing in Birmingham for my dissertation and the Southern
Oral History Program, I often found discussions circling back again and
again to the events of 1963 and the city's national moment. As I tried to
push the interviews forward to my own research topics, school desegregation in the 1970s or the recent Sixteenth Street Baptist Church bombing
trials, I faced a dilemma: how should I deal with this pervasive memory?
The power and importance of those days in spring 1963 and the memories
that accompany them cannot be denied. Yet they presented a serious challenge to a historian who wanted to study a more recent past. How could
I extend the narrative in interviewees' minds to explore civil rights in the
city's recent past rather than allow one iconic moment to tug the interviews
backward? When confronted by a history with such a strong hold over the
present, how does the researcher parse the events of yesterday from the
politics of today?

In both popular imagination and most historical treatments, Birmingham is frozen at the moment in 1963 when television cameras brought images of police dogs attacking civil rights demonstrators to a shocked national
audience. The product of decades of local organizing, as well as the media
savvy of national leaders, these protests and the violent white reactions they
provoked propelled Birmingham to the forefront of the civil rights movement. Just months later, the deaths of four children in the Sixteenth Street

Baptist Church bombing, an event that many see as assuring the passage of key civil rights legislation, cemented the city's position as a symbol of white resistance to desegregation. Histories, films, and television series have helped to enshrine a standard narrative arc of the civil rights movement in popular memory, with Birmingham taking its place as a necessary dark before the dawn of the Civil Rights Act of 1964.[1] Scholarly treatments of the city often suffer from the same stasis; Birmingham becomes a symbol in the larger civil rights struggle rather than the subject of its own history. Even the fullest and most thoughtful analyses stop when media attention shifted away from Birmingham and on to other flashpoints of the movement.[2] This choice of endings downplays the subsequent struggle toward integration that persisted well after 1963.[3] Ignoring the continuing fight over desegregation and the changing forms of racialized inequality does not allow for an evaluation of the most contentious part of the movement—the implementation of promised rights—and serves to trap Birmingham, in history and memory, under the weight of its own infamy.

Since the 1970s the use of oral history interviewing as a tool to research the recent past has become a widespread and well-accepted methodology. Yet this tool brings its own unique challenges. When historians conduct interviews, unlike using a set of materials in an archive, they enter into a conversation with the historical subject. This dialogue between interviewer and interviewee creates the dynamic force of an interview, giving this kind of source a rich power often lacking in the dry documents. However, this give-and-take also brings with it questions about the content of the interview—about who is controlling the subject and the tone, what questions are asked and what answers given. By conducting interviews, historians become part of the exchange and thus part of the history. How will they influence the story recounted in an oral history? What is or is not being created in this historical source because of their presence?

I conducted interviews in Birmingham for my undergraduate honors thesis and throughout graduate school, basing my dissertation, in part, on those oral histories. Growing up in Birmingham, I heard little of its civil rights history; however, when I left to go to college, I was constantly confronted with the image of the fire hoses and the dogs, along with questions about present-day race relations in the city. Traveling back to conduct interviews, I felt very keenly the challenge of how best to uncover the recent past. And as I introduced myself—a young, white woman from Birmingham—I began to wonder about my position as the interviewer and the story being told to me.

Although I looked for Birmingham's civil rights history after 1963, it kept slipping away under the weight of those famous events. The iconic nature of that moment posed methodological challenges that other historians working on similarly well-documented events may encounter: how to look beyond the usual story, how to excavate forgotten characters and institutions. While telling a new story from old material is the nature of historical practice, with more contemporary topics, historians must factor in another obstacle: the political investment of their subjects in that past.

Interviews of a Native Daughter

One Tuesday in November, I found myself navigating from Homewood to Fairfield to the Hugo Black Federal Courthouse downtown. Maps spread out all over the seat of the car, I had been crisscrossing Birmingham for hours, avoiding the interstates and marveling at the sprawl. I made each interview (and on time) but for every spare minute spent waiting in a hallway, hours had been logged driving around and around, lost. My parents could not believe that I grew up in Birmingham. Looking back, I cannot believe that I had spent years studying Birmingham, researching the city's changing landscape of race, yet still had to hang a left into a gas station in a desperate search for Arkadelphia Road that day.

I began conducting oral histories in Birmingham as soon as I first ventured into the archives to research my undergraduate honors thesis. When I spoke with the archivists about my project—the Sixteenth Street Baptist Church bombing—they immediately suggested several people to talk with about the subject. I was also lucky enough in that initial research trip to have access to the Birmingham Civil Rights Institute's extensive oral history project. So for me, interviewing was a natural outgrowth of a history topic recent enough to still linger in memory. The power of this source made itself immediately clear. Each interview, as well as the many in the years that followed, opened my eyes to a new aspect of Birmingham's history and prompted me to consider the way that history has been written. Most humbling, each interview impressed on me just how little I knew about the city that I called home. I thought about the limitations of my own understanding of Birmingham: physical zones of the city I had never been to, parts of the city's history I was teaching myself. I found myself lost, not just on the city's roads or in understanding its past, but in working from one narrow viewpoint, one life experience.

Many white southern writers, particularly those from Birmingham, wield their race and class as a kind of badge, proof of their liberalism.[4] The deeply personal allure of Birmingham's history for many of its residents or former residents is a fascinating topic in and of itself.[5] I had always hoped to avoid placing myself in the narrative while writing about the city; I had not, after all, been a civil rights lawyer or grown up in Birmingham in the 1960s. And the oral history interviews I conducted knocked the legs out from under any pretenses I might have had about my own importance in telling this story. Yet, the process of interviewing tangled me up in that history, if only as the questioner in the archived interviews I was creating.

Oral historians have theorized extensively about the relationship of the interviewer and interviewee.[6] Drawing on insights gained in sociology and anthropology, early oral historians, and in particular feminist oral historians, strove consciously to establish a democratic, creative space in which the interviewee controlled and guided the story being told. Gender theory has also informed oral history methodology, allowing for an analysis of the power dynamic within the interview in terms of the class, race, and gender signifiers brought to bear by both parties.[7] Historians, whether willingly or not, must at least consider their position relative to their sources and the way that position colors their reading of the history.[8] The palpability of that positionality when faced with another person as a historical source sparked in me, even as a college senior, an awareness of the way that race, class, and gender are all at play in the interview setting, influencing the questions asked, the answers given, and the way the interview is structured.

Birmingham's troubled history carries its own set of unspoken interpersonal dynamics. Even though I have not lived in the city for more than ten years, I would tell my interviewees that I was "from Birmingham," alerting them to the fact that I would "understand," that I was "one of them." Even as I attempted to establish that connection, assuring the interviewee of our shared understanding, I was constantly aware of how complicated a sense of belonging I had. In his classic oral history primer, *Voice of the Past*, Paul Thompson discusses the interviewer's "social presence." Interviewees shape answers based on a guess as to what is expected, their understanding of the interviewer, as well as the comfort level of the interview itself. Thompson warns against interviewers stressing insider status to gain information: "If the social relationship in an interview becomes, or is from the start, a social bond, the danger towards social conformity in replies is increased."[9] Social bonds specifically affect the narrative of Birmingham's civil rights history; however, they also encompass a well of racialized knowledge and assumptions brought to bear by both my African American and white interviewees, because I am "from Birmingham."

I have interviewed powerful (or formerly powerful) white conservatives, as well as African American foot soldiers in the civil rights movement and the struggles to desegregate Birmingham schools. In both cases, I quickly became aware of the way certain suppositions as to my opinions and knowledge hung in the air between us. Age was an interesting factor, leading many of my older African American female interviewees to size up what they considered to be my relative youth. They then began to lecture, to teach really, both the history of Birmingham from before my time, as well as aspects of life under segregation that they assumed I could not know because of my race and my age.

More chillingly, older racial conservatives reached out to me. Kathleen Blee discusses the unsettling ease of empathy established in her interviews with women formerly involved in the 1920s Klan.[10] She talks about how her interviewees simply assumed that she, as a white woman, held similar, if unspoken, attitudes about white supremacy. The conservative interviewees I have spoken with did not assume that I agreed with their ideology. My stated research subject—the civil rights movement in Birmingham—and, I believe, my standing as a member of a younger generation brought forth from the interviewees a defense, a desire for validation. While discussing the civil rights movement as something "in the past," a necessary evil imposed from without and now survived, one interviewee in particular sought to draw me out, by turning a question back and asking, "Don't you agree?" This dynamic turns as much on the need to justify oneself to history, here embodied by a historian, as well as to the next generation. However, I know that my age and race played a large part in his desire for consensus. Because I was a young woman, he also sought to tap any conception I might have of myself as a "southern lady," referencing that directly before our interview, as he tried to establish our mutual understanding.

I have consciously crafted a position of being "from Birmingham" over the years without fully thinking through the weight of the assumptions that came with it. Thompson expands on his concept of "social presence," moving it from the individual level to the role of community attitudes and censure in what is discussed in the interview: "Even when others are not present at the interview itself, their unseen presence outside may count. This is a particularly important influence in any tight-knit community."[11] Race works in this way in my interviews, manifesting as a wave of community attitudes and unstated understandings. I often was at a loss to combat these ideas and felt myself swept along, unwilling to break the bonds of empathy discussed by Blee in interviewing, for example, a defensive conservative, or even in hearing tales of what an interviewee assumed I could not have known because I did not grow up under segregation. Famous oral historian Alessandro Portelli insists that interviewers represent themselves truthfully, laying out their political position, even to the point of potentially antagonizing the interviewee.[12] Yet the weight of the color line I felt upon returning to Birmingham pressed me toward complicity with the interviewee's assumptions, even as I attempted to push past those attitudes.

My asserted position as from Birmingham also influenced the narrative of Birmingham's history as told to me by the interviewees. Oral history is a unique methodology in that it is a creative, joint project, what Portelli has called "the experiment in equality which is fieldwork."[13] Although historians may use personal charm or insider status to gain access to family papers or that last file in the archive before closing time, in so doing they cannot change the content of the source they may find there. Interviewing is different, as interviewees respond to the story they believe the interviewer wishes to tell and, sometimes, to the story they would rather have told. In a sense all historical sources have an agenda, something specific to convey. However, the unfinished nature of civil rights history, like many raw recent topics, draws the political investment of both historian and subject into sharp definition.

Dogs and Fire Hoses

I first decided to take Birmingham as my research subject in the late 1990s, when the newspapers reported preparations for another Sixteenth Street Baptist Church bombing trial. That famous bombing, timed to the beginning of school desegregation, killed four girls and wounded numerous other members of the congregation. Occurring just months after the famous mass demonstrations led by Martin Luther King Jr., and local civil rights leaders, the bombing and national horror in its wake have been interpreted by many as securing the passage of the Civil Rights Act. Yet local and federal officials arrested no suspects in the 1960s; no one was prosecuted for the crime until 1977. Although the case had been reopened on and off, when I began research for my undergraduate honors thesis, two of the original four suspects still remained at large.[14]

In beginning my research, I was already looking to the period following the city's most famous civil rights events, after the spring when Birmingham became the site of King's first major nonviolent victory and the scene of his now-iconic letter from jail denouncing white moderates and their calls for patience.[15] However, as I interviewed Birmingham residents about the bombing and the 1977 trial, the discussions would inevitably return to spring 1963 and the Children's Crusade. While I tried to steer the interviews to other topics, I was faced with the question of how to manage this prominent memory.

Portelli addresses the issue of an overbearing moment in memory, culled from his own work with student movement activists:

> We may also come across narrators whose consciousness seems to have been arrested at climactic moments of their personal experience: certain Resistance fighters, or war veterans; and perhaps certain student militants of the 1960s. Often, these individuals are wholly absorbed by the totality of the historical event of which they were part, and their account assumes the cadences and wording of *epic*.[16]

This sense of the "epic" nature of the civil rights narrative is further complicated by the canonization of the events of the movement itself, as enshrined in popular films, TV shows, histories, and monuments.[17] Oral history is especially vulnerable to the influence of the media on interviewees' narratives of past events; the way that the cultural zeitgeist manifests in interviews comprises one fascinating layer of this kind of source material. Birmingham's demonstrations and subsequent strategic importance in the national movement have become such an important part of local history and Birmingham's community identity that these events seep into many people's recollections of any past event. This fixation on the demonstrations is the result, in part, of intense media coverage and historical interest in that period of Birmingham's history, along with the drama, violence, and unquestionable power of that time.[18] In interviews many individuals would not willingly carry their memories forward to the Sixteenth Street bombing, stopping their story instead with the successful spring demonstrations or, as was the case with one interviewee, mentioning the bombing but quickly and uncomfortably moving on. This points to the therapeutic value of this narrative, particularly for former activists, and the way that the mind chooses to remember points of victory rather than pain.[19]

In these interviews, 1963 Birmingham emerges as a particular kind of *lieu de mémoire*, as described by Pierre Nora.[20] Deliberately created and maintained, sites of memory, which can be public displays and monuments, trials, archives, celebrations, or, in this case, the retelling of a specific set of events from the past, represent a moment of history removed from its context, showcased, and disputed.[21] While some southern historians resist the application of the lieu de mémoire conceit to the South generally, I invoke Nora's construct of a site of memory here not as a literal interpretation of this historical moment but rather as a way to interrogate the recurring image of 1963 that appears over and over in public discussions in Birmingham.[22] I choose the *lieux* as a theoretical tool to help make sense of the way certain moments of the city's past haunt it in the present.

The overwhelming influence of the events of that spring sometimes even impinged on my ability to conduct interviews. Interviewees sometimes protested that they were not worthy because they "were not there"—they did not march as children in the demonstrations in downtown Birmingham—although they were schoolteachers or community residents at the time. One former teacher directed me to videotaped interviews with "real" participants in the movement, explaining that those tapes would be more useful to me than her own perspective as a thirty-year veteran of Birmingham's public schools. Whether responding to what they perceive to be my research subject or their own sense of the important events of that time, or even repeating a story they have pieced together from the media and popular culture, my interviewees directed the narrative back again and again to Birmingham's place in the nationally televised civil rights movement. The moments of 1963 had become a pivot from which stories of individuals spun out, either willingly, as in the case of former activists or those sympathetic to the movement, or unwillingly, as with those who still feel victimized by civil rights demands.

In discussions with my interviewees, a refrain emerged, that the nation, or those outside the city, did not understand that Birmingham had moved forward. In 1963 Birmingham became, according to my interviewees, a symbol of African American organizing and white resistance to desegregation, but only the image of resistance remained, outweighing the victories and leaving the city frozen at a single moment in time. The city's reputation as "Bombingham" had become, according to Odessa Woolfolk, president emerita of the Birmingham Civil Rights Institute, "the elephant in the room": "So I tell people, Birmingham [today] is like the rest of America. Forty years ago we were an anomaly, but we are like the rest of America. We're progressive; we're struggling."[23] Some interviewees expected that I, having positioned myself as a historian from Birmingham, would tell a truer story than the one they felt existed of Birmingham's civil rights history, that is, a new history of civil rights victory and change rather than the old tale of resistance and stagnation.[24]

I, too, felt Birmingham's history after 1963 had not been adequately explored. I hoped that by focusing on the Sixteenth Street Baptist Church bombing I could extend the historiography and possibly use the recent bombing trials to investigate the city's relationship with its past. However, by choosing oral interviewing as a way of examining this history, I encountered several obstacles. First, it was sometimes difficult to compel interviewees to even talk about the events I was interested in—the bombing rather than the demonstrations, school integration rather than the early 1960s or the schools today. But beyond the exchange of the interview itself, my interviewees had distinct ideas about the larger story of Birmingham's history and how that story should be told. I had to address the classic, celebratory, and foreshortened popular narrative of the movement that leaves Birmingham in the spring of 1963 and has informed the way that citizens remember their past. In addition, I had to wrangle with my interviewees' sense that the city has been somehow misrepresented or misunderstood. In talking about their past, Birmingham residents were also thinking about the city's current image and the connection of its history to present-day political concerns.

Although within the interviews themselves I did not give up trying to move the discussion gently away from the demonstrations and toward other topics, at some point I realized that I could not prevail against the power of the dogs and fire hoses. So instead of resisting, I slightly changed course. My solution to these methodological problems was to explore the memory of the civil rights movement as a subject of inquiry. Rather than go searching for a particular story (which is exactly what our professors warn us against in graduate school) or letting my interviewees dictate the historical narrative, I decided to switch my focus to the conflict that had manifested in my interviewing experience: this battle over memory. I embraced the need to deal explicitly with this memory, to acknowledge its power and consider its ramifications for Birmingham's history and for Birmingham residents' reactions to that history today.

History and Memory

David Thelen recognized the value of oral history for memory studies in his 1989 article, "Memory and American History," arguing that attention to the individuals who participate in the "creation of a recollection" would push the field forward.[25] This attention to the individual—the individual subject, the individual narrative perspective, and the historian as a participating individual—changes not only the writing of history but its value as well. As Paul Thompson passionately explained,

> Finally, oral evidence can achieve something more pervasive, and more funda-
> mental to history. While historians study the actors of history from a distance,
> their characterizations of their lives, views, and actions will always risk being
> misdescriptions, projections of the historian's own experience and imagina-
> tion: a scholarly form of fiction. Oral evidence, by transforming the "objects"
> of study into "subjects," makes for a history which is not just richer, more vivid,
> and heart-rending, but *truer*.[26]

Oral histories point us toward "truer" narratives of the past, renderings in which individuals speak for themselves, showing us more definitively their experiences. The opportunity to conduct oral histories is a benefit of study-ing more contemporary topics. Oral histories as a source and methodology need not lead to a history of the memory of a certain event, but through my interviews I began to perceive the importance of the 1960s as a reoccur-ring theme for the story I would tell. I hoped these individual recollections could expose a longer history of the civil rights movement by looking be-yond demonstrations or the passage of legislation to the reverberations of those political and legal moves in individual lives.[27]

The revolution inherent in oral history as a methodology is precisely the individual voice. As Alessandro Portelli explains, "Oral history does not begin with one abstract person observing another, reified one, but with two persons meeting on a ground of equality to bring together their different types of knowledge and achieve a new synthesis from which both will be changed."[28] Through the relationship established in the room, the narrative between the interviewer and interviewee becomes a new addition to the source material and a new lesson of history. One of the great values of oral history interviewing is that it builds the historical record and, if shared in local archives, expands the efforts of all those looking to the recent past.

But interviewers must be aware of their own individual imprints on the interview. Portelli goes on to liken oral history's methodological impact on the profession to the influence of the point-of-view narration shift that occurred with the development of the novel in fiction; through interviewing the historian becomes an "I," another character in the story.[29] I, as a historian of Birmingham using oral history, cannot separate myself and my positioning—my age, race, gender, and class—from the version of the city's history that I wish to tell. As an interviewer, I am already in the story.

Ronald J. Grele explores the power dynamic of the interview session in an informative article, concluding that historians and interviewees are, "beneath the guise of politeness," in constant conflict as to the story being told.[30] He defines this conflict as the "political praxis" of interviews, meaning that the questions asked by interviewers, in which one version of history is sought, and the assumptions made by interviewees, including the desire to tell their often divergent or at least nonlinear version of events, both compete for dominance. I have felt this praxis in my own interviews as I, during college, went hunting for racists and villains in the city's history. I would probe for "change," delighting in sound bite–type nuggets from former politicians and lawyers as to the efforts of the good citizens of the city. Now, with some slight perspective, I hope, I am equally tangled in the praxis, as each interviewee challenges my understanding, opening a new viewpoint that demands to be heard. By fixing me in their gaze, I have responsibility to those whose story I would like to tell.[31] And because it is my own story as well, I have to find, if not comfort, at least a resting place within it.

Portelli explains, pressing his concept of the now-changed position of the historian further: "This is not a grammatical shift from the third to first person, but a whole new narrative attitude. The narrator is now one of the characters, and the *telling* of the story is part of the story being told. This implicitly indicates a much deeper political and personal involvement."[32] To that involvement I bring, of course, my own relationship to Birmingham as a hometown, along with the pressure of some interviewees—sometimes subtle, sometimes not—to craft a certain version of the city's past. I worry about how these influences might guide not only the history I write but, on a more fundamental level, the interviews I seek out, the questions I ask. While all historians should, at this point in the general historiography, be asking themselves much the same questions regarding their own subject position and wielding of a metanarrative of history, I have felt this dilemma very keenly within the push and pull of the interview setting.

This awareness of my own position has led me to individualize the story of Birmingham. Where I first went looking for the "Change" in Birmingham—the literal legacy of the civil rights movement in terms of legal and political advancement for African Americans—now I have shifted to lowercase *change*. The aftershocks of the movement, registering beyond failed attempts at school desegregation or depressing economic statistics, can be felt in a cultural change, a change in attitudes that is not uniform or unanimous, but that is palpable. Reception is one important, almost intangible, facet of the long civil rights movement. Changing attitudes temper the widespread understanding that the movement failed in some way, causing even the most angry to concede that something has changed in our perceptions of equal access and constitutional rights.

Oral history, used in combination with archival work in a focused local study, can illuminate these individual attitudes and how they change over time. Furthermore, individual memories as expressed through oral history can provide the theoretical intervention seen as necessary, at this point, to help anchor memory studies. Alon Confino, in his state-of-the-field article published in 1997, "Collective Memory and Cultural History: Problems of Method," explains that memory studies have become popularized and unmoored, ranging from subject to subject without the strong theoretical exploration needed to ground the new history. Confino calls not for analyses of cultural artifacts as evidence of social attitudes but to "look for memory where it is implied rather than said, blurred rather than clear, in the realm of collective mentality." Emphasizing reception of memory, Confino asks historians to examine the messy "multiplicities of memory" constantly made and received from an individual to a collective level. He calls for us to embrace this complexity, to allow it to serve "as a reminder to realize what is declared more often than practiced, namely the multiplicity of social experiences and representations, in part contradictory and ambiguous, in terms of which people construct the world and their actions."[33] Oral history can lead to a more complicated, more representative, and, dare I say, a truer history of memory.

Using oral history to reach the recent past forced me as a historian to broaden my scope, to examine both the version of history presented in the interviews and the way that story was told. The prominence of the famous demonstrations in my interviewees' minds led me to think about how and why 1963 surfaced in political, legal, and cultural battles in the city. As I compared newspaper accounts of a trial or the opening of a museum to an individual's memories of those events, I began to see challenges to the standard interpretation of the movement. Taking the memory of the civil rights movement as an explicit subject of inquiry led me to understand how a seemingly static moment of history is actually very much in flux in individuals' minds. This necessarily extends the movement's influence, as residents react to their past and express how that past interacts with their current identities. Furthermore, these alternative narratives of the civil rights movement offer tantalizing avenues for action today. By extending the legacy of that moment, a study of the memory of the civil rights movement pegged to the individual can expand the movement's political hold on the present.

Interviewing also impressed on me just how political the past can be. Oral history provides a valuable methodological tool for historians researching more contemporary events, but because these events reside in memory, they can become a part of interviewees' understanding of the present. The strong role historic moments play in shaping identity today presents a challenge for many researchers. The civil rights movement influences current questions of race and equality, making this a particularly fraught area; however, a scholar examining almost any recent topic may encounter powerful events lingering out of time. And by engaging with the recent past, a researcher's own sense of political placement may come to the surface. Consciousness of this can help the historian parse the dynamics within the interview room, understand the motivations for a subject's investment in iconic moments, and begin to navigate the presence of the past.

Notes

The author would like to thank Jacquelyn Hall, Larry Griffin, Beth Millwood, Horace Huntley, Laura Anderson, and Jim Baggett for all their help with this project. Thank you also to audience members and fellow panelists at the Oral History Association Meeting and the Southern Association of Women Historians Conference for your insightful comments on previous versions of this piece.

1. For this popular narrative of the movement, see Jacquelyn Dowd Hall, "The Long Civil Rights Movement and the Political Uses of the Past," *Journal of American History* 91, no. 4 (2005): 1233–63. For memory and the civil rights movement generally, see Renee C. Romano and Leigh Raiford, eds., *The Civil Rights Movement in American Memory* (Athens: University of Georgia Press, 2006).

2. David Garrow, *Birmingham, Alabama, 1956–1963: The Black Struggle for Civil Rights* (Brooklyn: Carlson, 1989); Glenn T. Eskew, *But for Birmingham: The Local and National Movements in the Civil Rights Struggle* (Chapel Hill: University of North Carolina Press, 1997).

3. Civil rights movement historians increasingly work within a long civil rights movement paradigm. See, for example, Timothy B. Tyson, *Blood Done Sign My Name: A True Story* (New York: Crown, 2004) and Glenda E. Gilmore, *Defying Dixie: The Radical Roots of Civil Rights, 1919–1950* (New York: Norton, 2008). Urban histories of integration in Birmingham have extended the city's civil rights story, emphasizing federal funding and urban renewal as themes. See Charles E. Connerly, *"The Most Segregated City in America": City Planning and Civil Rights in Birmingham, 1920–1980* (Charlottesville: University of Virginia Press, 2005) and Christopher MacGregor Scribner, *Renewing Birmingham: Federal Funding and the Promise of Change, 1929–1979* (Athens: University of Georgia Press, 2002).

4. These writers have produced historical accounts of Birmingham with ranging degrees of autobiographical content. Some examples include Diane McWhorter, *Carry Me Home: Birmingham, Alabama, the Climactic Battle of the Civil Rights Revolution* (New York: Simon and Schuster, 2001); Charles Morgan, Jr., *A Time to Speak* (New York: Harper and Row, 1964); Paul Hemphill, *Leaving Birmingham: Notes of a Native Son* (New York: Viking, 1993); and Elizabeth H. Cobbs / Petric J. Smith, *Long Time Coming: An Insider's Story of the Birmingham Church Bombing That Rocked the World* (Birmingham: Crane Hill, 1994).

5. Some fictionalized depictions of Birmingham's civil rights history include Christopher Paul Curtis, *The Watsons Go to Birmingham—1963* (New York: Bantam Doubleday, 1995); Anthony Grooms, *Bombingham: A Novel* (New York: Free Press, 2001); Sena Jeter Naslund, *Four Spirits: A Novel* (New York: Morrow, 2003); Hubert Grissom, "Bap-Bomb," unpublished play, premiered January 11, 2007, Tampa, Florida (see Susan Strickland, "Hubert Grissom Play to Premiere in Tampa," *Birmingham News*, December 26, 2006, 3D).

6. Most major studies of oral history methodology and theory include a discussion of this relationship. See, for example, Alessandro Portelli, *The Death of Luigi Trastulli and Other Stories: Form and Meaning in Oral History* (Albany: State University of New York Press, 1991) and Paul Thompson, *The Voice of the Past: Oral History* (Oxford: Oxford University Press, 2000). Many articles on oral history consider it as well, usually from an autobiographical stance. Some examples include Gwyn Prins, "Oral History," in *New Perspectives on Historical Writing*, ed. Peter Burke (University Park: University of Pennsylvania Press, 2001), 120–56; Kim Lacy Rogers, "Oral History and the History of the Civil Rights Movement," *Journal of American History* 75, no. 2 (1988): 567–76; and Kathleen Blee, "Evidence, Empathy, and Ethics: Lessons from Oral Histories of the Klan," *Journal of American History* 80, no. 2 (1993): 596–606.

7. See Blee, "Evidence, Empathy, and Ethics," 596.

8. This consciousness of historians' imprint on the writing of history developed from postmodern theory. See Peter Novick, *That Noble Dream: The "Objectivity Question" and the American Historical Profession* (Cambridge: Cambridge University Press, 1988).

9. Thompson, *Voice of the Past*, 139, 140.

10. Blee, "Evidence, Empathy, and Ethics," esp. 604–605.

11. Thompson, *Voice of the Past*, 140.

12. Quoted and discussed in ibid., 243.

13. Portelli, *Death of Luigi Trastulli*, xvi. See also, generally, chapter 2, "Research as an Experiment in Equality."

14. The final two suspects, Thomas E. Blanton and Bobby F. Cherry, were convicted in 2001 and 2002. Jamie Kizzire, "An End to an Era: Cherry Convicted in Killing of 4 Girls," *Birmingham Post-Herald*, May 23, 2002, A1. The fourth suspect, Herman Frank Cash, died in 1994 without ever standing trial. John Archibald and Jeff Hansen, "Death Spares Scrutiny of Cash in Bomb Probe," *Birmingham News*, September 7, 1997.

15. Martin Luther King, Jr., "Letter from a Birmingham Jail," in *Why We Can't Wait* (New York: Signet, 2000), 85–110.

16. Portelli, *Death of Luigi Trastulli*, 53 (emphasis in original).

17. See Hall, "Long Civil Rights Movement," 1234.

18. Some of my interviewees had already contributed to the Birmingham Civil Rights Institute's oral history project or met with other researchers. Because these interviewees in particular had probably already responded to a set of questions directed at the demonstrations, I believe they were more likely to reiterate a similar narrative to me.

19. For a discussion of the psychological effects of interviews on former activists, see Rogers, "Oral History," 569.

20. Pierre Nora, "Between Memory and History: *Les Lieux de Mémoire*," in *History and Memory in African-American Culture*, ed. Geneviève Fabre and Robert O'Meally (New York: Oxford University Press, 1994), 284–300.

21. Nora, "Between Memory and History," 289. Although Nora remains the touchstone for memory studies, his argument that historical memory, as manifest in *lieux de mémoire*, completely replaced collective memory has come under attack. See Susan Crane, "Writing the Individual Back into Collective Memory," *American Historical Review* 102, no. 5 (1997): 1375–76. She explains, "For if historical memory is only one form of collective memory, it may well be that collective memory has not been lost or supplanted but in fact has persisted in a way altogether unlike what has been proposed so far. In order to reconceptualize collective memory and show that it is not simply a historical artifact, I will suggest relocating the collective back in the individual who articulates it—the individual who disappeared in the occlusion of personal historical consciousness by the culture of preservation" (1375).

22. Bruce Baker cautions against applying Nora's model of history, memory, and *lieux de mémoire* to the U.S. South. Unlike France, the U.S. South never developed one dominant history, due largely to the lack of a centralized administrative state or even a leading center of culture. Bruce E. Baker, *What Reconstruction Meant: Historical Memory in the American South* (Charlottesville: University of Virginia Press, 2007), 5–6. Similarly, France's history of nationalization and then modernization in the context of the two world wars creates a very particular context for the disassociation of memory and history, something that Baker does not find in the U.S. South. I am not arguing for the application of Nora's work to the U.S. South generally or even during this specific period following the civil rights movement.

23. Odessa Woolfolk, interview with author, tape recording, Birmingham, Ala., June 4, 2003, *The Long Civil Rights Movement: The South since the 1960s; Remembering Bombingham, Remaking Birmingham*, 2003, series U.6, Southern Historical Collection, University of North Carolina at Chapel Hill.

24. Some interviewees referenced Diane McWhorter, a Birmingham native who published a best-selling book on the city's civil rights struggles. Some, particularly liberals, felt that her work revealed important aspects of the complicated web of white resistance.

Others, mostly conservatives, thought she reiterated a negative portrait of Birmingham. These interviewees pointed to oral history, especially, as a way to tell a more complete story.

25. David Thelen, "Memory and American History," *Journal of American History* 75, no. 4 (1989): 1118–19.

26. Thompson, *Voice of the Past*, 117 (emphasis in original).

27. On the state of the field for memory studies and southern history, see W. Fitzhugh Brundage, "Contentious and Collected: Memory's Future in Southern History," *Journal of Southern History* 75, no. 3 (2009): 751–66.

28. Portelli, *Death of Luigi Trastulli*, xii.

29. Ibid., 57.

30. Ronald J. Grele, "History and the Languages of History in the Oral History Interview: Who Answers Whose Questions and Why?," in *Interactive Oral History Interviewing*, ed. Eva M. McMahan and Kim Lacy Rogers (Hillsdale, N.J.: Erlbaum, 1994), 14.

31. Paul Thompson discusses at length the responsibilities of the interviewer to the interviewees and their community. See, for example, from *Voice of the Past*, 172, "If the study of memory 'teaches us that *all* historical sources are suffused by subjectivity right from the start', the *living* presence of those subjective voices from the past also constrains us in our interpretations, allows us, indeed obliges us, to test them against the opinion of those who will always, in essential ways, know more than ourselves" (emphasis in original).

32. Portelli, *Death of Luigi Trastulli*, 57.

33. Alon Confino, "Collective Memory and Cultural History: Problems of Method," *American Historical Review* 102, no. 5 (1997): 1395, 1398–1400.

CLAIRE BOND POTTER

When Radical Feminism Talks Back

Taking an Ethnographic Turn in the Living Past

ME: What I'm going to try to do throughout our time together is break down binaries.
SUSAN BROWNMILLER: You're going academic. It's like [the time] you said something about epistemology. I said, "Well, I don't know what this means, but . . ."[1]

As I sat down with feminist journalist Susan Brownmiller in the fall of 2009 to do the first oral history I had ever done, I could not help but be reminded of what different worlds we occupied in the mid-1980s. Coming off her best-selling book, *Against Our Will: Men, Women and Rape* (1975), she had become a prominent antipornography activist, working to close X-rated movie theaters and live sex shows in Times Square.[2] At the time I was in graduate school, dimly aware of this work, but mostly experiencing feminism through the impact it was having on traditional fields of scholarship. Sometime around 1985, I was invited to join a seminar of feminist academics and writers, many of whom were breaking new ground in their fields. It was an exciting moment to be a young historian associated with the emerging interdisciplinary field of women's studies. I remember reading portions of prize-winning monographs at their earliest stages, as well as debating some of the newest ideas and emerging fault lines in feminist thought.

The session I recall most vividly was a presentation by anthropologist Faye D. Ginsburg, who had done fieldwork among, and extensive oral histories with, female community activists battling one another over women's access to abortion in a small U.S. city far from our seminar room.[3] As the conversation wound down, we began to talk about the perils of doing research with living subjects. One member of the seminar said casually to another, "We anthropologists have a responsibility that you historians can't imagine. Our subjects are alive, will read our work, and could feel betrayed by it." The historians immediately leapt into the fray to assert our own deep commitments to ethical scholarship and respect for our subjects.

Not that any of us had worked with living subjects, you understand, or might have known how an ethical stance toward the living might differ from one's efforts to represent the dead. I, for example, was writing a dissertation about federal policing during the New Deal, almost entirely researched in government documents and police reports, a book that was later published as *War on Crime: Bandits, G-Men and the Politics of Mass Culture* (1998).[4] I had tracked down only one living participant, an elderly lady who had been a fugitive with Bonnie Parker and Clyde Barrow in 1933, and she had refused to be interviewed, fearing further publicity about a time in her life that she regretted. She was wise to turn me down: I was completely unfamiliar with research among living subjects, much less subjects who had a traumatic history of having been in gun battles with the police and incarcerated. Brushing aside my lack of experience, in the seminar that day I argued heatedly that it didn't matter that my subjects were in the graveyard—or that they would be by the time my book came out. Historians had a powerful obligation to represent people accurately and respectfully, I maintained, regardless of whether those individuals were still alive and able to hold us accountable for our views.[5]

Looking back on it, the only defense I can muster for my ignorance on this issue is that thirty years ago it was an abstract one for the vast majority of practicing historians. Few of us worked on the recent past. Colleagues who worked on far earlier periods than I did believed just as strongly that a commitment to representing the past accurately was at the core of an ethical disciplinary practice that was often wrongly accused of having a casual approach to empiricism. As feminist scholars, and as students highly influenced by what was then called the "new" social history, our research was driven by the fact that women and other marginalized groups had been overlooked or deliberately ignored by empirical practitioners in an earlier generation. We viewed our scholarship and the work of our mentors as a grand corrective to dominant historical narratives skewed by such exclusions. Feminism, we believed, *was* our ethical commitment to our subjects. That view only deepened when, in a 1986 essay that altered the practice of writing history, feminist scholar Joan W. Scott urged us to look beyond inclusion and to question the social binaries and paradigms that structured history itself.[6]

Fast forward twenty years from that argument to the day that I got my hands dirty with my first interview. As I sat in Susan Brownmiller's Greenwich Village penthouse, beginning my oral history practice with a woman who was a skilled interviewer in her own right, I had to work hard to push aside the growing realization that, although I had taken an intensive seminar in oral history and had fresh batteries in my digital recorder, I was wading into deep ethical waters as a researcher. As we sat there chewing over events three decades old, Brownmiller told stories that were familiar to me, but in her own way; she shared details about antipornography activism that I did not know and that other feminists were likely to dispute, and she allowed herself to be asked unusual and unfamiliar questions about the effect of antipornography politics on the feminist movement as a whole.

In the presence of this vibrant, witty, and generous woman, I felt my preinterview nerves drop away and a familiarity that might easily turn into friendship take over.[7] The tape is punctuated with laughter. As we cracked each other up, and then settled into a serious subject, Susan underlined many of her remarks by jabbing an often unlit cigarette through the air. Later, a member of my writing group read a first draft of this essay and sensed a connection that had developed during the course of the interview. He asked tactfully if I recalled Joan Didion's dark warning in *Slouching towards Bethlehem* (1968): "people tend to forget that my presence runs counter to their best interests," Didion wrote in the final lines of the introduction. "And it always does. That is one last thing to remember: *writers are always selling somebody out.*"[8]

Always selling somebody out: I never worried about this before I became a historian of the recent past, but I do now. I have typed Didion's sentences out and taped them next to my desk as a constant reminder that people on both sides of feminism's sex wars have a strong interest in what I am writing. But good intentions, I am afraid, are not enough, if living people who have helped me extensively hope, perhaps not even consciously, to see their own version of a contentious past vindicated. My research, begun with interviews among antipornography feminists, is perhaps the most exciting I have ever undertaken, and the most difficult. It has launched me into the practice of oral history and allowed me to meet and ask questions of historical actors. It has also taught me that the obligations that feminist social scientists felt bound by three decades ago in that seminar room addressed ethical obligations that we historians had barely begun to imagine.

I realize now that my naïveté on this issue was odd, since feminism had changed so much in my field already. Some of our foundational texts in the 1980s were critical accounts of a history that had barely passed or was still unfolding: Sara Evans's *Personal Politics: The Roots of Women's Liberation in the Civil Rights Movement and the New Left* (1980), Mary E. Berry's *Why ERA Failed: Politics, Women's Rights and the Amending Process of the Constitution* (1988), and Alice Echols's *Daring to Be Bad: Radical Feminism in America, 1967–1975* (1989) are a few prominent examples of books that would be published in that decade.[9] Echols's volume ends with a chapter on the split among radical feminists over pornography that I am currently researching, events that had occurred only a few years prior to publication and were still raging when *Daring to Be Bad* went to press. It is surprising that we historians who had such firm views about ethical representation scarcely viewed these volumes (all written by feminist activists who had become historians) as a living, recent past that might require something different from us than did the dead pasts we were used to.

We certainly did not anticipate that our own research might cause us to revise histories that we had admired as graduate students, ask new questions about what counted as feminism, or question why some social and political movements had been excluded from that history.[10] Feminist history's genealogy is not uniquely vulnerable to criticism in this regard. While scholars influenced by New Left social movements eagerly overturned some shibboleths about the past, highly focused dissertations and monographs that promise the inclusion of new evidence and new subjects can easily leave other exclusions firmly in place, or even create new ones.

Perhaps the greatest challenge presented by the new wave of feminist histories emerging now is that some will inevitably disrupt a consensus that an older generation of living activists has developed about its own past, and others will revive old animosities. Historians will have to tread carefully among opposing constituencies, be open to correction, and learn to negotiate obstacles to locating a stance that is both independent and respectful. Some of the research I have done in the archives of prominent white feminists has already turned up personal material that, if published, would risk exposing private lives that were concealed under carefully cultivated public personae, a methodological issue that has been discussed extensively by historians of African American women.[11] Oral histories present particular methodological challenges in this regard, particularly to those who are merely dipping into the practice as one of several methods of gaining access to a recent past: oral histories are not simply testimony or evidence but conversations and performances. As folklorist Katherine Borland argued in 1991, an interview consists of one "skillfully told tale" after another, "rooted in expressive social activity" and "artful talk." Oral histories also cannot be treated as raw, uninterpreted data. Interviews are shaped initially by their subjects and shaped again at the stage of the transcript in a "second-level narrative." They then become subject to scholarly interpretation that, in effect, reshapes an oral history for a third time. Each stage creates the possibility for what Borland calls "interpretive conflict": in other words, the interviewer and the subject may agree on what was said, but not on its meaning or significance.[12]

We who seek to tell these contentious stories also face institutional challenges that have emerged since these early accounts of second-wave feminism were published in the 1980s. University authorities today often keep a close eye on research involving human subjects, even that conducted by historians. Since the early 1990s, many institutions have required us to undergo approval from an Institutional Research Board (IRB). But unlike colleagues in the social sciences, graduate students in history who are casually advised by mentors to take advantage of the opportunity to include interviews with living subjects may be getting advice from those who have actually never done interviews, have never presented proposals to an IRB, and have never directly responded to formal questions about any of their methods.[13] Furthermore, the more recent the past, and the more controversial the episodes under study, the more likely it is that a book will engender controversy during the research process itself and the better planned that research needs to be as a consequence. More than once, I have talked to scholars working on some of the schisms that occurred among feminists during the 1970s and 1980s and heard some version of the following stories: "I did a great interview with ——— but when she saw what I was writing, she wouldn't let me use any of the quotes"; "she called her friends and told them not to talk to me"; and "she told me that she had decided to write her own memoir, and she wouldn't let me use the interview."

Few historians have been trained to handle heightened scrutiny by their own subjects. Unlike anthropologists and sociologists, historians—unless we are specialists in oral history—are not taught to take into account the relationship that exists between an author and an interview subject. The ethics of that relationship might properly ask us to "speak with" rather than "speak for" our subjects, as Karla Holloway puts it.[14] We are not taught to get a signed release before interviews, why we need to inform interviewees of their rights of joint ownership over the interview, or how to negotiate the contents of a final transcript. Writing contemporary history obligates scholars to take account not just of how persuasively and well documented our books are, but how our published work responds to the web of obligations and disagreements that we create in our wake. What effects does a historian's interpretation have on those who have donated their time to the project? Is it written in a language that they can accept and understand? Does it represent them honestly? Feminist activists from the 1960s, many of whom are living on the economic margins as they edge into retirement, may have less political influence than World War II veterans commanded when they challenged the Enola Gay exhibit at the Smithsonian in 1993. However, they have an established interest in their own representation and in the memory of their political causes, which many of them still work in. Taking on these topics represents a substantial ethical commitment to real people as well as to writing good history, whether the historian chooses to do oral interviews or not.[15]

What I Learned When I Stopped Arguing with the Anthropologists

As the story I began this chapter with suggests, when we are ready to listen, historians can look, not just to the scholars who have tackled questions of history and memory, but to colleagues in the social sciences who have the kind of methodological and ethical experience that many of our archive-based mentors did not teach us. Anthropologists and sociologists have a great deal to say about what they call "reflexive practice," a phrase that emerged several decades ago to describe the possibility of taking a critical approach to the social relationship between researcher and subject. For example, in "My Best Informant's Dress: The Erotic Equation in Fieldwork" (1993), anthropologist Esther Newton describes an ongoing flirtation with the elderly grande dame of Cherry Grove who made Newton's historical research possible by teaching her and connecting her to a network of old friends and ex-lovers.[16] In fact, Newton argues, eroticism might be central to the invention of ethnography, as the diaries of early twentieth-century ethnographer Bronislaw Malinowski reveal.[17]

Feminist scholar Kristin Luker helps us understand the process of creating social theory through interviews. Sociologists such as Luker collect stories not only to gather facts but also to understand and notice the patterns in the stories people tell about themselves, building theory in the process. "By and large," she argues in a way sure to make empiricist historians shift uncomfortably in their seats, "we are not so much interested in the veracity of the interviews, in some cosmic sense of the word, as we are in the deep truth of them." Following Barbara Myerhoff, Faye Ginsburg urges us to seek those patterns but also to watch for the life stories of subjects who are "atypical," teasing out important critiques of dominant narratives that might otherwise be lost in larger political and cultural struggles. Through such stories, distinct from life histories, subjects demonstrate narrative intent. Activists, and particularly those arguing from the margins, Ginsburg argues, are motivated by passionate conviction, "not just . . . cultural constructs or economic imperatives of which they have no awareness."[18]

Anthropological theory, particularly the work of Victor Turner, began to affect historians struggling with questions of representation and change over time as early as the 1980s.[19] The influence of cultural relativism on the discipline—which cannot be overstated—is embedded in historian John Lewis Gaddis's injunction that historians should attempt to grasp a larger sense of motion or drift in past events. Rather than put two contradictory, or just different, memories of the same events in competition with each other, Gaddis urges us to develop a sense of "how the parts interact to form the whole, not . . . focus on the parts at the expense of the whole."[20] However, this process cannot begin at the point of interpretation and writing, something that should cause us to note the differences between oral history and interviews done in the field. Historians do not have the opportunity to time travel and live among their subjects, and we usually find our subjects far too dispersed in the present to develop a sense of how they might talk to each other about their common history.

Ideally, historians trained to the paper archive would not, when seizing upon a new project in the recent past, simply run off with a digital tape recorder and start talking to people. And yet we do. Despite the fact that the practice of oral history is among the earliest of our traditions, dating back to the late nineteenth-century Johns Hopkins seminar room where Herbert Baxter Adams urged students such as Frederic Bancroft to interview a rapidly aging population of former slaves and slaveholders, many of us treat living subjects as just another kind of archive. There is an extensive

literature detailing the difficulties and responsibilities of oral history practice, although many scholars who want to do a few interviews do not consult it prior to embarking on living-subjects research. But this literature is
uneven in its attention to the historians' privilege of substituting their own
interpretations for those of the interview subjects. Again, this is not a new
problem. J. H. Hexter's admonition that all of us bring a "second record" of
acquired knowledge and experience to our research and Hayden White's
theories of narrative suggest that self-consciousness about method and interpretation behooves us all, whether the subjects are living or dead.[21]

It was researching and writing my book about the history of feminism's
"sex wars" during the 1980s that caused me to realize how little direction the
majority of historians have when it comes to collecting and interpreting the
interviews that must play a significant role in our writing about the recent
past. As I became enmeshed in a project that details a time of often bitter
conflict and diametrically opposed interpretations within radical feminism,
my research experiences among antipornography activists caused me to recall (with a sympathy I wish I had displayed at the time) Ginsburg's dilemma back in our feminist seminar room. Like her, I have been entrusted
with the stories of activist women for whom many contemporary feminist
scholars have had little or no sympathy, but all the same, they are women
who have trusted me to tell their story. That trust, and simultaneously at-
tending to the truths of those who dispute these stories and interpretations
(how radically different "parts interact to form the whole") is part of what
becomes compelling about research among the living.

While it was my expectation that my interviews with activists on both
sides would be exciting, my first interviews, those with antipornography
feminists, have already promised to deliver a new history of the sex wars
that links this moment to political phenomena beyond feminism, I began
with this group because many are significantly older than their opponents,
but also because I know their story has been less accessible. In the 1980s
activists and academics on the left who mobilized against antipornography campaigns wrote influential stories for the *Village Voice* and other local newspapers about antipornography activists' proposed changes in local
zoning and civil ordinances that they feared would have a significant impact on free speech as well as the sex trades. Extended analyses of the larger
dangers attendant to restricting sexual expression appeared in best-selling
and durable academic anthologies such as Carole S. Vance's *Pleasure and
Danger: Exploring Female Sexuality* (1993). Lisa Duggan and Nan Hunter's

influential work that explicated the dangers of censorship, *Sex Wars: Sexual Dissent and Political Culture* (1995), a collection that includes several essays from the ordinance struggle and contextualizes them in the conservative backlash of the 1980s, was recently rereleased in a tenth-anniversary volume.[22] In the classroom, where the use of works like these far exceeds coverage of materials from antipornography intellectuals such as Catherine MacKinnon and Andrea Dworkin, they have had an enormous impact on how the history of this period has been documented and understood.

Yet social movements are mostly made up of people who do not publish. How to tell the *whole* story of the sex wars, to produce my own interpretation and allow feminists on all sides of this divisive debate to be represented in a way they recognized as faithful to the truth? I now regret my naive view, expressed so many years ago in that seminar of experienced scholars, that bringing living people into one's research does not impose special obligations and problems. I certainly did not imagine in the 1980s, when I was involved in an argument about ethnography, that I would one day go to ethnography for help. I did not perceive that the "sex wars" referenced in that seminar would be one of the most publicly controversial episodes in the history of second-wave feminism, a breaking point that would end friendships, push some women out of movement politics, marginalize some intellectuals, and raise others to prominence in academic circles.[23] I did not understand that a contemporary conflict within radical feminism over violence, pornography, and representations of the erotic would become "history," much less one I would write.

I certainly did not dream that some of the people in that seminar room would actually be in the book.

Antipornography Feminism and the Problem of the Controversial Recent Past

The history of second-wave feminism is a volatile one, and antipornography activism may have been its most explosive and prolonged episode: they didn't call it the "sex wars" for nothing. (One historian to whom I described the project opened his eyes wide in mock terror and said, "Oooooh! You're writing *that* book!") Conflict over the status of pornography in the movement began in the mid-1970s, when radical feminists who had organized against rape began to publicly critique the connections between rape, domestic violence and depictions of sexual violence in the media. This analysis then led some activists to identify a burgeoning pornography industry as a central player in violence against women. In August 1978 radical feminists involved in the Bay Area, following the formation of Women against Violence against Women (WAVAW) in Los Angeles in 1975, established Women against Violence in Pornography and the Media (WAVPM). This organization's prior incarnations as the Women's Anti-Degradation Alliance (WADA) and Women against Media Violence and Degradation points to a critical connection between the broader themes of women's liberation and the antipornography movement: that gender was constructed and that "men" and "women" learned sex roles and behaviors from culture.[24]

The terrain of 1970s radical feminist mobilizations, collectives that formed and dissolved so quickly they are difficult to track, is genuinely confusing. The feminist antipornography movement, which continues to this day in some places, is a particular challenge to the historian's desire for closure and categorical unity, its interlocking, shifting, and sometimes incompatible agendas producing what anthropologist George E. Marcus might call "a messy text."[25] While California activists began with, and retained a high focus on, violent messages about women in the film, television, and music industries—particularly what they called "cock rock"—by 1979 San Francisco feminists had launched a focused antipornography movement by targeting the commercial sex industries in the Tenderloin and North Beach. These radical feminists soon imagined themselves as a vanguard for what might eventually be a national and international web of community-based antipornography collectives. They extended earlier campaigns against rape and domestic abuse from the 1970s to encompass an industry that was increasingly embraced by bourgeois consumers and that relied for its profits on *fantasies* about violence against women. Such fantasies, they pointed out, became real for many women, and not just because ordinary men might act on what they saw in magazines and on movie screens. Actors, models, and even porn "stars" employed in the industry were managed and robbed of their fees by men who were petty crime figures, pimps who maintained control over actors and models through drugs, financial dependency, and physical (as well as psychological) abuse.[26]

The first feminist media activism groups were founded in Los Angeles and New York; some WAVAW chapters evolved into antipornography groups, while others did not. But it is no accident that San Francisco, a city that was famous for sex tourism and radical lesbian activism, housed the first WAVAW group to make this shift. The transformed chapter, which became WAVPM, was also the first to concentrate its efforts on street actions against peep shows, live sex acts, and pornography.[27] For decades, the lives of lesbians, gay men, and other sex radicals had been imbricated in vast red-light districts that had only recently been relieved of police scrutiny because their gay, lesbian, and transgender residents had learned to resist, organize, and demonstrate. Some feminists within WAVPM turned these skills on pornographers, at the same time raising concerns about free speech and the repression of free sexual expression that would later be more characteristic of the opposition to antipornography activism. As WAVPM began to target sexual commerce, this feminist opposition emerged within a radical leather dyke community that had organized first as Cardea in 1977 and then as the Samois Collective between 1978 and 1983.

Intellectuals, writers, and radical sex practitioners found support among former WAVAW members as well. Distressed with an intensified antiviolence activism that they feared would restrict consensual forms of sexual expression, these latter activists were also in the process of crafting a new lesbian sexual citizenship from the bottom up, one based on feminist interrogations of shame, power, and pleasure.[28] Furthermore, S/M lesbians relied heavily on kinky men and on gay male sex clubs, both of which were potentially threatened by WAVPM feminist activism in the Tenderloin, to develop their praxis and to learn techniques of bondage, domination, and pain. Anticipating queer theory, which would emerge in the 1980s, they understood gender as a fluid category, one that intersected with sexuality in unexpected ways. S/M was not just a form of sexual expression but allowed women to enact forms of power that could be gendered male or female by choice. In this context, pornography, along with the sex clubs that WAVPM saw as sites for the abuse of women, were valuable spaces for fantasy and responsible sociality, a precondition for the formation of community.[29]

These early developments in San Francisco were crucial to the emergence of the sex wars of the 1980s. However, subsequent organizing in New York City—particularly the ordinance movement after 1983, when antipornography activists pursued a strategy of defining freedom from pornography as a civil right, and the Feminist Anti-Censorship Task Force (FACT) made a coalition with the American Civil Liberties Union and other groups to block them—has dominated interpretations of the movement's earliest period. New York antipornography feminists' accounts, and those of Samois's allies elsewhere, have also tended to underplay the importance of the organizations that emerged in all the cities in between the two coasts.

In most accounts, the sex wars began at the moment this conflict became visible when Women against Pornography (WAP) opened its Times Square storefront in 1979. The struggle over censoring sexual expression intensified at the 1982 Barnard conference, "The Scholar and the Feminist," which included leather activists, explicitly sexual programming, and a panel on BD/SM. WAP picketed the conference and demanded that Barnard withdraw the program (Barnard did so). Activists also harassed featured speakers, actions that some claim continued long after the conference and played a key role in making the dangers of censorship clear to feminists who were otherwise conflicted about pornography. The sex wars intensified after 1983, when FACT mobilized to oppose the model ordinance written by radical antipornography feminists Catherine MacKinnon and Andrea Dworkin, which eventually became influential outside the United States as well. The sex wars ended in 1993, when WAP (which had survived a decade beyond the collapse of the San Francisco group in 1983) closed its doors. Some of its remaining activists continued their work in locations as diverse as the battered women's shelter movement, nongovernmental organizations devoted to the fight against sexual trafficking, anti-incarceration activism, and the State Department under George W. Bush.

Needless to say, in such contested and confusing terrain it is easy to take a step likely to offend or distress former activists: each story, and the meaning of that story, is easily countered by someone else's truth. One way I have devised to tell the stories of antipornography activists without, as Didion puts it, "selling somebody out," is to ask feminists to make sense of their activism as part of a longer life-history narrative. This broader context is easy to miss in a narrowly directed day in the archives, but it can be elicited using standard oral history practices through which the interviewer puts subjects at ease by asking personal questions designed to stir memory. Rather than violating subjects' sense of "who they are" by taking them directly to that disputable moment, the interviewer can ask for more complexity and depth by digging into a further past and returning to that moment in context. Who were your parents? Were they political? What was your introduction to politics? Were you always a feminist? How did you come to name your politics "feminism"? I discovered, for example, that many of the defining figures in the early movement moved on quite quickly and made only token appearances during the most difficult moments of the sex wars. Brownmiller was involved in antipornography activism for less than five years and rarely present by 1982 (many activists were attached to the movement for even less time). But those years are also informed by a longer trajectory: New Deal left politics, the civil rights and peace movements, Brownmiller's critical role in the antirape and antibattering movements, and her continuing commitment to progressive politics.

Understanding the relationship between conventional politics and feminist activism through these conversations has helped me break out of a paradigm that locates antipornography feminism in what some scholars have, until recently, perceived as an almost entirely self-referential cultural feminist world.[30] As I now understand it, by the 1970s radical feminists, like other social activists, tended to prefer membership in engaged, chosen communities as an alternative to, and in active opposition to, national citizenship. However, they also saw their work as vitally connected to the larger communities in which they were based, resulting in more diversity and internal dissent within the early phase of the movement than has been previously understood. Like Brownmiller, most radical feminists had histories with several political movements, and they urged one another to be aware of possibilities for potential alliances with other oppressed groups. Understanding this fact allowed me to make sense of otherwise unimportant and seemingly quaint details in the paper archives of antipornography collectives. In New York, WAP acquired significant community support from some small business owners in Times Square who were not involved with the sex trades and who had as large a stake in the redevelopment of the district as any of the larger corporate or government interests. San Francisco, a critical site for the antiwar and gay liberation movements, offered rich opportunities for feminists to have dialogue and make alliances with a variety of black, Asian American, and Latino/a community groups; radical elderly citizens (the Gray Panthers); and a radical sex workers' movement (Call Off Your Old Tired Ethics, or COYOTE).[31]

It is not impossible that the international trajectory of antipornography activism was shaped as much by these early alliances, however vexed they were, than by the national phase of the movement after 1983. In 1977, before it found a home at the Berkeley Women's Center, WAVPM met at COYOTE's storefront. By 1975 COYOTE founder Margo St. James had already attended a UNESCO-sponsored meeting of the International Abolitionist Summit, later claiming that she was "the first whore ever in its one hundred year history to take the floor." In turn, WAVPM may have also inspired other identity-based activists to address violence more seriously. Already overextended with its own projects, WAVPM repeatedly called on its membership to support antiviolence organizing that was not confined to issues of women's sexuality. "Patsy and Elmo, who recorded the hit song 'Grandma Got Run Over by a Reindeer' will be performing . . . at S.F's Boarding House," one set of Action Committee minutes from 1979 notes. "Action was taken to support the Gray Panthers in their protest of this event."[32]

Understanding this movement context eventually led to seeing myself as activists saw me: an academic, with little background in the grassroots work and coalition building that former antipornography feminists valued. In fact, when I first began my interviews, I failed to realize that my self-identification as a university-based scholar put me at a disadvantage for doing this research at all among women who valued engaged intellectual labor in the community. As I came to know Brownmiller and other activists, I also realized, to my horror, that I had overlooked a crucial feature of my own history: that I had attended graduate school at New York University, where many activists who saw antipornography activism as a threat to free speech and women's sexual freedom were employed. They had been key organizers of the seminar I described at the beginning of this chapter, where many of the preexisting views that I brought to this topic had been shaped. Once I grasped this, I also came into possession of an important point of insight about the lingering resentment antipornography feminist activists bore toward their opponents. Scholars and theorists, many of them university-based, had produced nearly all the critical accounts of this phase of the modern women's movement in the 1980s and 1990s. Although numerous antipornography feminists were accomplished writers, this was a moment in which the independent feminist publishing collectives that had published their work were dissolving, and major publishing houses were no longer interested in publishing self-identified feminist work. In this commercial atmosphere, academics and intellectuals admired by academics, supported by a comparatively well-financed network of university presses, were acquiring increasing influence over what ideas counted as "feminist." Although many other intellectuals were silenced by the collapse of independent publishing, academics shaped the feminist classroom and acquired new influence over which ideas would reach a broader progressive public.

Antipornography feminists had built a broad-based social movement, and many have since pursued their commitments in other influential spheres. However, a few intellectuals, not unlike myself, have had a greater opportunity to construct the historical memory of the sex wars and to define the legacy of radical feminism. Several of these pieces—for example,

Gayle Rubin's classic 1984 article "Thinking Sex" (1984), a critical approach to stigma and sexuality derived from her struggles with antipornography feminism—anticipated new intellectual directions for the movement, as has Duggan and Hunter's *Sex Wars*. Both are widely acknowledged today as turning points for the emergence of queer theory from feminism, even as these authors' activist connection to the events of the sex wars grows more obscure to younger readers.[33]

Conversely, antipornography feminists (with the exception of MacKinnon and Dworkin, neither of whom ever joined an antipornography group) had little interest in the research or theory that were beginning to define academic feminism by the 1980s. Brownmiller, for example, left Cornell prior to completing her bachelor's degree, went to work as a civil rights organizer, became a public writer, and found her intellectual home in radical feminist politics. She has taught off and on, but the university has never been instrumental to her work, as it has been to mine. Many antipornography feminists also believe that those who sought to discredit them did so in part by publicizing what they believed to be strategic, incidental, or accidental connections with conservatives. As a consequence many, although not all, have a deep distrust of unknown historians and documentary filmmakers who show up swearing that they will tell the "real story." Who can blame them?

The scenario I just sketched only highlights something that all researchers who stick their toes in the water of living-subjects research need to be aware of: interviews are always inflected by power dynamics and by history itself. What feminist legal theorist Janet Halley has called "power over," the capacity to impose one's own desires on a subject, story, or relationship, is something that even feminist historians discuss too little in relation to either the act of research or the act of interpretation.[34] Unlike working in paper archives, in an ethnographic approach to recent history, living subjects get to interrogate the historian as well, to try to anticipate how their stories might be understood and used. This interrogation can continue long beyond the interview. The unspoken question on the table from all veterans of the sex wars is always: "What kind of feminist are you?" This has been a hard question for me, a lifelong feminist, to answer, given the virtual absence of a contemporary social movement in which to make myself legible. But when the terrain of the interview is defined by our mutual interest in a prolonged political episode so divisive and traumatic that many other scholars and former activists believe that it destroyed second-wave feminism as a movement, my answer—and my ongoing engagement of the question—will be vital to how I am understood, the kind of interview I walk away with, and the permission to use it.[35]

Of course, no one has ever just come out and asked what kind of feminist I am. However, to create honest relationships with former antipornography activists, I have had to wrestle with this useful intellectual question, as well as with my historical connection to the research I have chosen. Such lessons will serve me well, as my oral history project expands to include the opponents of antipornography activists as well. This form of self-reflection is what anthropologist Ruth Behar calls "vulnerable observation": the recognition that a scholar is drawn to topics for a reason and has an a priori relationship to living subjects that needs to be explored and honored as she works toward interpretation. Arguing against detachment and an insistence on interpretive autonomy that can set us at odds with the interests of our subjects, she cites Clifford Geertz's advice that the ethnographer become "enmeshed" as an alternative to exploitation. This too is a balancing act: as Behar asks, "But just how far do you let that culture enmesh you?" Contemporary historians need to be constantly aware that new evidence may carry new ethical responsibilities with it, as we navigate the relationships that make research possible. Behar notes, "the worst of it is that not only is the observer vulnerable, but so too, yet more profoundly, are those we observe."[36] Aside from the possibility of doing harm or, the reverse, simply channeling subjects' point of view without interpretation, angry interviewees have recourse and agency to talk back to the researcher. If they have not already signed permissions that allow us to publish freely, or quote from archived collections to which they have retained copyright, living subjects can refuse to do so, putting a historian in the awkward position of being unable to document major arguments that have shaped the book.

And have I mentioned that they can also sue? This is why publishers will ask for releases for the evidence drawn from interviews. But I do not wish to focus on the power that subjects can muster to enforce their point of view, at the expense of emphasizing the collaborative work that an oral history can, and should, be. Katherine Borland resolved a conflict with an elderly relative, offended that Borland had called her a feminist, by talking to her about the misunderstanding. "After a long and fruitful discussion," Borland writes, "she declared that if I meant by feminist a person who believed that a woman has the right to live her life the way she wants to regardless of what society has to say about it, then she guessed she was a feminist."[37] Staying in relationship to my subjects, crafting a final transcript together, and asking for criticisms of what I have written offer crucial strategies for honoring subjects' points of view while placing their stories in a larger narrative of my own construction. Remembering John Gaddis's useful reminder that historians need to explore how the parts form a whole, we must also be vigilant that the whole does not emerge at the expense of the parts.

Assuming this posture led me to the critical insight that the sex wars may have been as much a contest about the structures of feeling through which sex might be articulated as they were about deep divisions about questions of censorship within feminism. This analysis, derived from my work with antipornography feminists, can sharpen my approach to subsequent interviews with their opponents. It has also given me a new perspective on the secondary literature produced in response to efforts to suppress sexual geographies. As sex radicals such as Samuel Delaney and Patrick Califia have implied, feminists and queers who fought the antipornography movement had an erotic attachment to local, urban spaces that were being transformed and homogenized by global capital, HIV and AIDS, and the reimposition of state efforts to police sex in public during the 1980s.[38] Similarly, to understand the urgency and sincerity with which antipornography feminists undertook their task, I have had to take seriously the fear that feminists felt moving through the same public spaces during the 1970s, a period of deindustrialization and declining urban civility. In other words, I have had to inhabit something that complicated feminist activism at the moment I am scrutinizing: the presence of real violence against women existing alongside the forms of power-exchange eroticism that sex radicals and gay men sought to protect as they mounted a broader campaign against sexual censorship.

Antipornography feminists testified repeatedly, orally and in writing, how much they dreaded moving through urban public space in the 1970s, following the emergence of a legal commercial framework for marketing live and filmed sex acts. Although today this revulsion and fear is often caricatured or dismissed, a great many radical and liberal feminists who are not commonly associated with antipornography politics experienced it too. Barbara Deming, a longtime antiviolence and civil rights activist and a feminist who had recently come out as a lesbian, wrote to Bella Abzug in

1976 on this very topic. Before she had become involved in picketing the movie *Snuff* in 1975, she said that she

> took it for granted that we had no right to defend ourselves against pornogra-phy—though it is clearly an assault against women. But now I begin to have second thoughts about all of it. . . . Yes free speech is vital. But so is the com-mon defense. And if you look at rape, at wife battering, at the treatment of prostitutes etc. etc. etc. etc. doesn't one have to admit that there is a war against women? Can one ask the government to come to our defense? A fascinating question.[39]

Listening to activists also shifted my perspective on what has become a standard truth about the sex wars: that it broke the back of a feminist move-ment already strained by the rise of conservatism and the massive resources poured into passing the Equal Rights Amendment during the 1970s. Ar-guably, antipornography politics may have actually extended the life of a grassroots movement at a time when energy and funding was shifting quickly toward liberal politics and institution building. Deming, Dworkin, and the poet Leah Fritz, among others, appear to have shifted their activism from other left politics and toward feminism *because of new concerns about the connections between violence against women and legalized pornography.* Similarly, Susan Brownmiller viewed campaigns against pornography as in-jecting new life into a movement that had lost its radical edge. "I felt that the steam had run out of the Women's Movement," remembers Brownmiller, one of the founders of WAP, about why she attended a WAVPM conference in 1978. "I felt that we'd make more headway against prostitution, but we didn't because we ran into prostitutes," she said, interrupting herself with a laugh. WAP acknowledged the agency of working-class women who resisted being spoken for, and by doing so altered feminist history. In a preview of what was to come from a broader range of women, sex workers "were . . . giving us what for. Yes, they were a very vocal group, and it was too volatile; it was too hot to handle."[40]

Oral histories have also provoked me to address the roots of the anti-pornography movement in histories that its opponents claim and honor too. Both groups understood their activism as a continuation of the anti-rape movement and saw themselves in alliance with the sensibilities that drove antibattering, women's shelter, and anti-incest activism. Far from the unconscious conservatives they were later depicted as, antipornogra-phy feminists spoke in early collective meetings of their longing for more openly revolutionary tasks that sustained their commitments to New Left politics. Over time, antipornography work channeled activists in institutional directions that they did not foresee but that brought them into alliance with the state in unexpected new ways, such as running international anti-trafficking organizations. By the 1990s others went to work for NGOS dedicated to relieving violence against women, lobbying for legislation to protect battered women and abused children, and fighting new policies that incarcerated women at dramatically higher rates.

Furthermore, by asking antipornography feminists to retell iconic stories in their own words, I have often been able to hear shifts in emphasis that reveal movement dynamics the same stories have previously obscured. For example, the concluding session of the 1979 WAP conference in New York dissolved into "a blur of tearful statements and harsh accusations" of homophobia in New York leadership circles when Brownmiller, whose long-term relationship with a man had just ended under the pressure of her activism, was criticized for her heterosexual privilege and for using the movement to become a media star. "I'm sick and tired of this," Brownmiller recalls a butch named Frog shouting at her. "We do all the work in this Movement. You go home and suck cock." Brownmiller remembers this as "a breaking point. . . . Since I was going home alone to an empty apartment, I exploded." She responded sharply, "If you hate men so much, why are you wearing men's clothes?"[41]

This well-known incident is usually understood as yet more evidence of a split in radical feminism based on sexual orientation. Placing it in a broader frame produces a different interpretation. Although some lesbians were alienated from antipornography politics as a result of an incident Brownmiller deeply regretted, many others were not. Andrea Dworkin was prominent among those who felt that the episode had been blown out of proportion, and Lynn Campbell, a West Coast organizer who had come to New York, remained in a leadership position in WAP until illness prevented her from continuing. This larger picture points us to a promising focus for future research: that the sex wars intersected with a complex struggle among lesbians that had long roots in radical feminism. In the early years of antipornography politics, divisive struggles over ideologies of desire were a way of moving oneself to the far left of the radical feminist spectrum, sometimes at the expense of heterosexual or bisexual women. As frequently perhaps, it was at the expense of other lesbians. In *Heresies #6*, Andrea Dworkin reported that at a conference in 1977, she "had been trembling, more afraid to speak than I ever had been . . . in a room of 200 sister lesbians" who accused her of political deviationism as a practicing bisexual.[42] Similarly, a movement committed to grassroots action produced multiple sectarian struggles within a politics of sexuality, not a neat, dichotomous separation between feminists who sought to control the sex lives of others and feminists who fought those efforts for control.

An ethnographic approach to written as well as oral sources suggests that one underrecognized movement dynamic within the ranks of antipornography activists was the disagreements about radical feminism's relationship to state power. Women's access to an authentic sexuality free from censorship was a topic of immense concern in collective meetings. At the same time, antipornography feminists failed to achieve a stable theory of what constituted an acceptably feminist erotica or how articulating erotic as "not obscene" would not inevitably make other forms of sexual expression vulnerable to prosecution. Minutes from sessions that lasted well into the night as activists tried to achieve consensus are an excellent example of Marcus's "messy texts." A 1977 WAVPM meeting saw the formation of study groups "to clarify what pornography and erotic art is, in addition to other subjects." At another meeting, a collective member announced that she was "opposed to all pornography whether or not it is violent, but is concerned about the problem of censorship." Reassured that "censorship is not what we're about," the group turned to an extended discussion about the differences between erotica and pornography, and whether the name of the group ought to reflect that they opposed only *sexist* pornography.[43]

A methodological principle I have adopted is to look for, honor, and interrogate such documents for conflict and indecision about movement goals as well as for the decision making that pushed antipornography activism forward. When juxtaposed with archival sources, interviews with antipornography feminists suggest that scholars need to be wary of representing the history of any radical social movement from its most public and widely distributed pronouncements. This caveat should be intensified when an activist organization made its decisions by consensus, as many radical feminist groups still did as late as the mid-1980s. Expressions of doubt and dissent were often rendered invisible when the group took its statement or action into the public sphere. Minutes of WAVPM meetings reveal not only the specific harm that might be done to lesbians by demanding enhanced scrutiny of San Francisco's red-light districts but the real doubts that many women in the organization expressed about whether similar sexual acts, including BD/SM, transferred to different ideological contexts and power hierarchies, were still violent. Unsure about this point, even after four years of discussion, in 1980 WAVPM invited Samois collective members to a steering committee meeting, ostensibly to discuss the realities of lesbian power exchange. Following the Samois presentation, which may have clarified differences rather than commonalities, the committee decided to approve a strong, negative response to an article in the *Advocate* by Pat Califia. Paradoxically, that same evening, they also agreed to invite two Samois collective members to participate in a panel on S/M that was intended to draw a paying audience and apologized to the collective for mounting "a fundraising event when we don't have a position on real-life consensual SM."[44]

How to understand such contradictions?

My new ethnographic imagination suggests one possible solution to this problem of interpretation: reject a historicism more appropriate to the distant past and less sensitive to opportunities, in favor of what Clifford Geertz called "thick description." Including contradictory evidence enhances our sense of milieu and the different positions available to activists by taking account of confusion, dissent, and uncertainty.[45]

This approach requires that historians be aware of where they are, who they are, and the effect that this can have on both the research and the interpretive process. Such awareness should occur during the interview; it should develop further in the course of writing multiple drafts. For example, as I reread the transcript of my oral history with Susan Brownmiller a year after the interview, I came upon the exchange that I used at the beginning of this chapter but read it differently. I now understand her observation that I was "going academic" as a gentle but firm signal that I was engaged in an act of interpretation, even prior to asking her a question, perhaps making it less likely from her perspective that she would be heard and understood. A veteran of many interviews and of feminist consciousness raising, she also may have wanted to know whether I was listening. Brownmiller knew perfectly well what I was talking about when I suggested that we "break down binaries" but was insisting on having a more nuanced conversation, one that the language I was using might even prevent. Since I reached this conclusion, I have tried to avoid the use of theoretical language in all my interviews. Despite the fact that feminist theory is part of the interpretive architecture of the book, much of it is, in fact, a legacy of the history I am trying to write, and its introduction immediately suggests a path for interpretation.

The lesson is this: absent any other evidence about my intentions or trustworthiness as an interlocutor, the language that I use defines me to my subjects. Attention to what I say is a methodological preoccupation that is not particular to the oral history process with antipornography feminists. It should be foundational to planning interviews with all subjects and may even be more important to the process of interviewing those people (like my former seminar colleagues and other academics who opposed the anti-pornography movement) with whom I have a preexisting or personal connection. Language conveys whether the historian has come to an interview *prepared* to share interpretive space and indicates whether the book or the film that will come from that conversation has already attached itself to a political stance on pornography that will be critical or supportive of the subjects' commitments. Like other scholars I have talked to who have worked on this difficult topic, I have been brought up short by carelessness on this point. For example, prior to launching the oral history project for this book, an important antipornography activist chided me sharply in an e-mail for the use of the phrase "sexual counterrevolution," which I had written without thinking carefully about what it might mean to someone who identified publicly as a Marxist-feminist. More recently, I shared a draft of this chapter with a scholar-activist who had opposed antipornography activism, and she pointed out instances of language use that, in her view, dismissed principled opposition to groups such as WAP and WAVPM.

For similar reasons, in my interviews with antipornography feminists I have trained myself not to use the terms "antisex" and "prosex," unless I am actually discussing the emergence of this language as a terrain for conflict and its use as a popular description, however inaccurate, that made the sex wars legible to a larger public. The characterization of those who opposed the antipornography agenda as prosex had a positive resonance, immediately calling to mind the National Organization for Women's articulation of itself as "pro-ERA," and abortion activists' articulation of their own movement as "prochoice," a euphemism that surfaced as women's reproductive freedoms under *Roe v. Wade* began to erode in the Carter and Reagan administrations. The emergence of these terms to describe participants in the sex wars not only flattens what was at stake, it stigmatized antipornography feminists as willing allies of the movement conservatives who were shaping social policy after 1980. Understanding this has allowed me to move toward a method for rethinking the sex wars outside the binaries that have defined their history until now.[46]

Taking a reflexive stance means constant vigilance, something I am not used to as a historian. My own use of language can easily convey that I perceive myself as an interested player in the sex wars—as many journalists and documentarians have been—rather than as a student of the conflict. I cannot truly understand this moment if feminist activists on all sides believe that their theoretical and interpretive insights and their memories will be occluded by mine. This creates a very different experience from the normal trajectory of historical research, in which the scholar moves toward completion with growing self-confidence. In her introduction to *Contested Lives*, the book about the struggle over abortion among feminists in Fargo, North Dakota, that started me on this path three decades ago when she presented it in our seminar, Faye Ginsburg writes about the potential for a research experience that is "schizophrenic," one in which ethnographers fear that they will find themselves at political odds with their subjects. And yet, Ginsburg argues, during her own fieldwork she found that "the layers of my own thought and unexamined beliefs began to shift and collide and take new shape in relation to the people I was trying to understand." Her ideas, she says, "changed and deepened."[47]

Mine have too. I would resist any claim that the oral histories I am collecting are like fieldwork; they are not even fieldwork "lite." But they do require that historians attend to the dangers that accompany such rich—and for many of us, novel—intellectual opportunities. Studying conflicts over sexuality that have a highly political valence can, as Didion put it, cause historians, in the name of scholarly detachment and interpretive independence, to "sell out" the subjects who have helped make the research possible. That is one danger. Another is that scholars are positioned in a defensive posture in relation to feminist colleagues who actually think that they *should* sell (at least some of) their living subjects out and see the failure to do so, when others have, as inexplicable.

In *Unlimited Intimacy: Reflections on the Subculture of Barebacking* (2009), literary scholar Tim Dean alludes to the shocked, and often negative, responses he received from colleagues and referees about his work. While studying gay men who aggressively reject "safer" sex practices, actively court the transmission of the HIV virus, and participate in rituals of kinship and community that can provoke disgust in others, Dean befriended these men, socialized, and had sex in their communities. Answering those who had stigmatized their conduct and his participatory research as "indefensible," Dean asserted his own desire not to "pathologize" men who had taught him so much. As Dean argued, *Unlimited Intimacy* was "far from an apologia for barebacking. I contend that an unclouded view of this subculture may be gained only by checking the impulse either to criticize or to defend it."[48]

I would go further than this: scholars working on recent history should aggressively seek out intellectual identities that are not their own and try them on, as rigorously as possibly. Whether we see our subjects as intellectual forebears or not, are the identities and ideas of all living subjects not fundamentally different from ours? Our temporary identities can also be methodological, despite the fact that we cannot have the training in or confident grasp of fields that we are merely dipping into. I can, for example, think about my evidence, interpretative methods, and positioning from an ethnographic perspective even if I am not actually "doing" ethnography.

Such experiments have rewards that go well beyond the project at hand. Gaining access to, and learning from, a living archive has taught me a great deal about how to do historical research. Historians should also be alert to formal opportunities to retrain and to learn at least something about methods not their own. In the summer of 2009, I attended an intensive institute at the Regional Oral History Office (ROHO) at the University of California, Berkeley. In five days, I received a short course in everything from navigating IRBs to choosing recording devices, producing a transcript, archiving the interview, understanding ethical practices, negotiating ownership, and recognizing the intimacy of the interviewing relationship. This short, formal training by professionals in the field was well worth the time, both in terms of increasing my own confidence and ethical sensibility and in gaining access to a community of colleagues who understand the challenges of these research methods.[49]

But engagement with my living archive has changed my view of my field as well. It has conveyed lessons I will carry into a larger project that grapples with all participants in the sex wars. Those of us who undertake the project of writing the history of the recent past don't just have to overcome difficulties. Our reward is the pleasure of access to historical actors as a source of information, evidence, and critical perspective. This means we have the opportunity, even the responsibility, to work *with* our subjects in framing and testing our arguments. Like ethnographers, when we historians listen to people tell their stories, attend to the language they use, and take note of the life events that they privilege, we cultivate allies for our research. These allies can help us rethink difficult problems and direct us to others who can pick up the story where they left off. They affirm, reject, and ask us to rethink our methods, our arguments, and even our facts.

The ongoing process of conversation and connection to radical feminists has caused me to believe that in some circumstances scholarly detachment not only is unnecessary for the historian but can be detrimental to the truest story. I now understand that it is irrelevant whether I agree with my subjects about positions they did—or did not—take thirty years ago, but it is necessary to understand that they sincerely believed in the work they did. Ultimately, from my perspective, it was not the sex wars but AIDS, urban renewal, and a new media landscape that permanently altered both urban sexual geographies and the multibillion-dollar pornography industry.[50] However, that is visible only as I write in 2011. What is more important is that by working in the recent past, and with living subjects, I have discovered anew my ability to think across the barrier of time.

Notes

I would like to thank Renee Romano, Nancy Barnes, Beverly Gage, Edward Ball, Paul Sabin, and Alice Echols for their advice and criticism; and Susan Brownmiller for her support and wisdom. Portions of this article were originally presented at the Center for Humanities, Wesleyan University, in May 2009; the 2011 American Historical Association Annual Meeting; and the University of Massachusetts–Amherst.

1. Susan Brownmiller, oral history, interview by author, August 27, 2009, 5, in the author's possession.

2. Brownmiller, *Against Our Will: Men, Women and Rape* (New York: Simon and Schuster, 1975).

3. Faye D. Ginsburg, *Contested Lives: The Abortion Debate in an American Community* (Berkeley: University of California Press, 1989).

4. Claire Bond Potter, *War on Crime: Bandits, G-Men and the Politics of Mass Culture* (New Brunswick: Rutgers University Press, 1998).

5. As it turned out, I was wrong about the persistence of people with a stake in the far past. Well over a decade later, I received an agitated telephone call from a John Dillinger descendant who objected to my revelation, found in FBI reports on the federal campaign to capture this bandit, that one of his great-uncles had become an informant in exchange for the family's safety.

6. Joan W. Scott, "Gender: A Useful Category of Historical Analysis," *American Historical Review* 91, no. 5 (1986): 1053–75. See also Karen Offen, "The History of Feminism Is Political History," *Perspectives on History* 49, no. 5 (May 2011): 22–24.

7. Valerie Yow, "'Do I Like Them Too Much?' Effects of the Oral History Interview on the Interviewer and Vice-Versa," *Oral History Review* 24, no. 1 (Summer 1997): 55–79.

8. Joan Didion, *Slouching towards Bethlehem* (New York: Farrar, Strauss, and Giroux, 1968), xvi.

9. Sara Evans, *Personal Politics: The Roots of Women's Liberation in the Civil Rights Movement and the New Left* (New York: Vintage Books, 1980); Mary E. Berry, *Why ERA Failed: Politics, Women's Rights and the Amending Process of the Constitution* (Indianapolis: Indiana University Press, 1988); and Alice Echols, *Daring to Be Bad: Radical Feminism in America, 1967–1975* (Minneapolis: University of Minnesota Press, 1989).

10. Christina Greene, *Our Separate Ways: Women and the Black Freedom Movement in Durham, North Carolina* (Chapel Hill: University of North Carolina Press, 2005); Annelise Orleck, *Storming Caesar's Palace: How Black Mothers Fought Their Own War on Poverty* (Boston: Beacon, 2006); Anne M. Valk, *Radical Sisters: Second-Wave Feminism and Black Liberation in Washington, D.C.* (Urbana-Champagne: University of Illinois Press, 2010); Nancy A. Hewitt, ed., *No Permanent Waves: Recasting Histories of U.S. Feminism* (New Brunswick: Rutgers University Press, 2010).

11. Darlene Clarke Hine, "Rape and the Inner Lives of Black Women in the Middle West: Preliminary Thoughts on the Culture of Dissemblance," *Signs* 14 (Summer 1989): 912–20; Deborah Gray White, "Private Lives, Public Personae: A Look at Early Twentieth-Century African American Clubwomen," in *Talking Gender: Public Images, Personal Journeys and Political Critiques*, ed. Nancy Hewitt, Jean O'Barr, and Nancy Rosenbaugh (Chapel Hill: University of North Carolina Press, 1996), 106–23; Evelynn M. Hammonds, "Toward a Genealogy of Black Female Sexuality: The Problematic of Silence," in *Feminist Theory and the Body: A Reader*, ed. Janet Price and Margaret Shildrick (New York: Routledge, 1997), 249–59.

12. Katherine Borland, "'That's Not What I Said': Interpretive Conflict in Oral Narrative Research," in *Women's Words: The Feminist Practice of Oral History*, ed. Sherna Berger Gluck and Daphne Patai (New York: Routledge, 1991), 63.

13. John Lewis Gaddis, *The Landscape of History: How Historians Map the Past* (New York: Oxford University Press, 2002), xi.

14. Karla Holloway, "Classroom Fictions: My Tongue Is in My Friend's Mouth," in Hewitt, O'Barr, and Rosenbaugh, *Talking Gender*, 125.

15. John Bodnar, "Saving Private Ryan and Postwar Memory in America," *American Historical Review* 106, no. 3 (2001): 805–17; Richard H. Kohn, "History and the Culture Wars: The Case of the Smithsonian Institution's Enola Gay Exhibition," *Journal of American History* 8, no. 3 (1995): 1036–63.

16. Esther Newton, "My Best Informant's Dress: The Erotic Equation in Fieldwork," *Cultural Anthropology* 8, no. 1 (February 1993): 3–23.

17. Pierre Bourdieu, *Invitation to a Reflexive Sociology* (Chicago: University of Chicago Press, 1992); Paul Rabinow, *Reflections on Fieldwork in Morocco* (Berkeley: University of California Press, 1977); Ruth Behar, *The Vulnerable Observer: Anthropology That Breaks Your Heart* (Boston: Beacon, 1997); Esther Newton, *Margaret Mead Made Me Gay: Personal Essays, Public Ideas* (Durham, N.C.: Duke University Press, 2000), 243–58; Bronislaw Malinowski, *A Diary in the Strictest Sense of the Term* (Palo Alto, Calif.: Stanford University Press, 1989); Michael Young, *Malinowski: Odyssey of an Anthropologist, 1884–1920* (New Haven, Conn.: Yale University Press, 2004).

18. Kristin Luker, *Salsa Dancing in the Social Sciences: Research in the Age of Info Glut* (Cambridge, Mass.: Harvard University Press, 2008), 167; Barbara Myerhoff, *Number Our Days: A Triumph of Continuity and Culture in an Urban Ghetto* (1978; repr., New York: Touchstone Books, 1980); Ginsburg, *Contested Lives*, 12.

19. See Victor Turner, *Dramas, Fields and Metaphors: Symbolic Action in Human Society* (Ithaca, N.Y.: Cornell University Press, 1975), and Carroll Smith-Rosenberg, "Davy

Crockett as Trickster: Pornography, Liminality and Symbolic Inversion in Victorian America," in *Disorderly Conduct: Visions of Gender in Victorian America*, ed. Carroll Smith-Rosenberg (New York: Oxford University Press, 1986), 90–108.

20. Gaddis, *Landscape of History*, 61.

21. John David Smith, *An Old Creed for the New South: Proslavery Ideology and Historiography, 1865–1918* (Westport, Conn.: Greenwood, 1985); Donald A. Ritchie, *Doing Oral History* (New York: Oxford University Press, 2003); Valerie Yow, *Recording Oral History: A Guide for the Humanities and Social Sciences*, 2nd ed. (Lanham, Md.: Altamira, 2005); Robert Perks, *The Oral History Reader* (New York: Routledge, 2006); J. H. Hexter, *The History Primer* (New York: Basic Books, 1971), Hayden White, *The Content of the Form: Narrative Discourse and Historical Representation* (Baltimore: Johns Hopkins University Press, 1990).

22. Carole S. Vance, *Pleasure and Danger: Exploring Female Sexuality* (New York: Routledge and Kegan Paul, 1993); Lisa Duggan and Nan Hunter, *Sex Wars: Sexual Dissent and Political Culture* (New York: Routledge, 1995); and Ann Snitow, Christine Stansell, and Sharon Thompson, eds., *Powers of Desire* (New York: Monthly Review Press, 1983).

23. Several university-based scholar-activists who opposed the antipornography movement have objected to my characterization of them as having achieved academic prominence through the writing they did during the sex wars. Variously, they argue that their careers were impeded, that they have remained marginalized within academia in part because of their defense of and intellectual commitment to radical sex theory and practice, and that other intellectuals who were equally deserving have never had the security of pursuing their work as academics.

24. See Carolyn Bronstein, *Battling Pornography: The American Feminist Antipornography Movement, 1976–1986* (New York: Cambridge University Press, 2011).

25. George E. Marcus, "What Comes (Just) after 'Post'? The Case of Ethnography," in *Handbook of Qualitative Research*, ed. Norman K. Denzin and Yvonna S. Lincoln (Thousand Oaks: Sage, 1994), 567.

26. Linda Lovelace, *Ordeal*, with Mike McGrady (New York: Citadel, 2006).

27. Nan Alamilla Boyd, *Wide Open Town: A History of Queer San Francisco to 1965* (Berkeley: University of California Press, 2003).

28. For notions of top-down sexual citizenship, see Margot Canaday, *The Straight State: Sexuality and Citizenship in Twentieth-Century America* (Princeton, N.J.: Princeton University Press, 2009).

29. Gayle Rubin, "Elegy for the Valley of the Kings: AIDS and the Leather Community in San Francisco, 1981–1996," in *In Changing Times: Gay Men and Lesbians Encounter HIV/AIDS*, ed. Martin P. Levine, Peter M. Nardi, and John H. Gagnon (Chicago: University of Chicago Press, 1997), 101–43; Pat Califia, *Public Sex: The Culture of Radical Sex* (San Francisco: Cleis, 1994).

30. For contemporary history that is starting to make these larger connections, see Amy Erdman Farrell, *Yours in Sisterhood: Ms. Magazine and the Promise of Popular Feminism* (Chapel Hill: University of North Carolina Press, 1998) and Susan Ware, *Game, Set, Match: Billie Jean King and the Revolution in Women's Sports Feminism* (Chapel Hill: University of North Carolina Press, 2011).

31. This builds on work that addresses the critical importance of the sex wars within feminism; see Alice Echols, *Shaky Ground: The Sixties and Its Aftershocks* (New York: Columbia University Press, 2002), and Jane Gerhard, *Desiring Revolution: Second-Wave*

Feminism and the Rewriting of American Sexual Thought, 1920–1982 (New York: Columbia University Press, 2001).

32. Margo St. James, "Economic Justice for Sex Workers," *Hastings Women's Law Journal*, Winter 1999, http://heinonline.org/HOL/LandingPage?collection=journals&handle=hein.journals/haswo10&div=7&id=&page=; Minutes of the WAVPM Action Committee, n.d., Committee Records, Action Committee, 1979–89, Administrative files, WAVPM Papers, WAVPM record no. 1996-21, box 1, GLBT Historical Society, San Francisco.

33. Gayle Rubin, "Thinking Sex: Notes for a Radical Theory on the Politics of Sexuality," in *Pleasure and Danger*, ed. Carole Vance (New York: Routledge, 1984); Duggan and Hunter, *Sex Wars*. For a reflection on the importance of intellectuals associated with FACT queer theory, see Henry Abelove, *Deep Gossip* (Minneapolis: University of Minnesota Press, 2003).

34. Janet Halley, *Split Decisions: How and Why to Take a Break from Feminism* (Princeton, N.J.: Princeton University Press, 2006).

35. Susan Brownmiller, *In Our Time: Memoir of a Revolution* (New York: Dial, 1999), 295.

36. Behar, *Vulnerable Observer*, 5, 12, 24.

37. Borland, "Not What I Said," 74.

38. Samuel Delaney, *Times Square Red, Times Square Blue* (New York: NYU Press, 2001); Patrick Califia, *Public Sex: The Culture of Radical Sex* (Berkeley, Calif.: Cleis, 2000). Califia's volume reprints some essays originally published in the 1970s and 1980s in community newspapers.

39. Draft of letter to Bella Abzug, n.d., Deming notes about prosecution of *Snuff*, March 25, 1976, folder 676, "WAVAW—Thoughts 1967–77," Deming Papers, box 34, Schlesinger Library, Harvard University, Cambridge, Massachusetts.

40. Brownmiller, interview.

41. Ibid.; Brownmiller, *In Our Time*, 309–10.

42. Andrea Dworkin, "Biological Superiority: The World's Most Dangerous and Deadly Idea," *Heresies #6* (1978): 46.

43. Women against Media Violence and Degradation minutes, January 29, 1977, Committee Records, General Meeting, 1977–83, GLBT Historical Society; "Women against Media Violence and Degradation" was a proposed name for WAVPM that lasted for only a meeting. See also WAVPM Minutes, February 12, 1977, Committee Records, Steering Committee, 1980–83, Administrative files, folder 6, box 1, GLBT Historical Society.

44. Minutes of Steering Committee, April 15, 1980, Committee Records, Steering Committee, 1980–83, GLBT Historical Society.

45. Clifford Geertz, "Thick Description: Towards an Interpretive Theory of Culture," *The Interpretation of Cultures: Selected Essays* (New York: Basic Books, 1973), 3–30.

46. Ann Snitow, "A Gender Diary," in *Conflicts in Feminism*, ed. Marianne Hirsch and Evelyn Fox Keller (New York: Routledge, 1990), 9–43.

47. Ginsburg, *Contested Lives*, x–xi.

48. Tim Dean, *Unlimited Intimacy: Reflections on the Subculture of Barebacking* (Chicago: University of Chicago Press, 2009), x, 180.

49. The ROHO Advanced Oral History Summer Institute can be found at http://bancroft.berkeley.edu/ROHO/education/institute/ (Regional Oral History Office, Regents of the University of California, last modified April 4, 2011).

50. Delaney, *Times Square Red*, 1–108.

PART FOUR

Technology and the Practice of Recent History

DAVID GREENBERG

Do Historians Watch Enough TV?

Broadcast News as a Primary Source

THOMAS J. SUGRUE'S *SWEET LAND OF LIBERTY*, published
in 2010, has been praised as a "major contribution to our understanding"
of the struggle for racial equality in the United States and a "bold . . . rewriting of civil rights history."[1] Interpretively, the book argues powerfully
for expanding the focus of the familiar civil rights story beyond the South
to northern states, where racial discrimination was less egregious but still
deeply pernicious. Empirically, it rests on heroic labors in scores of archival
collections, oral histories, hard-to-find newspapers, government reports,
and sociological studies. To browse its 117 pages of endnotes is to surmise
that Sugrue must have looked at everything.[2]

Or almost everything. Comb those 117 pages and you will find almost no
references to the news broadcasts produced by ABC, NBC, or CBS that illuminated the movement, and the era, for a national audience. Although the
text of *Sweet Land of Liberty* includes one mention of the "unprecedented"
three-hour documentary *American Revolution of '63*, which ran on NBC in
September of that year, and one of *The Harlem Temper*, which ran on CBS
in December, Sugrue neither describes these prime-time specials nor indicates whether he watched them. A two-paragraph discussion of media
coverage on the continuing black struggle for equality during the 1960s
and 1970s refers to the spread of black public affairs programming and to
the "superficial and usually sensationalistic" treatment of racial issues on
the network news. But the only video source cited is the website of *American Black Journal*, a Detroit-based public television show that was focused
on African American concerns.[3] Sugrue also notes in passing that "Black
revolutionaries made for 'good TV,'" but without having employed that programming as primary source material, the book doesn't convey why. What

made those revolutionaries so telegenic? What was it like for a viewer at home to watch them?[4]

Historians, like most intelligent people, tend to think that we have better things to do than to watch TV. But the above gloss on *Sweet Land of Liberty* raises the question: would watching more television in this case have been a bad idea? Broadcast media, as we know, formed a key part of the civil rights struggle. Television cameras turned events such as the desegregation of Central High School in Little Rock into nightly soap operas and brought political dramas such as the 1964 fight to seat the Mississippi Democratic Freedom Party at the Democratic convention into people's living rooms. Civil rights leaders, aware of the medium's impact, crafted their political and public relations strategies with television in mind. Throughout the 1960s the vexing racial issues that divided the nation pervaded news and discussion shows. For many Americans, the civil rights movement and television are and were inextricably bound together.

To point out that such an important and comprehensive work as *Sweet Land of Liberty* hasn't consulted or encompassed even more material than it does will strike many people as captious, if not perverse. No book can do everything. But these comments about the author's neglect of television are meant not so much to criticize the book as to raise a larger set of questions for all historians of the recent past. For if a book of such industry and ability has paid comparatively little attention to TV as a source, it's a good bet that others in the field have too.

Indeed, a random check of recent political histories covering the years since television's emergence bears out this hypothesis. Donald Critchlow's biography *Phyllis Schlafly and Grassroots Conservatism* (2005) alludes to television's importance but betrays little actual television watching. Its footnotes mention a libel case filed by Schlafly against NBC, but the book doesn't examine the broadcast that sparked the case; the book's treatment of television's coverage of Barry Goldwater's 1964 campaign, meanwhile, is drawn from secondary sources. David Kyvig's fascinating *Age of Impeachment: American Constitutional Culture since 1960* (2008) lists several films in its bibliography but no TV programs, even though both Watergate and the Clinton impeachment were nothing if not long-running television spectacles. Kim Phillips-Fein's *Invisible Hands: The Making of the Conservative Movement from the New Deal to Reagan* (2009), an excellent account of businessmen's role in the rise of conservatism, contains no section for television news in its bibliography and no discussion of TV in its bibliographical essay, though Phillips-Fein cites a few television transcripts, such as those for the commentaries delivered by Jesse Helms for a local North Carolina station. For *The Rebellion of Ronald Reagan: A History of the End of the Cold War* (2009), a story about the consummate television president, journalist-historian James Mann conducted Freedom of Information Act searches and reviewed State Department cables, but his notes name only a few news transcripts and don't indicate whether he watched the broadcasts.[5]

It's fair to say that while standard historical practice includes time-consuming, demanding research of many kinds, television is typically ignored. This statement, I should make clear, applies to my own work no less than the works cited earlier. In writing *Nixon's Shadow: The History of an Image* (2003), about another president to whose career TV was crucial, I screened only a small amount of footage, and when I did so, I relied on it more to inform my general sense of Nixon as a person and a politician than to examine specific appearances or news programs for whatever new information they might provide.[6]

All of this adds up to a collective methodological blind spot of major proportions for scholars of the recent past. Although we may seek insight from television, we rarely think of television programs as evidence, as we do with printed documents, or apply the same critical standards to them. Oddly, this is not a mistake we make when we take off our historians' hats and write or even think about the world around us. In judging contemporary figures, we rely heavily on impressions drawn from having watched them on the screen, sometimes from clips that originate on television and are recirculated many times over in the virtual world. When we talk about major events such as the terrorist attacks of September 11, we naturally assume that the television coverage of this event serves as a shared national reference point. Yet when historians write about people or events from earlier periods, we often deprive ourselves of the knowledge, understanding, and perspective gained from having seen them on TV. And so it strikes me that if we really want to do justice to the past—to capture it as it was and as it was understood—maybe we should put down our books, sit down on the sofa, and start watching more TV.

The tendency to ignore television as a primary source is not universal. Historians of culture—especially historians of television itself—are duty-bound to immerse themselves in the programming they discuss. Books such as Michael Kackman's *Citizen Spy: Television, Espionage, and Cold War Culture* (2005) and Daniel Marcus's *Happy Days and Wonder Years: The*

Fifties and Sixties in Contemporary Cultural Politics (2004) delve into the guts and gristle of TV shows that took hours to view. But these are mainly works of textual interpretation rather than narrative reconstruction. Their authors are subjecting televisual artifacts to close readings to tease out the ideas that these texts contain, rather than mining them for evidence about the people or events that they document. The authors of these kinds of works frequently teach in departments of communications, journalism, media studies, or English, not history, and travel in those interdisciplinary orbits; their work is often unfairly ghettoized, walled off from the mainstream of historical studies. In the same vein, there are many good books about the history of news coverage, such as Craig Allen's *Eisenhower and the Mass Media: Peace, Prosperity, and Primetime TV* (1993) or Daniel Hallin's *The Uncensored War: The Media and Vietnam* (1989), which rely on close examination of on-air sources. But, again, these books take television and news, not politics, as their direct object of study. A historian writing a general history of the Eisenhower presidency or of the Vietnam War is much less likely to have worked extensively in televisual sources.[7]

It remains the case that for the vast majority of postwar historians, television is too easily—and too commonly—avoided. When we do cite television, it tends to be cursory—making reference to well-known, one-time broadcasts, such as Walter Cronkite's program questioning the Vietnam War or the popular miniseries "Roots," instead of conducting a systematic review of segments from the nightly news shows, prime-time magazines, or Sunday roundtables. And the sources that we do physically examine and cite are seldom the video documents themselves. More often we work with the published transcripts, which are easier to browse through, highlight, and mine for quotes.

One might ask how much is truly lost in shortchanging television as a source. Television, after all, is notorious for conveying relatively little information compared to print. According to an oft-told story, Richard Salant, president of CBS News, found that the number of words that Walter Cronkite spoke in one broadcast filled only three-quarters of a single page of the *New York Times*.[8] Other shortcomings of television programming are also widely acknowledged. Broadcast news in particular, we have been reminded for years, is brief and superficial, obsessed with images and aesthetics, inclined to cover events and crises more than persistent conditions, and devoted to a contrived "balance" between the viewpoints of the political parties rather than to true objectivity. Given these abundant failings, should we really ask historians to suffer through old reruns of Tim Russert or Peter Jennings when much more information, intelligence, and insight can be found in old issues of the *New York Times, Congressional Quarterly*, or the *New Republic*?

I think the answer is yes. Although manifestly flawed as a primary means of keeping abreast of current affairs, television footage is still a unique and important primary source for historians, and we have hardly begun to exploit it. There are good reasons for this neglect; the challenges to making full use of television are considerable. But there is also a lot to be learned.

Were it not for the widespread disregard of television as a source for political history, it might seem unnecessary to point out that watching TV, like examining any archive, can teach us a great deal about the past. Most obviously, television can educate us about people, places, and times in ways that reading about them simply can't. Like photographs, it can tell us basic things about the way a person looks, but with the voice and motion conveying additional information. To hear the voice and speech patterns and to watch the body language of a figure can impart, for example, an appreciation of political skill or, conversely, the limits of popular appeal. Think of footage of George Wallace, which conveys his angry appeal as his words alone might not, or of the laconic bearing of Eugene McCarthy, which can convey in a flash his ambivalence toward politics. Alan Brinkley's biography of Henry Luce, *The Publisher* (2010), opens with a descriptive account of a television interview with Luce in which Brinkley describes how Luce "sat slouched in his chair through most of the hour, his clothes slightly rumpled, his tie askew, his pants pulled up over his crossed legs. . . . He rambled in conversation, often stopping in midsentence and starting over again, circling around questions before actually answering them, sometimes speaking so fast that he seemed to be trying to outrace [his childhood] stammer." For the reader, the description is compelling for the subtleties of Luce's physical appearance and manner that it conveys. For the historian, it holds a second lesson as well, because it makes clear that the experience of studying Luce on TV has enriched the author's understanding of him.[9]

What is true for people is also true for events: our understanding of political occurrences profits from seeing them with our own eyes. There are details to be learned that reporters may have neglected to record: where people sat in a congressional committee room, or which junior aide fed a grandstanding politician his remarks; how a crowd responded to an orator, or which snippet of a speech was featured and replayed on the nightly news. But to observe that television imparts factual information, detail, and perspectives that print sources may omit is merely to begin to appreciate its value. Television can also convey, if intuitively, the multiple layers of meaning contained in a person's body language and vocal inflection in the fine details of a physical setting and in the subtle reactions of individuals to an incident. To witness the moon landing can impart the tingling sense of awe enjoyed by spectators at the time. To behold a cityscape such as Watts during the 1965 riots can convey the feelings of fear it produced among participants and viewers that simply reading about an episode of urban violence may not. One can read about Chicago mayor Richard Daley calling Connecticut senator Abraham Ribicoff a "fucking kike" at the 1968 Democratic National Convention after Ribicoff denounced Daley's "Gestapo tactics," but only the actual footage conveys the power and feel of the incident itself. Visual and aural context helps us as historians to furnish our readers with the kind of thick description of historical events that we desperately seek in our writing. Using televisual sources thus also confers another benefit: instilling confidence in ourselves and in our audience that we know our material with an otherwise elusive intimacy, emboldening us to write about it with familiarity and authority.

Besides allowing us to see historical figures and events in full motion and in three dimensions, using TV as a source also teaches us as historians how television journalists covered these events, which has often differed from how print journalists did. Countless political developments of the past half century unfolded spontaneously before the cameras, and many others were reported and analyzed on the air within hours or days. Long before the Internet, the electronic media was breaking major stories before they appeared on paper; other stories received more thorough coverage from TV than they did from print. Just as a historian wouldn't want to write about Watergate without reading Bob Woodward's and Carl Bernstein's reports in the *Washington Post*, so a chronicler of the Iranian hostage crisis would be derelict without watching Ted Koppel's late-night shows on ABC—a pathbreaking set of broadcasts that became the basis for the long-running news show *Nightline*. From John F. Kennedy's assassination to Barack Obama's election, there has been truth in the cliché that television served as a national hearthside, the place to which millions of Americans instinctively turned to find out what was happening, to put frightening or confusing or meaningful news in perspective, or to feel connected to their fellow citizens amid crisis or celebration.

The events that have drawn this kind of blanket coverage, moreover, haven't been only those of indisputable, objective significance. The explosion of the *Challenger* space shuttle in 1986, as a *New Republic* editorial remarked at the time, was transformed by television coverage from a significant occurrence in space travel into a national obsession. Quarreling with the widespread comparisons to the Kennedy and King murders, the magazine noted that "what the assassinations and the explosion truly had in common was the presence of the camera and the swarm of anchormen. They must spend a day inviting us to the titillation of watching a toy explode in the sky. That is what it became: television had launched a toy and made it explode—before our very eyes. The comparison to Dallas was made, in some cases explicitly, to exalt television as the legitimate creator of a common national emotion."[10] By the 1990s TV was regularly serving up a stream of what the critic Frank Rich dubbed "mediathons"—unending waves of hype, graphics, and commentary enfolding small shards of trivial news, on frivolous topics as well as serious ones, transfixing large swaths of the public and, all by themselves, making issues important.[11] Some of these topics wouldn't be of interest to historians at all if television hadn't invested them with cultural significance in the first place.

To consider national developments even more broadly, Americans have for decades experienced even quotidian occurrences primarily through TV. In 1963 both NBC and CBS expanded their evening news broadcasts from fifteen to thirty minutes, and according to polling, more people began turning to television that year than to newspapers as their main source of news. The Roper Organization, which has regularly polled Americans about which media they consult, found in 1963 that 55 percent of respondents ranked TV first, with newspapers a close second at 53 percent. Since then, television has widened its lead. Today the reliance on TV for information is overwhelming. The Roper surveys now break down "television" into two categories— network and cable—but television still dominates both the Internet and print as a vehicle for conveying political information. The numbers in a 2010 audience survey remained similar to those of the 1980s and 1990s: 62 percent of those interviewed accessed their news through television, with newspapers falling to 14 percent, and the Internet at only 13 percent. Television has clearly remained integral to the process by which Americans learn about and interpret public events. It stands to reason that historians, who strive to understand how people experienced their own worlds, should explore how TV portrayed the developments they are writing about.[12]

The question of where Americans have gotten their news matters because, as I have suggested, the content can be quite different and because the way in which the content is conveyed shapes how we understand it. Media theorist Marshall McLuhan put this idea most succinctly when he postulated that "the medium is the message." Although McLuhan's body of work—opaque, cryptic, and oracular—has unfortunately retained for historians a discrediting whiff of the cultish, his core insight, that the medium itself matters independent of what it conveys, was certainly sound; it was indisputably influential at the time and ought to remain so.[13]

For several decades now scholars from a range of fields have proposed plausible and provocative hypotheses as to how television differs from print. Some of these hypotheses are fairly intuitive or commonsensical. It seems obvious that the images people see on their television screens— dogs and fire hoses in Birmingham, hippies protesting the Vietnam War, famine-ravaged children in Africa—stir up sentiments that might well be absent, or felt much more faintly, had people only read about them. It is equally obvious that television news at times fixes on and directs attention to incidents that print reporters ignore or discount. One relatively recent instance of this phenomenon occurred when former Vermont governor Howard Dean, in a speech after his disappointing finish in the 2004 Iowa caucuses, let out a guttural roar. Although the next day's newspaper stories didn't make much of the growl, regarding it as the cry of an exhausted, hoarse campaigner trying to rally his troops, the cable news channels replayed the speech fragment over and over, spreading the idea that Dean had lost his moorings. Here was a case where the TV coverage had consequences for history. Only later did newspapers hurry to cover the newly minted controversy of what is now known as "the scream," and the negative fallout dashed whatever slim chances Dean still had of winning the Democratic presidential nomination.

Beyond these straightforward differences between print and television, several scholars have advanced more elaborate ideas about the different psychological effects of these two forms of communication that might be useful to historians as they begin to make use of televisual sources. McLuhan suggested that TV, as what he called a "cool" medium, allows more sensory and cognitive participation from the consumer than does the "hot" medium of print.[14] Subsequent scholars have tried to develop those ideas with greater precision and concreteness. In the 1970s Michael J. Robinson called attention to the manner in which TV news is watched. Television viewing, he argued, is frequently "inadvertent": many people don't set out to watch a news broadcast but end up seeing it because it's on the air when they turn on the TV or they pass by a TV that someone else has turned on. The TV news audience also, at the time of Robinson's study, came disproportionately from less well educated and less socially connected segments of the population. TV news, he found, was frequently consumed in a fragmentary form—not watched from start to finish but tuned into for brief bits and snatches, while the viewer was simultaneously doing other things. Of the consequences that might flow from this kind of viewing experience, Robinson emphasized especially the phenomenon of "videomalaise"—the sense of anomie and disaffection that political scientists began to discern among citizens in the 1970s, which gave rise to the angry conservative populism that has afflicted American politics since.[15]

In the 1980s sociologist Joshua Meyrowitz proposed a different theory. He argued that television collapsed a long-standing distinction between public and private, or what he called the "onstage" or "front region" and the "backstage" or "back region" of political life. Fostering an illusion of intimacy, TV encouraged viewers to believe that they grasped dimensions of political figures that they actually didn't. It also led them to expect an impossible level of consistency from their political leaders, giving rise to enhanced skepticism about politics as a practice.[16]

Not all scholars, of course, will agree with these particular arguments. But it's clear that in myriad ways, watching news on television can produce different experiences from reading a paper or magazine and that historians—if they explore insights developed in other disciplines—could make use of television sources better than we now do. At the least, these ideas lend weight to the argument that historians need to think more about the ways that television, directly or indirectly, has shaped popular understandings of public events. Even if some historians decline to theorize about television's psychological and social effects, they will almost certainly agree that television has had political and historical consequences, if only because journalists, politicians, and their aides have for decades taken television's importance for granted and have acted accordingly. However television news affected citizens and voters, it clearly affected political actors.

It hardly needs stating that political leaders and professionals have long recognized the power of TV to communicate with and perhaps to influence the public, and they have tailored their behavior to exploit that power. As early as 1952, when comparatively few Americans had televisions, Dwight

Eisenhower pioneered televised campaign "spots"; as president, he experimented with televising his cabinet meetings. John F. Kennedy debuted live presidential press conferences in 1961. Lyndon Johnson moved the State of the Union address to prime time. Virtually every subsequent president has tried to develop new uses for television, sometimes quite self-consciously. In *The Selling of the President 1968*, the journalist Joe McGinniss reported that Nixon's aides actually read McLuhan's works and tried to fashion, if a bit comically, a media strategy that would exploit the properties of this "cool" medium. One memo read, "the bobby [Kennedy] phenomenon: his screaming appeal to the tv generation . . . thousands of little girls who want him to be president so they can have him on the tv screen and run their fingers through the image of his hair."[17] By the 1980s television was of such self-evident importance that Ronald Reagan kept on hand a slew of full-time media advisers who focused intently on what stories might lead the nightly news broadcasts each day and how the White House might shape those segments to render the president and his policies in the best possible light.

If television and television news are so clearly important, to viewers and politicians alike, then why haven't historians used video broadcasts more as a source? The most basic reason is the sheer difficulty of obtaining video copies of broadcasts. Television networks, as private companies, have the right to restrict access to their tapes and charge prohibitive rates for their use. Geared toward wealthy commercial researchers, and not scholars husbanding comparatively small research budgets, news archives have never been widely accessible. Any attempt to examine TV news as a historical source will be fraught with frustration, as Todd Gitlin vividly recounted in *The Whole World Is Watching* (1980), a study of news coverage of the anti–Vietnam War movement:

> CBS would grant outside researchers limited access to their Newsfilm Archive, *which is the only archive even halfway open for news broadcasts made before August 1968* (when Vanderbilt University began videotaping all three networks' nightly news shows). NBC was closed to outsiders. So was ABC. I could not use their news even as secondary objects of comparison.
>
>   . . . When I got to the CBS Newsfilm Archive in New York City, I found that it was impossible to find and to see—let alone study—a large proportion of CBS News footage on the movement. Some material had been recorded on videotape, not on film, especially when it had been "fed" into the network from an out-of-town bureau; once the report had been transmitted, the tape had been

reused and, in the process, wiped clean. If any copy was left in the world, it was the CBS "aircheck" copy, which CBS would not show. One would have to buy a copy to see it, I was told, and the cost was prohibitive. But more important, much film was simply lost. . . . Sometimes one day's coverage was there and the next day's was nowhere to be found. . . . I was told, "We can only keep so much, because of space, so obviously someone decided back then not to save these."

. . . Finally, I was not permitted to see all the footage I succeeded in locating and asked to see. And because I could get an archive clerk assigned to me only briefly, I saw each news piece only once or twice. I took detailed notes, but it would surely have been better if I had been allowed to return to the clips in order to review them.[18]

Amid these difficulties, Gitlin does point out, if only in passing, one bright spot and opportunity for historians. Vanderbilt University's Television News Archive, a collection of network news shows compiled systematically since 1968, is now the most complete collection of TV news broadcasts in existence. Here, ironically, we have politics to thank. The archive was created amid the turbulence of the late 1960s, when Paul C. Simpson, a politically conservative insurance executive from Tennessee, had come to regard the network news shows as biased toward left-wing views and began compiling the archive to hold the networks accountable to public scrutiny. The archive had to fend off a lawsuit by CBS in its early years before establishing itself as the preeminent video resource for scholars of TV news.[19]

Though of great potential value, the Vanderbilt archive has notable shortcomings. For one thing, it only recently began taping cable news—a delay that has left large omissions in its coverage of the 1980s and 1990s.[20] The archive's location in Nashville hasn't exactly made it a magnet for researchers, and grants to support travel to Vanderbilt (as well as other repositories of TV news shows) are hard to come by. In a promising turn, the university recently made some of its materials from NBC and CNN available online, and institutional libraries can subscribe to the database, much as they can subscribe to JSTOR or Lexis/Nexis. But a researcher without institutional access, who is in search of broadcasts from CBS, ABC, or Fox News, or who can't get to Tennessee has just one other option: to submit a request for a specific program, which is copied and mailed at a cost of $10 per programming hour. That price may be affordable for someone conducting highly targeted research but not for the painstaking review of weeks or months of material that is necessary to gain a sense of how an event or issue was conveyed over time to audiences.

Despite these limits, Vanderbilt sets an important standard for video archiving. A few other good repositories also exist, although they have smaller or fragmented collections. Perhaps second to Vanderbilt as a destination for historians is the UCLA Film and Television Archive, which along with substantial holdings in entertainment television, owns several collections focused on news, including both the Edward R. Murrow and the News and Public Affairs collections; the latter includes more than 100,000 news programs and broadcasts taped between 1979 and 2003, including *Nightline*, the PBS *News Hour*, and the *Today Show*.[21] UCLA also collects local news broadcasts from Los Angeles—another valuable source largely ignored by libraries and historians alike.

There are only a few other archives with significant holdings. The Museum of Television and Radio in New York, recently renamed the Paley Center, owns roughly 150,000 television and radio programs and advertisements, but its collection relies on donations for its materials and is far from comprehensive. Similarly incomplete is the collection of CBS nightly news shows at the National Archives, which covers from the mid-1970s through the 1980s. Finally, the University of Georgia has a collection of videos submitted for the Peabody Awards, an important sampling of high-quality news programming but, again, a decidedly partial one. Taken together, these collections do offer historians opportunities that we have only begun to exploit; yet in the end they are tiny in number compared to the abundance of places a researcher can go to read a comparable print source, say, the entire run of *Time* magazine.

Although access poses major problems for historians seeking to use TV as a source, there are larger obstacles inherent in the nature of the medium and the very work of studying it. It is no wonder that most work in TV history has been done by cultural historians who have only to watch a finite set of discrete episodes of a handful of shows. It is much more demanding to consume episode after episode, day after day, or week after week, of a variety of programs. For reasons of time alone, few historians ever undertake such an exhausting effort. Yet for those who do, it can pay off. Thomas Doherty's study of Red Scare–era television, *Cold War, Cool Medium* (2003), is illuminating in part because the author screened certain materials that no one else seems to have looked at in decades. Some of Doherty's revisionist conclusions—for example, that journalists were not timid in standing up to Joe McCarthy's demagoguery, as is typically alleged, but pressed him hard when he came on the Sunday shows—were easily drawn from evidence that was sitting in plain view, unwatched.[22]

Television also challenges historians in another important way: unlike print, it can't be easily skimmed. Working through a sheaf of newspaper articles or other documents can be tedious, but historians know (or quickly learn) how to sift familiar from unfamiliar material, sort the important from the unimportant, and breeze past paragraphs or pages that seem at a glance unlikely to be of use. But TV has to be watched in real time to hear the audio tracks and appreciate the images. A researcher might get away with a small amount of fast-forwarding, but to watch only a fast-motion whir with a squeaky soundtrack is to lose the whole reason for examining a television broadcast in the first place. Watching footage at high speed, a historian simply isn't able to grasp how audiences originally experienced the show.

The final reason that historians overlook television as source material may simply be habit. None of the profession's institutional structures— from the formulation of job descriptions to the design of conferences to the awarding of prizes—place much value on the use of television as a source. Few books even exist that consider television as a source that demands its own methods and contains its own unique rewards. Graduate students aren't trained to think about television's distinctive qualities, and courses in research methods seldom devote much or any time to questions of using video or film in research—where to look for sources, how to read them, and how to assess their importance. When professors use visual sources in the classroom, their role is mainly as a cosmetic enhancement to perk up blasé undergraduates in a lecture hall, not as sources to be deeply explored in their own right. This tendency, in turn, stems from a larger lack of concern with the methodological and epistemological questions associated with broadcast media—the larger unfamiliarity on the part of most historians with media scholarship as a whole.

Although I have framed the historical profession's neglect of televisual sources as a methodological critique, in every critique there lies an opportunity. In truth, we are quite lucky to have a television record of our times. Historians of the pretelevision, precinematic past are at a disadvantage in having no video or cinematic record of George Washington or Frederick Douglass, no moving pictures of the Constitutional Convention or the battles of the Civil War (however great the pleasures of recreating what it was like to live in places and times and conditions very different from our own). In contrast, future generations of historians who study our own era will be fortunate in this respect, and may have more access to these sources than we do now because of DVD and Internet archives. Blessed with extensive film and video documents of so many people and events of our times, they will be free of many of the difficulties of trying to imagine subjects as they were.

To make fruitful use of this abundant audiovisual material, however, they will need to develop practices for gaining better access to these sources, judging their quality and reliability, using them efficiently, and thinking through what they teach us. They will need a body of literature that explores these important questions. Now is a good time for us to start writing one.

Notes

1. Robert H. Zieger, "Northern Exposure," review of *Sweet Land of Liberty: The Forgotten Struggle for Civil Rights in the North*, by Thomas J. Sugrue, *Reviews in American History* 37, no. 4 (2009): 572–77; Scott Saul, "Off Camera," review of *Sweet Land of Liberty: The Forgotten Struggle for Civil Rights in the North*, by Thomas J. Sugrue, *The Nation*, June 22, 2009, 25–31.

2. Thomas J. Sugrue, *Sweet Land of Liberty: The Forgotten Struggle for Civil Rights in the North* (New York: Random House, 2008).

3. Ibid., 288–89, 405, 496, 653.

4. Ibid., 339, 405.

5. Donald Critchlow, *Phyllis Schlafly and Grassroots Conservatism* (Princeton, N.J.: Princeton University Press, 2005); David Kyvig, *The Age of Impeachment: American Constitutional Culture since 1960* (Lawrence: University Press of Kansas, 2008); Kim Phillips-Fein, *Invisible Hands: The Making of the Conservative Movement from the New Deal to Reagan* (New York: Norton, 2009); James Mann, *The Rebellion of Ronald Reagan: A History of the End of the Cold War* (New York: Viking, 2009).

6. David Greenberg, *Nixon's Shadow: The History of an Image* (New York: Norton, 2003).

7. Michael Kackman, *Citizen Spy: Television, Espionage, and Cold War Culture* (Minneapolis: University of Minnesota Press, 2005); Daniel Marcus, *Happy Days and Wonder Years: The Fifties and Sixties in Contemporary Cultural Politics* (New Brunswick, N.J.: Rutgers University Press, 2004); Craig Allen, *Eisenhower and the Mass Media: Peace, Prosperity, and Primetime TV* (Chapel Hill: University of North Carolina Press, 1993); Daniel Hallin, *The Uncensored War: The Media and Vietnam* (Berkeley: University of California Press, 1989).

8. Robert MacNeill, *The People Machine: The Influence of Television on American Politics* (New York: Harper and Row, 1968), 40.

9. Alan Brinkley, *The Publisher: Henry Luce and His American Century* (New York: Knopf, 2010), vii–viii.

10. "When Challenger Fell from the Sky," *New Republic*, February 17, 1986, 7.

11. Frank Rich, "The Age of the Mediathon," *New York Times Magazine*, October 29, 2000.

12. Television led newspapers by 59 to 49 percent in 1968, 66 to 36 percent in 1986, and 81 to 35 percent in 1991. Burns W. Roper, *Public Attitudes toward Television and Other Media in a Time of Change*, fourteenth report in a series by the Roper Organization (New York: Television Information Office, 1985), 1–3; "Topics at a Glance: News Media," *Public Opinion Archives*, Roper Center, University of Connecticut, 2011, http://www.ropercenter.uconn.edu/data_access/tag/News_Media.html. For the 1991 statistics, see *America's Watching—Public Attitudes toward Television, 1991*, December 1990, I-POLL Databank, Roper Center for Public Opinion Research, University of Connecticut. Besides Roper, other surveys have found a similar reliance on TV more than other news media. See, for example, Time/CNN/Yankelovich Partners Poll, October 1996; Pew Global Attitudes Project Poll, August 2002; and Pew Research Center for the People, December 2009. I-POLL Databank, University of Connecticut.

13. See, for example, Marshall McLuhan, *Understanding Media: The Extensions of Man* (New York: McGraw-Hill, 1964).

14. Ibid.

15. Michael J. Robinson, "Public Affairs Television and the Growth of Political Malaise: The Case of 'The Selling of the Pentagon,'" *American Political Science Review* 70 (June 1976): 409–32; Michael J. Robinson, "Television and American Politics, 1956–1976," *Public Interest* 48 (Summer 1977): 3–49.

16. Joshua Meyrowitz, *No Sense of Place: The Impact of Electronic Media on Social Behavior* (New York: Oxford University Press, 1985), 268–304.

17. Joe McGinniss, *The Selling of the President 1968* (New York: Trident, 1969), 179.

18. Todd Gitlin, *The Whole World Is Watching: Mass Media in the Making and Unmaking of the New Left* (Berkeley: University of California Press, 1980), 297–98.

19. The story of the Vanderbilt Television Archive is recounted by its founder, Paul C. Simpson, in *Network Television News: Conviction, Controversy and a Point of View* (Franklin, Tenn.: Legacy Communications, 1995).

20. CNN footage has been taped since 2005, Fox News footage since 2004. "Vanderbilt Television News Archive," Library of Congress, National Science Foundation, and National Endowment for the Humanities, accessed September 1, 2010, http://tvnews.vanderbilt.edu/.

21. "News and Public Affairs (NAPA) Collection," UCLA Film and Television Archive, 2011, http://www.cinema.ucla.edu/collections/napa.html.

22. Thomas Doherty, *Cold War, Cool Medium: Television, McCarthyism, and American Culture* (New York: Columbia University Press, 2003).

JEREMY K. SAUCIER

Playing the Past

The Video Game Simulation as Recent American History

IN MARCH 2003 THE FIRST RECON BATTALION (nicknamed First Suicide Battalion) of the U.S. Marine Corps entered Iraq as part of the effort to oust Iraqi leader Saddam Hussein from power. Much like the characters of so many Hollywood combat films, elite soldiers from different socioeconomic backgrounds, races, and hometowns composed the battalion. Despite these differences, they all shared similar training and the extraordinary ability to fight and destroy their enemies. As the battalion approached another resistant Iraqi town, their Humvees dodged burned-out vehicles, enemy gunfire, and dropped wire cables meant to decapitate turret gunners.

For Corporal James Trombley, the scene was at once deadly, yet familiar. Trombley had experienced something like this well before he ever set foot in the Iraqi desert. As the nineteen-year-old marine explained, "I was thinking one thing when we drove into that ambush . . . *Grand Theft Auto: Vice City*." Thrown into a moment of crisis, Trombley recalled the spectacularly violent and popular video game *Grand Theft Auto* (2003). Set in the drug-fueled underworld of 1980s Miami, players of *Vice City* control Tommy Vercetti, an ex-convict who narrowly escapes a drug deal gone sour and then spends the rest of the game searching for stolen drug money, killing the men who double-crossed him, and trying to achieve his ambition of becoming the city's crime lord. Though Trombley was a soldier, not a drug-dealing criminal, the game resonated with him. "I felt like I was living it when I seen the flames coming out of the windows, the blown-up car in the street, guys crawling around shooting at us. It was fucking cool."[1] Men such as Trombley, as well as the millions of people who play the army's online recruiting game *America's Army* or other war-themed and violent video games, are *virtual veterans*, actively training for and experiencing battle, whether or not some of them ever cross oceans to fight, kill, or die on behalf of their country.

Historians have shown that cultural representations of war and violence have long played an important role in shaping soldiers' sensibilities.[2] Historian Joanna Bourke notes that between 1914 and the end of the Vietnam War, combat films were officially and unofficially used to "excite men's imaginations," as well as "reassure them" before battle.[3] At the end of the twentieth century, video games have played a similar role. Many young soldiers who graduated from basic training and were sent to fight in Afghanistan and Iraq in the first decade of the twenty-first century likely grew up playing combat video games such as the World War II first-person shooter game *Medal of Honor* (1999) or the violent survival horror game *Resident Evil* (1996). The U.S. Supreme Court's 2011 ruling that the 2005 California law prohibiting the sale or rental of exceptionally violent video games to minors was unconstitutional likened video games to literature and film, which have been protected by the first amendment to the Constitution.[4] Yet although video games borrow from and share much with literature and film, they are fundamentally different. Video games immerse players in interactive virtual worlds that push the boundaries of novels and movies. As such, the use of video games as sources for historians of recent U.S. history raises difficult questions and poses several challenges. Can video games designed for young people with quick reflexes and the skills to play various games and game systems with different rules and controls be viably studied by mature scholars? How do historians locate earlier video games, game systems, ephemera, and other industry and game-related materials? What methodological strategies can we use to employ video games as historical sources?

This essay considers the problems and prospects of using video games as sources for writing recent U.S. history. Video games have proven crucial sources for my own research on post-Vietnam military advertising. The army has successfully employed video games as recruiting, marketing, and training devices, and as such, they offer a powerful lens to explore the cultures of late twentieth- and early twenty-first-century warfare and violence. Combat video games such as *America's Army* have helped *militarize* millions of Americans. But video games can be a rich source for historians working on a wide range of recent topics. This essay begins by discussing what video games are and focusing on their development as a medium that feeds on film. It offers methods for "reading" video games in ways that will make them familiar to historians and poses *Resident Evil* as an example of the kinds of cultural and political work that one video game performs while demonstrating its potential as a rich source for a variety of recent histories. Finally, I provide information about how historians can locate games and how they can use older games that play on systems that are no longer readily available, before briefly discussing how I use video games in my research.

A History of Video Games and Video Games as History

From their birth during the late 1950s to their massive expansion into U.S. homes and institutions since the late 1970s, video games have become enormously popular and influential cultural products. Since Willy Higinbotham designed *Tennis for Two* for an analog computer at Brookhaven National Lab in 1958, millions of young boys and girls have slayed dragons in preprogrammed fairy tales and hit home runs on virtual baseball diamonds, ambitious high school students have studied for their SATs, overweight men and women have exercised, and soldiers have trained for the psychological stresses of combat with the help of video games and what the military calls video or computer "simulations."[5]

According to media theorist Marshall McLuhan, games are "popular art, collective social reactions to the main drive or action of any culture." McLuhan argues that games of all sorts are reflections of a particular culture and are "extensions of man."[6] Yet video games, which have become increasingly more sophisticated than many predigital games, are difficult to define. Critic Janet H. Murray writes of the boundary-blurring nature of video games:

> They include elaborate rule systems, rely on active intervention by the interactor and convene large numbers of simultaneous players, include vast amounts of information and multiple media forms, and offer complex spaces to move through. One might argue that digital games are becoming the assimilator of all earlier forms of media culture. They allow players to take on the characters of print fantasy literature or popular films. They incorporate cinematic characterization, lighting, camera angles, and even allow players to make their own movies within the game environment. . . . They include music, graphic design, and dialog, and they make wide use of narrative genres such as adventure, romance, gangsters, and superheroes and are rapidly assimilating other new media formats such as bulletin boards, chat rooms, and in-game newspapers and radio stations.[7]

Video games and video game storytelling, then, cast a wide cultural net, combining and relying on old and new popular forms, narratives, technologies, and techniques. As such, they are hybrids of literary and visual culture, blurring the line between play or entertainment and work or training.

Despite the complex nature of video games, they are often associated with children and are sometimes considered juvenile cultural products.[8] Many American children growing up during the 1970s had their first video game experience while playing *Pong* (1972), a virtual tennis or ping pong–like simulator, which allowed players to bounce a circle (virtual ball) back and forth between two lines (rackets/paddles). Nevertheless, video games have come a very long way since *Pong*, or even the now iconic arcade game *Pacman* (1980). Few popular cultural forms can rival the rapid technological evolution and artistic elevation that video games and video simulations have enjoyed since the 1970s. Today, video games have become one of the fastest-growing, most influential, controversial, and profitable mass cultural mediums. In 2008 alone the U.S. video game industry earned more than $21 billion, far surpassing the Hollywood box office.[9]

Ignoring the presence of video games in recent America is akin to writing the history of the late nineteenth and early twentieth centuries without noting the significance of the dime novel or writing the history of postwar America without acknowledging the importance of television. Historians such as Thomas Cripps, John E. O'Connor, Robert A. Rosenstone, Robert Brent Toplin, and Richard Slotkin have demonstrated the importance of films in U.S. culture, whether acting as disseminators of historical narratives, as expressions of changing cultural myths, or as a medium in which Americans work out their anxieties.[10] Although they are interactive, it is useful to think of and approach video games in some of the same ways that historians have examined films.

By the end of the twentieth century, video games had become increasingly complicated and were more closely associated with the film medium. From the early days of *Pong*, where players manipulated virtual paddles or tennis rackets, video games have developed to allow players to act for a character. Video games had become narrative-driven experiences that often fused players with characters who had already been portrayed on film. Not surprisingly, the video game industry relied heavily on Hollywood's technical knowledge; fashioned itself after the giants of the film industry; and forged a symbiotic relationship where films spawned video games, and video games became the basis for new films. In 2004 software company Electronic Arts (EA) opened EALA, a video game development complex outside of Los Angeles, modeled after neighboring Hollywood studios such as Paramount Pictures and Universal Studios. As Rick Giolito, executive producer of EA game *Medal of Honor* explained, "We're bringing people who have worked on movies like *Spider-Man*, *Spider-Man 2*, *I, Robot*, and *Titanic* into the studio and what they've done is brought in the practices that have been honed over 80 or 90 years of filmmaking." Giolito believed that collaborating with Hollywood was vital as games became "more and more complex," and the "consumer expect[ed] a deeper, more immersive, emotionally moving experience."[11]

The video game industry also looked increasingly to Hollywood for creative content, producing games based on famous film characters such as Indiana Jones (Harrison Ford) and "Dirty" Harry Callahan (Clint Eastwood), as well as successful film franchises such as *Star Wars*.[12] The movie *Star Wars* epitomizes film and media industry efforts toward synergy, or a kind of brand expansion that invests in creating and marketing multiple products from a single film or series of films. Lucas Licensing, a division of *Star Wars* creator George Lucas's company Lucasfilm Limited, is responsible for licensing and merchandising the *Star Wars* brand and a massive list of products as diverse as video games, General Mills cereal, and Pottery Barn duvets and sheets. According to Lucas Limited, licensing for *Star Wars*, *Indiana Jones*, and other Lucas films has generated more than $20 billion in consumer sales worldwide, 100 million books in print, and one of the best-selling boys action toys of all time.[13]

During the late 1980s and 1990s, new technologies, producing sharper and more realistic graphics, increased memories and processing speeds, and better home game consoles, drove the relationship between the film and video game industries to new heights.[14] By the turn of the twenty-first century many new blockbuster films followed the *Star Wars* model, spinning off dozens of products and new video game projects. For instance, by 2011 director Peter Jackson's *The Lord of the Rings* (LOTR) trilogy of fantasy films (*Fellowship of the Ring*, 2001; *The Two Towers*, 2002; and *The Return of the King*, 2003) based on the novels of J. R. R. Tolkien had provided the backstories for more than a dozen video and computer games, including LOTR: *The Fellowship of the Ring* (2002), LOTR: *The Third Age* (2004), LOTR: *The Battle for Middle Earth II* (2006), and LOTR: *Aragorn's Quest* (2010). Much like the *Star Wars* video games, game players can effectively wield the same weapons, fight against similar enemies, and act for favorite characters in a virtual world already imagined in literature and on film.

If the video game industry turned to Hollywood for assistance, these collaborations produced new film projects as well. Beginning in the early 1990s Hollywood released a growing list of movies based on best-selling video games and game franchises, including *Super Mario Bros.* (game, 1985; film, 1993), *Street Fighter* (game, 1987; films, 1994 and 2009), *Mortal Kombat* (game, 1992; films, 1995 and 1997), *Tomb Raider* (game, 1992; films, 1995 and 2003), *Doom* (game, 1993; film, 2005), *Hitman* (game, 2000; film, 2007) and *Prince of Persia: The Sands of Time* (game, 2003; film, 2010). Some of the film adaptations helped earn video games added legitimacy, but few were box office successes.[15] The collaborations proved more vital as a bridge between Hollywood and the video game industry. With screenwriters, directors, producers, musical composers, and actors often contributing their filmmaking talents and techniques to new simulations and games, many video games became more like narrative-driven interactive films.

Reading Resident Evil

A video game such as *Resident Evil* (1996) demonstrates the many ways in which games have developed cinematic qualities since the 1970s, as well as the cultural and political work video games can perform. In *Resident Evil*, players enter a postapocalyptic world, where they are part of a Special Tactics and Rescue Squad police force struggling to survive in an old mansion where zombies lurk in the shadows. The game begins much like the prologue of a film, cutting between live action and computer-generated imagery, as the narrator describes the situation in Raccoon City in July 1998.

> As players hear the sound of typing and a helicopter, the narrator, Chris, explains, "Alpha Team is flying around the forest zone situated in northwest Raccoon City, where we're searching for the helicopter of our compatriots, Bravo Team, who disappeared during the middle of our mission." After the team tells a police officer by radio that they still have not found their comrades, Chris states, "Bizarre murder cases have recently occurred in Raccoon City. There are outlandish reports of families being attacked by a group of about ten people. Victims were apparently eaten. Bravo Team went to the hideout of the group and disappeared." As we hear helicopter blades again, a female member of the team, Jill, exclaims, "Look, Chris!" The scene cuts to the team discovering Bravo Team's helicopter, but, as Chris tells us, "Nobody was in it. But

strangely, most of the equipment was still there. However, we soon discovered why." Another member of the team, Joseph, shouts, "Hey! Come here," as the scene quickly cuts to a doglike animal growling. Seeing something in the grass, Joseph reaches in and pulls out a human hand. Suddenly, he is attacked. As Joseph screams in pain, the team opens fire while they run away into a nearby mansion.

The scenario in part recalls such horror films as director George Romero's *Night of the Living Dead* (1968), *Dawn of the Dead* (1978), and *Day of the Dead* (1985), which center on small groups of Americans (barricaded in a farmhouse, mall, and underground bunker, respectively) making last stands against undead hordes. Every aspect of *Resident Evil*, from its scenario, music, and sound effects to its gory visuals and multiple perspectives, immerses players within a horror film.

> You (acting for Chris), Jill, and Captain Wesker hear a gunshot and decide you will investigate it while the others stay in the main hall. You walk through an empty hallway, turning a corner as you hear the sounds of chomping and gnawing over a suspenseful musical score. Looking down, you view a close-up of what seems to be making the sound: a white-faced zombie creature with blood dripping from its mouth. Frightened, you step back and search for a weapon. Unable to find your gun, you draw your combat knife, but the creature attacks, grabbing, moaning, and biting at your neck and shoulder. You push it away and run back to the main hall, where you find Jill's Beretta, but Jill and Captain Wesker are gone.

The changing perspectives, moving from behind the avatar to across the room, occur as quickly as switching film camera angles to enhance the storytelling, suspense, and game-playing experience. As one reviewer observed, *Resident Evil* was "Part mystery, part killfest, part puzzler," incorporating "the best elements of many genres to create an experience that is both unique and universally appealing. . . . At times it's easy to forget that *Resident Evil* is just a video game."[16] *Resident Evil* may be "just a video game," but its interactive format allows players to virtually inhabit characters who do not know what they might encounter around the next corner or behind the next door they open. Unlike a film, and more like real life, the player shapes and reshapes the game's story depending on what choices they make during the game.

But how does one make sense of or "read" an interactive game that resembles film but has several narrative possibilities with no sure conclusion?

One answer is that because most video games draw so heavily from cinematic sources, it is useful to incorporate the insights of film studies and read them frame by frame for their narrative elements. Semiotician and film theorist Jurij Lotman writes, "Everything which we notice during the presentation of a film, everything that excites us, has meaning. In order to learn how to understand these meanings it is necessary to master the system of meanings, just as we do in the case of classical ballet, symphonic music or any other sufficiently complex, traditional art form."[17] Semiotics, then, provides us with a potential method for reading a new and unexplored video game text in a way familiar to many historians.

Looking beyond *Resident Evil*'s mimicking of film form and genre, its interactive narrative expresses deep cultural concerns with capitalism and gender roles, which offer a potentially rich source for cultural histories that address popular representations of women, feminism, the zombie, warriors, and the national security state. The game's story line was seemingly so compelling to Hollywood producers and marketers that they adapted it into a feature film starring actress Milla Jovovich in 2002, spawning three sequels, *Resident Evil: Apocalypse* (2004), *Resident Evil: Extinction* (2007), and *Resident Evil: Afterlife* (2010); a line of comics; action figures; and other merchandise.[18] As the films later reveal, this virtual world of preying scavengers and flesh-eating zombies was accidentally unleashed by the ruthless Umbrella Corporation, a manufacturer of everything from sunblock to weapons. In this way, *Resident Evil* expresses long-standing tensions within the capitalist system, as well as postwar anxieties about a military industrial complex that, out of the public eye, produces biological and chemical weapons.

Jovovich's role as Alice in the film version also constructs a strong female heroine who fights zombies and the corporation. In becoming the world's best chance for survival and the franchise's super warrior-hero, she also displays the same victimhood and psychological trauma expressed in representations of soldiers since World War II.[19] Much like a drafted soldier, Alice is a victim of fighting a war she has not asked for. As a biogenetically enhanced Umbrella experiment with superior physical strength, agility, and telekinetic powers, she has been *made* into a weapon or super soldier. Struggling to take control of her own body from the company—perhaps a metaphor for the fight for women's reproductive rights—her frequent flashbacks (or posttraumatic stress) depict her as a psychologically wounded veteran who has been through far too many battles and Umbrella experiments.

Those working on recent American political histories examining debates over censorship, children, and violence could also find a valuable source in *Resident Evil* and the political debate it generated. While the themes found in the games and films may have resonated with many U.S. consumers, who purchased 2,750,000 copies, the original game was also the target of controversy.[20] The game hit store shelves in the wake of presidents Ronald Reagan's and George H. W. Bush's initiatives to promote conservative values, initiatives that unleashed new battles over gay rights, abortion, education, and the arts. Many conservatives cited higher rates of out-of-wedlock pregnancy, divorce, and abortion as evidence of the United States' cultural decline since the 1950s. At the same time, both conservatives and liberals worried about the increasing prominence of politically driven acts of violence aimed at doctors and abortion clinics by antiabortion extremists, extreme right-wing hate groups who attacked racial minorities and gay men and women, and the kind of antigovernment militias that led Timothy McVeigh and Terry Nichols to kill 168 people when they blew up the federal building in Oklahoma City in 1995.[21]

In this political and cultural context, new technologies allowing the video game industry to produce more narrative-driven home-console games with more realistic thirty-two- and sixty-four-bit graphics appeared potentially dangerous.[22] Some politicians and critics publicly denounced the increasingly violent content of many new games. The vast majority of reviews of *Resident Evil* noted the game's "grotesque imagery," "lots of spilled blood," and "extreme violence."[23] In 1993 Senator Joseph Lieberman (D-Conn.) was among the first politicians to voice concerns over the release of *Mortal Kombat*, a one-on-one fighting game that rewarded players for "fatalities" achieved, among other ways, by decapitating or ripping out the heart of one's opponent. At the same time, psychologist David Walsh's jeremiad against video games and other media, *Selling Out America's Children*, argued that U.S. society exploits children for profit.[24] By 1996 Walsh founded the National Institute on Media and the Family, a media watchdog group who regularly released video game report cards. With the 1996 release of *Resident Evil* and nearly twenty other video games deemed unsuitable by Walsh and his institute, Lieberman joined Walsh and Senator Herbert Kohl (D-Wisc.) in a campaign to inform Congress and American parents about video game content they deemed inappropriate for children. "Despite the concerns first raised by the likes of Mortal Kombat and Doom years ago," Lieberman explained, "too many games now on the market . . . are more violent, more antisocial and generally more disgusting than ever."²⁵ *Resident Evil* has already become a subject of political debate; along with other video games, it should also be considered an important topic for historical research.

The Challenge of Using Video Games as Historical Source

Video games offer potentially rich sources for historians of the recent past, but examining video games and integrating them into historical projects is not without methodological challenges. Perhaps the biggest problem with employing video games as sources is that they are difficult texts to learn and eventually master. For historians to adopt video games such as *Resident Evil* as sources, they must first become versed in an often unfamiliar, if not completely foreign, language with many dialects. That is, even if one acquires the basic skills needed to advance through one game, those skills may or may not help one decipher, understand, or even play another game.

The best way to engage games as texts is to "play" them.²⁶ Yet this too demands a certain amount of skill that goes well beyond the basic and more advanced levels of literacy needed to observe film and television or to read many more traditional written sources. The interactive nature of video games requires historians to be at least literate in the fundamentals of video game play. More often than not, players will have to master a given game—beat all opponents, overcome every obstacle, locate all the treasures, open all doors and levels—to unravel everything the game's narrative has to offer. Watching even fifty films can be a daunting task for historians, but playing fifty video games from beginning to end would be truly Herculean.

In such a case, one must consider a more ethnographic approach focusing on observing experienced players as the next best option to game play. Observing and discussing game play with experienced gamers familiarizes historians with the contours of the game and the virtual world the players enter. Moreover, game play itself can be read as text, much in the same way that anthropologist Clifford Geertz read the "deep play" of the Balinese cockfight. By reading the cockfight as a text, Geertz demonstrates what this ritual or game means to Balinese men. As Geertz observes, "Balinese go to cockfights to find out what a man, usually composed, aloof, almost obsessively self-absorbed, a kind of moral autocosm, feels like when, attacked, tormented, challenged, insulated, and driven in result to the extremes of fury, he has totally triumphed or been brought totally low."[27] Ethnographers, such as Tom Boellstorff, have even examined game play and players' interaction with virtual worlds in the online game *Second-Life* (launched in 2003). He argues that ethnography "has a special role to play in studying virtual worlds because it has *anticipated* them. Virtual before the Internet existed, ethnography has always produced a kind of virtual knowledge."[28] For historians employing video games as sources, this ethnographic approach creates an avenue for examining the kinds of people who play games, how they interact with games or online communities of players, what these games mean to them, and how they are used.

Even if one is able to gain the skills necessary to play a video game or find a skilled player to watch, locating the sources necessary to tell a particular story is an entirely different challenge. Where does one find video games and other sources associated with the video game industry? Historians can track down skilled players and serious hobbyists who often amass large collections of games and may possess a wealth of knowledge about the development of video gaming. Researchers can also troll online auctions, flea markets, and garage sales for old game consoles, games, and popular gaming magazines such as *Game Informer*, *Electronic Gaming Monthly*, and *GamePro*, but this is an expensive and potentially frustrating enterprise. Fortunately, at the turn of the twenty-first century some universities, museums, and archivists instituted ambitious projects focusing on collecting and preserving video games and related materials. These institutions are the best places to begin serious research. Among the four most notable in the United States are as follows:

1. The International Center for the History of Electronic Games at the Strong National Museum of Play in Rochester, New York. Their holdings include arcade games, handheld games, and home consoles dating back to the early 1970s, a collection of more than ten thousand console games, as well as trade catalogs, advertising, strategy guides, and the papers of Ralph H. Baer, inventor of the first home game system.
2. The UT Video Game Archive at the Dolph Briscoe Center for American History, University of Texas at Austin. The archive includes growing collections of games, papers, and files from video game developers such as Richard Garriott and Warren Spector and from composer George Sanger.
3. The Stephen M. Cabrinety Collection in the History of Microcomputing, Stanford University, California. The collection is composed of ephemera, printed materials, 400 pieces of computer hardware, 200 pieces of

computer-related realia and peripherals, and 6,300 pieces of computer software, of which two-thirds are computer games.

4. Computer and Video Game Archive, University of Michigan, Ann Arbor. The archive holds hundreds of video game titles dating back to the 1970s.[29]

There are also several excellent "online archives," such as the Internet Archive, YouTube, and the Digital Game Archive, which allow players and researchers to view video game footage and download playable games.[30]

Because video games and simulations borrow much of their visual and generic motifs and storytelling techniques from Hollywood filmmakers and other popular cultural sources, historians should begin to look to film studies, communications, media studies, and the burgeoning field of game studies for insight and assistance. Leading game-studies journals include *Game Studies: The International Journal of Computer Game Research*, *Simulation and Gaming*, and *Games and Culture: A Journal of Interactive Media*, though other media studies and communication journals often include articles on interactive media, video games, and simulations.[31] Ultimately, if historians are to employ video games as sources, they should understand the grammar of video games through play and observation, while employing the theories and insights of film, media, and game studies. Such an approach could lead to innovative interdisciplinary studies that incorporate the video game into histories of recent America.

Combat Simulations and the Rise of the Virtual Veteran in Recent America

One arena that provides an example of how video games can serve as valuable historical sources is that of the recent histories of American warfare and cultures of violence. Although some politicians have labeled many violent video games as dangerous, video games have become increasingly important recruiting, marketing, and training tools for the U.S. military. By combining readings of games with archival research and industry, government, and military materials found in the public domain, we can better understand how games are made, received by players, and used by soldiers.

When American soldiers returned home from the Vietnam War, some publicly reflected on how their combat experiences were very different than the films they grew up watching. For marine Ron Kovic, movie heroes such as John Wayne and Audie Murphy defined courage, heroism, and masculinity during war. Marine Philip Caputo wanted to experience "the romance of war, bayonet charges, and desperate battles against impossible odds." He wanted to live out what he "had seen in *Guadalcanal Diary* and *Retreat, Hell!* and a score of other movies."[32] For many soldiers of the Vietnam War generation, the hero of the Hollywood combat film, particularly the John Wayne image, was at times a "recruiting poster" and at other times an example that no man could live up to. The "John Wayne thing," as psychologist Robert Jay Lifton calls it, "meant military pride, lust for battle, fearless exposure to danger, and prowess for killing."[33] The internalization of the Wayne image, Lifton tells us, caused soldiers to feel guilt and shame over their failure to live up to their big screen counterparts. Yet for a new generation of soldiers fighting in Iraq and Afghanistan and potential soldiers battling friends and enemies in virtual worlds, John Wayne is a distant memory if not a cliché. In a new military culture, video games instead serve as recruiting, preparation, and training tools, producing millions of *virtual combat veterans*.

Video games are different from conventional forms of media used to recruit young men and women into the military. Janet Murray contends that digital storytelling, like the kind created by video game designers and consumed by millions of players, offers people the opportunity to enact stories rather than observe them. "Enacted events," Murray asserts, "have a transformative power that exceeds both narrated and conventionally dramatized events because we assimilate them as personal experiences."[34] The power of video game storytelling is that it immerses players in a world of their choosing, where they can be a soldier, police officer, doctor, professional athlete, drug dealer, assassin, or whoever else they want to be. The idea that people identify with the characters or alternate selves constructed on video screens has been at the center of psychologist Sherry Turkle's work on computers, digital games, and the Internet. She describes computers as a "second self" and video games as something more than play. "Television is something you watch," Turkle writes. "Video games are something you do, something you do to your head, a world that you enter, and, to a certain extent, they are something you 'become.'"[35]

For many of the soldiers who fought in Afghanistan and Iraq, combat video games were something they did for entertainment and in preparation for battle before and while they were overseas. Sergeant Sinique Swales, a national guardsman, described firing on a group of insurgents in Northern Mosul, Iraq, as "a big video game. It didn't faze me." Like many of his comrades, Swales spent his off-hours playing Xbox and Playstation 3 combat games such as *Full Spectrum Warrior* (2004)—a game developed by the army to train soldiers for urban combat—and the futuristic first-person shooter game *Halo 2* (2004). Swales's friend Sergeant Sean Crippen recalled that he was scared the first time he fired his M249 automatic machine gun at another person, "but once I pulled the trigger, that was it, I never hesitated. . . . it felt like I was playing 'Ghost Recon' at home."[36] Much like Swales, Crippen imagined himself playing a video game, in this case, the Tom Clancy–inspired special-operations combat game franchise *Ghost Recon*. Video game magazines, such as *Game Informer*, have published "candid photos" of soldiers such as Swales and Crippen stationed in Iraq playing video games, while the army's newspaper, the *Army Times*, regularly reviews video games of interest to its soldiers in the paper's entertainment section.[37] With soldiers crowding around game consoles before they go on patrol and military psychologists using games to treat combat stress, the video game experience is often inseparable from modern warfare.[38]

The concept of employing the virtual to prepare for the real has not been lost on the army. The way that many soldiers compare their actions in combat to playing a video game recalls Orson Scott Card's science fiction novel *Ender's Game*, a book that Michael Macedonia, director of the army's simulation and technology center noted, "has had a lot of influence on our thinking."[39] The novel follows Ender Wiggins, one of a number of children who are trained to battle aliens in a video game universe before learning that the game was real and they had saved humanity. For the army, *Ender's Game* suggested that video games could perhaps effectively train soldiers by blurring the line between virtual reality and reality.

Whether the purpose of playing a particular video game is to escape from one reality, or to train for another, the player must at least act for or even "become" someone else—in this case, a soldier. Indeed, the marketing for *Medal of Honor: Frontline* (2002), a game that invites players to replay the opening scenes of *Saving Private Ryan* (1998) by storming the virtual blood-soaked beaches of Normandy on D-Day, claims, "You don't play, you volunteer."[40] The slogan constructs the combat simulation as more than a game. In striking down the word "play," the line expresses the seriousness of the player's task. Quoting the language of the current volunteer military, it suggests that the player is a soldier voluntarily engaged in a noble effort. Note that the slogan is not "You don't play, you get drafted."

The most widely played and popular of these new realistic combat video games is the army's own online recruiting game, *America's Army*. Released in 2002, the combat simulation, as one army spokesperson explained, was meant to "not only enhance kids'—and adults'—Army game–playing experiences and spark interest in the Army as a potential career, but to reintroduce the Army to the population at large."[41] The original combat simulation, available for download online, features two distinct games. "Soldiers" focuses on cultivating a player's character through training and various missions that provide the player with information about the army. The second game, "Operations," is a first-person combat game that places players in virtual service to the army. During online play, virtual soldiers from all over the world can come together to fill roles as squad leaders, grenadiers, riflemen, and automatic riflemen, carrying out missions such as protecting an Alaskan pipeline or recovering a prisoner of war from behind enemy lines.

Game developers combined these combat scenarios with realistic portrayals of virtual environments and renderings of army weaponry meant to "suspend disbelief through immersion." According to the developers, they accomplished this "immersion" through such approaches and innovations as accurate "weapon functionality" and sound effects that precisely reproduce the sound that one kind of bullet makes when it hits concrete versus the very different sound another kind of bullet makes when it blasts through wood. Through the use of motion capture, a technology that records the actions of individuals and uses it to animate digital characters, players are able to quite literally copy and act out movements recorded by actual soldiers. The game's weapons, sound effects, and motion capture animation provide players with what designers called "a cinematic experience."[42] But in some ways, the experience is more than cinematic, because players inhabit characters that move, shoot, and throw grenades just like the soldiers whom designers have recorded.

With the third generation of the game, *America's Army 3*, launched online in 2009, game developers hoped to blur the distinction between game play and combat even further. As the game's lead designer, Ace Aubuchon, explained, "Something that we've always said, and we've always had as a goal, is that you would play your in-game character as if you were really in combat."[43] As I watched a video recording of *America's Army 3* posted by a self-described high school freshman, it appeared that was exactly how this online group of players experienced it.

The members of the fire team run across the urban landscape, ducking in and out of alleys, pausing only to make sure the area is clear or to look through their sniper scopes. A teen boy's voice continually lets other people in the unit know when they should move and whether particular areas are clear, calling, "I got the alley," or "I got your back." Before the soldiers enter a diner named Buckets (the rallying point), the teen says, "Seems clear, move quick." But they have walked into an ambush. After taking several shots, a soldier falls to the floor and the teen shouts, "This is not clear! This is not clear!" After being helped by a medic, the soldier survives, and the unit moves toward their objective.[44]

If *America's Army* is a just a game to these online players, it is a very serious game that provides them with an outlet to participate in an interactive cultural experience that realistically simulates combat. Although it is difficult to say whether any of the people playing with the teen are veterans or currently enlisted, or have any military experience at all, they operate as a military unit, following cues and speaking the language of combat. Players are connected visually by watching their unit's actions on-screen and verbally by listening to others' commands over their computer's speakers or through their headsets. As another teenager commented about an earlier version of the game, "It's a way cool game. I personally don't think it compares with any other in the world. . . . The realism is simply stunning. . . . The developers have worked hard on this aspect of the game, and it certainly shows through."[45]

With game graphics becoming nearly as realistic as they can be, developers have already turned to expert consultants to add a new level of realism. For instance, EA's *Medal of Honor* employed Captain Dale Dye, a technical adviser for *Saving Private Ryan* and a number of other films and television programs. For the army, consultation came from within the ranks of its own soldiers. The use of soldiers' input, however, also became a marketing strategy and a way to extend the army brand. As a 2007 print ad for *America's Army: True Soldiers* for Xbox 360 claimed, the game was "Created by Soldiers. Developed by Gamers. Tested by Heroes." The ad presented a close-up image—with the viewer looking almost directly over the shoulder and right down the profile of a rifle—of army Sergeant Tommy Rieman peering down the hallway of a bombed-out building. Rieman, who earned a Silver Star during Operation Iraqi Freedom, acted as a game "development consultant" and as one of the first four "*America's Army* Real Heroes." In 2007 the army and toy maker Jazwares created action figure likenesses of Rieman, Sergeant Matthew Zedwick, Sergeant First Class Gerald Wolford, and Major Jason Amerine and sold the toys with a copy of an updated version of *America's Army*. By 2011 the *America's Army* website showcased nine "real heroes" profiles, including a white woman and a black male, as examples of "dedication and gallantry in action."[46]

As real soldiers create, test, and train with *America's Army*, the distinction between the training and conditioning of the actual and the virtual soldier blurs. Military psychologist David Grossman forcefully argues that violent video games contribute to a desensitization toward killing, especially in children. Drawing on B. F. Skinner's theory of "operant conditioning," Grossman contends that the Vietnam-era armed forces trained soldiers to overcome their resistance to killing by shooting at human-shaped pop-up targets, with devastating results.[47] Psychological studies examining the effects of video game violence also suggest that children and young adults who play violent video games are more likely to have more angry thoughts, more physiological arousal, and more overtly aggressive behavior.[48] U.S. Supreme Court justice Stephen Breyer's dissenting opinion in *Brown v. Entertainment Merchants Association* (2011) relied on many of these studies, noting that "video games can help develop habits, accustom the player to the performance of the task, and reward the player for performing that task well. Why else would the Armed Forces incorporate video games into its training?"[49] With the rise of video games, the same combat simulations used by the military to ready their soldiers for war are socializing millions of America's new warriors daily.

With one in four of all American males between the ages of thirteen and twenty-four having played *America's Army*, and with 10 million registered users—more than the population of the entire army during World War II—*America's Army* has built a massive online army of virtual veterans. Claiming 29 percent of players are more likely to be interested in military service, *America's Army* has also prepared, trained, and "volunteered" a generation for combat well before they volunteer for the actual military.[50] Indeed, as game theorist Ian Bogost suggests, while *America's Army* draws interested youth to recruiters, the game also "encourages players to consider the logic of duty, honor, and singular global political truth"—one in which the United States is right and there is little explanation for its enemies' behavior save evil—"as a desirable worldview."[51] If cinematic and literary representations of war and violence had helped forge an image of an "Indian country" in the imaginations of many Vietnam-era soldiers, interactive video games and simulations have proven to be the official and unofficial virtual training grounds of a new generation of militarized Americans.

Driven by new research, new technologies, and new markets at the end of the twentieth century, video games, with their ever-growing narrative and visual sophistication, stand posed to rival the art forms of the nineteenth and twentieth centuries. Like other cultural products, such as film, literature, or music, video games express cultural tensions and anxieties. Their subjects and narratives speak to a particular society's place and time and are thus important sources for historical work. Video games are potentially the most powerful storytelling medium of the twenty-first century. Not only are simulated experiences becoming more commonplace, but they are being woven into the fabric of American social, economic, and political institutions. Political battles have been and will continue to be waged over the psychological and cultural costs of video games, at the same time they are used to recruit and train a new generation of soldiers. The game industry will no doubt continue to grow and produce more innovative simulations. Video games, then, hold a special promise for historians of recent America, and the benefits of utilizing them, I hope, far outweigh the challenges.

Notes

1. Evan Wright, *Generation Kill: Devil Dogs, Iceman, Captain America and the New Face of American War* (New York: Putnam's Sons, 2004), 5.

2. See, for instance, Michael C. C. Adams, *The Great Adventure: Male Desire and the Coming of World War I* (Bloomington: Indiana University Press, 1990); Richard Slotkin, *Gunfighter Nation: The Myth of the Frontier in Twentieth-Century America* (Norman: University of Oklahoma Press, 1998); Craig M. Cameron, *American Samurai: Myth, Imagination, and the Conduct of Battle in the First Marine Division, 1941– 1951* (New York: Cambridge University Press, 1994); Joanna Bourke, *An Intimate History of Killing: Face-to-Face Killing in Twentieth-Century Warfare* (New York: Basic Books, 1999); David Kennedy, *Over Here: The First World War in American Society* (New York: Oxford University Press, 2004), ch. 3; John Pettegrew, *Brutes in Suits: Male Sensibility in America, 1880–1920* (Baltimore, Md.: Johns Hopkins University Press, 2007), ch. 4.

3. Bourke, *Intimate History of Killing*, 12.

4. See Brown v. Entertainment Merchants Association, no. 08–1488, S. Ct. 2011, Supreme Court of the United States, June 27, 2011, http://www.supremecourt.gov /opinions/10pdf/08–1448.pdf. The majority's opinion, in part, relied on the logic that the country has no tradition of restricting children's access to depictions of violence. In associate justice Stephen Breyer's dissenting opinion, he noted that the state's prohibition of the sale of depictions of nudity to minors while protecting the sale of violent interactive video games "creates a serious anomaly in first amendment law."

5. David H. Ahl, "Mainframe Games and Simulations," in *The Video Game Explosion: A History from Pong to Playstation and Beyond*, ed. Mark J. P. Wolf (Westport, Conn.: Greenwood, 2008), 32.

6. Marshall McLuhan, *Understanding Media: The Extensions of Man* (New York: New American Library, 1964), 38.

7. Janet H. Murray, "Toward a Cultural Theory of Gaming: Digital Games and the Co-evolution of Media, Mind, and Culture," *Popular Communication* 4, no. 3 (2006): 187.

8. The history of childhood itself is just beginning to be elaborated as a specialty. With its own set of methodological problems and archival challenges, it has, not surprisingly, found more acceptance among literary scholars, ethnographers, and sociologists examining such topics as children's literature and toys. See, for instance, Ann duCille, "Toy Theory: Black Barbie and the Deep Play of Difference" in *Skin Trade*, ed. Ann duCille (Cambridge, Mass.: Harvard University Press, 1996), 8–59; Roni Natov, *The Poetics of Childhood* (New York: Routledge, 2002); and Christine L. Williams, *Inside Toyland: Working, Shopping, and Inequality* (Los Angeles: University of California Press, 2006), esp. ch. 5. Nevertheless, since the 1990s, some social and cultural historians of the United States have begun to examine children's roles as producers, consumers, members of families, political and cultural symbols, and members of distinct groups and cultures. See, for instance, Joseph M. Hawes and N. Ray Hiner, eds., *American Childhood: A Research Guide and Historical Handbook* (Westport, Conn.: Greenwood, 1985); William M. Tuttle, Jr., *Daddy's Gone to War: The Second World War in the Lives of America's Children* (New York: Oxford University Press, 1993); Gary Cross, *Kid's Stuff: Toys and the Changing World of American Childhood* (Cambridge, Mass.: Harvard University Press, 1997); Paula Fass, *Kidnapped: Child Abduction in America* (New York: Oxford University Press, 1997); Joseph E. Illick, *American Childhoods* (Philadelphia: University of Pennsylvania Press, 2002); Lisa Jacobson, *Raising Consumers: Children and the American Mass Market in the Early Twentieth Century* (New York: Columbia University Press, 2004); Steven Mintz, *Huck's Raft: A History of American Childhood* (Cambridge, Mass.: Harvard University Press, 2004); and Peter Stearns, "Challenges in the History of Childhood," *Journal of the History of Childhood* 1, no. 1 (2008), 35–42.

9. Mike Snider, "Video Game Sales Hit Record Despite Economic Downturn," USAtoday.com, January 18, 2009, http://www.usatoday.com/tech/gaming/2009-01-15-video-game-sales_N.htm.

10. See, for instance, Thomas Cripps, *Making Movies Black: The Hollywood Message Movie from World War II to the Civil Rights Era* (New York: Oxford University Press, 1993); John E. O'Connor and Martin A. Jackson, eds., *American History/American Film: Interpreting the Hollywood Image* (New York: Continuum, 1988); Robert A. Rosenstone, *Visions of the Past: The Challenge of Film to Our Idea of History* (Cambridge, Mass.: Harvard University Press, 1995); Robert Brent Toplin, *History by Hollywood: The Use and Abuse of the American Past* (Chicago: University of Illinois Press, 1996); Robert Brent Toplin, *Reel History: In Defense of Hollywood* (Lawrence: University Press of Kansas, 2002); and Slotkin, *Gunfighter Nation*.

11. "Lights, Camera, Action! EA Combines the Glamour and Glitz of Hollywood with the Power of Video Games," *Game Informer* 137 (September 2004): 57.

12. Examples include *Indiana Jones and the Temple of Doom* (film, 1984; game for the Nintendo Entertainment System, 1985) and *Dirty Harry: The War against Drugs* (films, *Dirty Harry*, 1971; *Magnum Force*, 1973; *The Enforcer*, 1976; *Sudden Impact*, 1983; and *The Dead Pool*, 1988; game for Nintendo Entertainment System, 1990). The list of *Star Wars* computer and video games spans nearly three decades and includes *Star Wars: The Empire Strikes Back* (Atari 2600, 1982), *Star Wars* (Atari arcade, 1983), *Star Wars*

(Nintendo Entertainment System, 1991), *Super Star Wars* (Super Nintendo Entertainment System, 1992), *Star Wars: Shadows of the Empire* (Nintendo 64, 1996), *Star Wars: Jedi Starfighter* (Playstation 2, Xbox, 2002), *Star Wars: The Clone Wars* (Playstation 2, Xbox, Game Cube, 2002–3), *Star Wars: Republic Commando* (Xbox, 2006), *Star Wars: The Force Unleashed* (Playstation 2, Playstation 3, Playstation Portable, Nintendo Wii, Nintendo DS, Xbox 360, 2008), LEGO *Star Wars: The Clone Wars* (Playstation 3, Playstation Portable, Nintendo Wii, Nintendo DS, Nintendo 3DS, Xbox 360, 2011).

13. See Lucasfilm Limited, Licensing Division, accessed June 29, 2011, http://www.lucasfilm.com/divisions/licensing/.

14. See Mark J. P. Wolf, "Imaging Technologies," in Wolf, *Video Game Explosion*, 9–12.

15. Authors Kwan Min Lee, Namkee Park, and Seung-A Jin argue that the relatively small box office yields of films adapted from games may be the result of players' disappointment with discrepancies between their own creative, interactive experiences and the narratives constructed by film directors. See "Narrative and Interactivity in Computer Games," in *Playing Video Games: Motives, Responses, Consequences*, ed. Peter Vorderer and Jennings Bryant (Mahwah, N.J.: LEA, 2006), 268.

16. Aaron Curtiss, "Resident Evil Ushers in New Set-Top Standards," *Los Angeles Times*, June 3, 1996, 4.

17. Jurij Lotman, *The Semiotics of Cinema*, trans. Mark Suino (Ann Arbor: Michigan Slavic Contributions, 1976), 41.

18. "The History of Resident Evil," ComputerAndVideoGames.com, March 7, 2009, http://current.com/11qva4c.

19. See, for instance, Andrew J. Huebner, *The Warrior Image: Soldiers in American Culture from the Second World War to the Vietnam Era* (Chapel Hill: University of North Carolina Press, 2008).

20. Chris Faylor, "Capcom Releases Lifetime Sales of All Franchises: Resident Evil, Mega Man, Disney Top Charts," *Shack News*, May 23, 2008, http://www.shacknews.com/onearticle.x/52832.

21. See James T. Patterson, *Restless Giant: The United States from Watergate to Bush v. Gore* (New York: Oxford University Press, 2005), chs. 4 and 8; and Graham Thompson, *American Culture in the 1980s* (Edinburgh, Scotland: Edinburgh University Press, 2007), 31–36.

22. Home consoles are commonly categorized by "generation," including first-generation consoles (early to mid-1970s), which were nonprogrammable systems (e.g., Magnavox Odyssey); second-generation consoles (mid-1970s to mid-1980s), which upgraded consoles to programmable eight-bit systems (e.g., Atari and ColecoVision); third-generation consoles (mid-1980s to early 1990s), which were more advanced eight-bit systems (e.g., Nintendo Entertainment System); fourth-generation consoles (early to mid-1990s), which featured sixteen-bit systems (e.g., Sega Genesis); and fifth-generation consoles (mid-1990s to early 2000s), which depending on the system showcased thirty-two- or sixty-four-bit graphics (e.g., Sony Playstation and Nintendo 64). The sixth-generation (early to mid-2000s) and seventh-generation (mid-2000s) of consoles, which included the Sony Playstation 2, Microsoft Xbox, Nintendo Game Cube, Sony Playstation 3, Microsoft Xbox 360, and Nintendo Wii, respectively, brought graphics and online game play to new heights. See Mark J. P. Wolf, ed., *The Video Game Explosion: A History from Pong to Playstation and Beyond* (Westport, Conn.: Greenwood, 2008), chs., 9, 26, 36.

23. Lisa Ferguson and Jay Ferguson, "Resident Evil by Capcom," *San Diego Union-Tribune*, April 16, 1996, 11; Vox Day, "Horror Game Is a Little Too Graphic for Kids," *St. Louis Post-Dispatch*, September 5, 1996, 40; "Violence Mars Evil Game," *Sunday Star-Times* (Wellington, New Zealand), September 8, 1996, F8.

24. David Walsh, *Selling Out America's Children: How America Puts Profits before Value—and What Parents Can Do* (Minneapolis, Minn.: Fairview, 1995).

25. Mike Snider, "Senators' No-No List of Violent Video Games," *USA Today*, December 6, 1996, 1D; Laura Eveson, "Video Games Rated, Guide for Parents Notes Violence, Nudity," *San Francisco Chronicle*, November 26, 1997.

26. Any discussion of the anthropology of play must begin with Johan Huizinga's 1938 book, *Homo Ludens*, and Roger Caillois's 1958 work, *Man, Play, and Games*. See Huizinga, *Homo Ludens: A Study of the Play-Element in Culture* (New York: Routledge, 2000) and Caillois, *Man, Play, and Games* (Urbana: University of Illinois Press, 2001).

27. Clifford Geertz, "Deep Play: Notes on the Balinese Cockfight," in *The Interpretation of Cultures* (New York: Basic Books, 1973), 450.

28. Tom Boellstorff, *Coming of Age in Second Life: An Anthropologist Explores the Virtually Human* (Princeton, N.J.: Princeton University Press, 2008), 6.

29. International Center for the History of Electronic Games, accessed June 29, 2011, http://www.icheg.org/; UT Video Game Archive, Dolph Briscoe Center for American History, accessed June 29, 2011, http://www.cah.utexas.edu/projects/videogamearchive/index.html; Brenda Gunn, "Preserving Video Game History, the Time Is Now," *Game Informer* 174 (October 2007): 52; Stephen M. Cabrinety, "Collection in the History of Microcomputing," Department of Special Collections, Stanford University, accessed June 29, 2011, http://library.stanford.edu/depts/hasrg/histsci/index.htm; Computer and Video Game Archive, University of Michigan, accessed June 29, 2011, http://www.lib.umich.edu/aael/cvga.

30. See Internet Archive, http://www.archive.org/details/gamevideos; YouTube.com, http://www.youtube.com/; Digital Game Archive, http://www.digitalgamearchive.org/home.php; all accessed September 1, 2009.

31. For helpful introductions to video game study, see Simon Egenfeldt Nielsen, *Understanding Video Games: The Essential Introduction* (New York: Routledge, 2008); Mark J. P. Wolf, ed., *The Medium of the Video Game* (Austin: University of Texas Press, 2001); Wolf and Bernard Perron, eds., *The Video Game Theory Reader* (New York: Routledge, 2003); and Steven E. Jones, *The Meaning of Video Games: Gaming and Textual Strategies* (New York: Routledge, 2008).

32. Philip Caputo, *A Rumor of War* (New York: Ballantine Books, 1986), 14.

33. Robert Jay Lifton, *Home from the War, Vietnam Veterans: Neither Victims nor Executioners* (New York: Simon and Schuster, 1973), 219.

34. Janet Murray, *Hamlet on the Holodeck: The Future of Narrative in Cyberspace* (New York: Free Press, 1997), 170.

35. Sherry Turkle, *The Second Self: Computers and the Human Spirit* (New York: Touchstone, 1985), 66–67. See also, Turkle, *Life on the Screen: Identity in the Age of the Internet* (New York: Touchstone, 1995). For a study focusing on video games and their potential as a model of human learning, see James Paul Gee, *What Video Games Have to Teach Us about Learning and Literacy* (New York: Palgrave Macmillan, 2007).

36. Jose Antonio Vargas, "Virtual Reality Prepares Soldiers for Real War: Young Warriors Say Video Shooter Games Help Hone Their Skills," *Washington Post*, February 14, 2006, A01.

37. See, "GI SPY: Candid Photos from the Seedy Underbelly of the Video Game Industry," *Game Informer* 162 (October 2006): 12; and "Video Games," *Army Times.com*, accessed September 1, 2009, http://www.armytimes.com/entertainment /video_games/.

38. Kristen Kalning, "Playing 'Outside the Wire': Video Games Provide Relief, Therapy for Soldiers in Iraq," msnbc.com, February 12, 2008, http://www.msnbc.msn.com /id/23114125/.

39. Orson Scott Card, *Ender's Game* (New York: Doherty Associates, 1994); Amy Harmon, "More Than Just a Game, but How Close to Reality?" *New York Times*, April 30, 2003, G1, G6.

40. The first user comment on the *Medal of Honor: Frontline* page found on Internet Movie Database (IMDB) states, "It's just like being in Saving Private Ryan . . . Wow!!," September 8, 2002, http://www.imdb.com/title/tt0289330/#comment. After the success of *Frontline*, the "You don't play, you volunteer" tagline became the slogan for the entire *Medal of Honor* franchise.

41. Heike Hasenauer, "The Army Game: The Next Best Thing to Being There," *Soldiers* 57, no. 8 (August 2002): 23.

42. Margaret Davis, ed., *America's Army PC Game, Vision and Realization: A Look at the Artistry, Technique, and Impact of the United State's Army's Groundbreaking Tool for Strategic Communication, produced by the U.S. Army and the MOVES Institute in conjunction with the America's Army presentation at the Game Scenes exhibition, Yerba Buena Art Center, San Francisco* (Monterey, Calif.: Wecker Group, 2004), 37.

43. "America's Army 3 HD-Trailer-Interview-Gameplay," YouTube video, 5:12, posted by "PureInsanity00," April 11, 2009, http://www.youtube.com/watch?v=4g-VW _xuKEs.

44. See "America's Army 3 Gameplay," YouTube video, 7:25, posted by "xxAllNight-Longxx," June 22, 2009, http://www.youtube.com/watch?v=4gdvABtzBeo.

45. Quoted in Zhan Li, "Fans and Clans: Who's Playing America's Army?" in Davis, *America's Army PC Game*, 27.

46. See "America's Army, Real Heroes," United States Army, accessed June 29, 2011, http://www.americasarmy.com/realheroes/.

47. Dave Grossman, *On Killing: The Psychological Cost of Learning to Kill in War and Society* (New York: Back Bay Books, 1995), 299–332; Grossman, *On Combat: The Psychology and Physiology of Deadly Conflict in War and in Peace* (Millstadt, Ill.: PPCT Research, 2007), 74–93; and Grossman and Gloria DeGaetano, *Stop Teaching Our Kids to Kill: A Call to Action against TV, Movie and Video Game Violence* (New York: Crown, 1999). For a counterargument to Grossman, see Gerard Jones, *Killing Monsters: Why Children Need Fantasy, Super Heroes, and Make-Believe Violence* (New York: Basic Books, 2002), esp. ch. 10.

48. Dorothy G. Singer and Jerome L. Singer, *Imagination and Play in the Electronic Age* (Cambridge, Mass.: Harvard University Press, 2005), 100–109; Kwan Min Lee and Wei Peng, "What Do We Know about Social and Psychological Effects of Computer Games? A Comprehensive Review of the Current Literature," in Vorderer and Bryant, *Playing Video Games*, 327–345; Rene Weber, Ute Ritterfeld, and Ann Kostygina, "Aggression and Violence as Effects of Playing Violent Video Games?," in Vorderer and Bryant, *Playing Video Games*, 347–361.

49. Brown, 08–1448, S. Ct. 2011, Breyer's opinion, 12.

50. David Goodman, "War Games: The Army's Teen Arsenal," *Mother Jones*, September/October 2009, http://www.motherjones.com/politics/2009/09/war-games-armys -teen-arsenal.

51. Ian Bogost, *Persuasive Games: The Expressive Power of Video Games* (Cambridge, Mass.: MIT Press, 2007), 79. Bogost argues that video games have a unique persuasive power because they are a form of "procedural rhetoric," or the art of persuasion through rule-based representations and interactions rather than the spoken word, writing, images, or moving pictures. See esp. preface and chs. 1 and 11.

ALICE YANG AND ALAN S. CHRISTY

Eternal Flames

The Translingual Imperative in the Study of
World War II Memories

THE INSTALLATION OF AN "ETERNAL FLAME" is a com-
mon feature of memorial sites around the world. The symbol captures the
ephemerality of the past in the immateriality of fire and highlights the en-
during significance of the past for the present and the way that the past can
illuminate the present. The eternal flame also captures the incendiary con-
tentiousness of the past and the responsibility of the present to remember
and sustain the past. All of these aspects of the symbol resonate in relation
to historical memories of World War II. Few question that World War II
was a cataclysmic event that dramatically transformed the societies of the
Pacific Rim and continues to have a deep impact, even among those generations with no experience of the war. The war redrew the political and
economic landscape of East Asia and catapulted the United States to its role
as global hegemon. It fundamentally restructured not only state-to-state relations but also relations between states and their national subjects.

Since 1999 we have been studying the impact of memories of World War
II in the United States and Japan. We have been building an archive that
includes not just accounts of World War II in the Pacific but also the ways
in which people interacted with World War II in the recent past. Examining
historical memories of the war articulated in the 1990s is not used to engage
in historical research on the 1940s but on the 1990s. Just as we need to understand historical events in their proper contexts, our study of historical
memories, or historical consciousness, is properly an examination of the
context of the memory act. What the war means to someone in the 1990s is
really a statement about the 1990s and not the 1940s.

Many scholars have analyzed how historical memories affect perceptions of the present. In 1998 Roy Rosenzweig and David Thelen noted that

although many Americans shun "academic" history, they "pursue the past actively and make it part of everyday life" by keeping diaries, talking with relatives, visiting museums, and collecting memorabilia.[1] Our comparison of interpretations of the Pacific War in the United States and in other nations is designed to create new mechanisms for stimulating transnational conversations about historical memories. In other words, we hope our collaborative scholarship can be extended to the larger public to examine the interaction, construction, and translation of memories across national lines.[2]

Our research shows that memories of events such as the Rape of Nanjing and the Battle for Iwo Jima powerfully affect people in the present and will continue to do so even after the generation that experienced the war passes on. Comparing American and Japanese views of these two particular war events reveals a multitude of methodological issues scholars need to confront when examining historical memories. Like other researchers studying the recent past, we need to historicize and contextualize the creation and reception of the sources we use. We need to recognize the impact of larger political, cultural, and economic factors on interpretations of the war. There is a wealth of scholarship on the war, but research on historical memory cannot assume that war survivors and other members of the public know about or accept this research. Instead, we need to critically analyze the interaction between different constituencies in promoting, dismissing, and revising historical memories. As a result of this collaboration, we have begun developing an innovative website—named Eternal Flames: Living Memories of the Asia Pacific War—that can function as a repository of memory artifacts in multiple media and as a site to develop a collaborative translingual community among scholars, students, institutions, activists, and the general public around the world.

Even if one limited research to a single country, this is a daunting goal given the proliferation of possible sources on war memories in our digital age. For example, a Google web search on the "Nanking Massacre" on January 29, 2011, yields 484,000 results, which include photos, memorial exhibits, memoirs, personal testimony, news accounts, documentary footage taken during the war, and clips from recent popular films. If we search for the "Nanjing Massacre," a term used now by most scholars because of a preference for pinyin romanization, we get 406,000 results.[3] If we were traditional historians interested only in the war itself, we might dismiss many of these sources as "unreliable." Our interest in historical memory, however, requires us to consider these sources, including those that distort or misrepresent scholarly research, as potentially valuable. Although many of these sources may lack citations or even clear authors, they often present influential polemical arguments about the causes and consequences of war events that reveal more about the creator's assumptions about the nature of war and national groups than about the war itself. One can find accounts insisting that Japanese atrocities in Nanjing prove that the Japanese are a savage race that deserved the dropping of atomic bombs on Hiroshima and Nagasaki. Others insist that a few examples of faked photographs of Nanjing atrocities show that the whole massacre is a myth and that accounts by survivors are nothing more than Chinese communist propaganda. Many of the accounts indicting Americans for failing to prosecute war crimes in Nanjing or to demand apologies from Japan are cited as evidence of how the postwar alliance allowed the United States "to win the war" and let Japan "win the peace."

In this essay, we discuss three examples that illustrate how memories of World War II circulate across the Pacific region, and across linguistic boundaries, in ways that undermine the idea of fixed national narratives. These examples highlight the importance of developing new methods of transnational collaboration that will enable historians to better contextualize and understand sources and their meanings to different groups of people. First, we discuss the case of Iris Chang's bestseller *The Rape of Nanking: The Forgotten Holocaust of World War II* to consider what happens in both the United States and Japan when popular history and the media ignore scholarship. Chang's book catapulted what had been a dispute at the level of popular nationalist memory between Chinese and Japanese into American popular historical consciousness. In projecting this dispute into the United States, Chang failed to recognize the depth of historical and popular scholarship on Nanjing that had taken place in Chinese- and Japanese-language sources, thus reducing a complex discourse into simple binaries of truth tellers versus deniers. The Chang controversy provides an example of a common disjuncture between popular and professional historical consciousness.

If Chang's work served to heighten the sense of conflict between national memories, Clint Eastwood's paired films, *Flags of Our Fathers* and *Letters from Iwo Jima*, attempted to bridge and heal this presumed divide. By using Japanese language (with English subtitles) in *Letters from Iwo Jima*, Eastwood emphasized the need for American audiences to engage with

Japanese perspectives. Moreover, in the film's credits, and in Eastwood's publicity, much was made of his reliance on Japanese primary and secondary sources. But these perspectives were harnessed to a universalist message about the common humanity of young men at war. Some critics, unaware of Japanese popular discourses, read this as a simple Americanization of another nation's experience, yet we question the degree to which it derived from Eastwood or his sources.

Chang's and Eastwood's interventions in the transnational circulation of war memories were conducted in the realms of mass media popular culture. But popular culture and popular historical consciousness reside in other forms as well. For our third example, we consider how the Eternal Flames website we are developing can help us interpret a popular cultural war-memory artifact in a way that retains its complexity. During the war, there was a lively trade in war souvenirs among American soldiers, primarily of articles taken from the bodies of dead Japanese soldiers. Tucked away in many attics and basements in the United States today, this genre of war memorabilia continues to percolate into the popular consciousness in places like eBay or as donations to research centers such as our own. Using a Japanese flag we received from a veteran, we examine how digital technology can help us explore the multiple meanings that such objects can have for diverse groups in several countries.

Analyzing and comparing the role that different historical groups play in shaping memories of the war is no easy task. Historical memory sources within just the United States keep growing at a rate that makes it impossible to give anything close to a comprehensive view of national memories. We argue, however, that historical memory scholars need to be even more ambitious and go beyond the nation-state, because war memories are not hermetically sealed within each society. Instead, American memories circulate in Japan and Japanese memories circulate in the United States, and collective memories in *both* societies have been transformed as a result. Consequently, we need to develop new research methods to capture this global process and its intersections with multiple local networks in all its complexity.

Emerging work in the digital humanities can offer us new methodologies to examine this circulation of war memories and address the problem of communicating across languages and cultures. Traditionally, historians have wrestled with the problem of insufficiency. The passage of time destroys records and traces, leaving historians the difficult task of reassembling a past from few sources. Contemporary history, as a field that examines a past that can be digitally archived, has a fundamentally different problem: overabundance. Much of the work in the emerging field of digital humanities directly addresses this problem. How can we manage the enormous archives of the recent past? How can we search, organize, and analyze a seemingly endless array of historical sources? We suggest that new technologies can provide historians with tools to address these vexing issues.

The Chang Controversy and the Misrepresentation of Japanese Memories

The controversy over Iris Chang's 1997 bestseller *The Rape of Nanking* and its fraught translation into Japanese provides a compelling example of the need to critically analyze the role of scholars, media, and the general public in the circulation of memories of World War II within and between countries. Heated accusations leveled by both Chang and her critics about misrepresentations and distortions of Nanjing history illustrate how memories of the war continue to be highly charged for groups within both countries. American media accounts of Japanese denial of and amnesia about Nanjing also reflect judgments about perceived "national memories" of the war. U.S. scholars of Japan increased their efforts to publicize to Americans the long history of Japanese scholarship on Nanjing to counter the image of Japanese historical amnesia about the war. That both right-wing and left-wing groups in Japan responded to the publication of Chang's book with a flurry of new accounts in Japanese and English shows an analogous interest in Japan over how public memory is presented in both countries.

In 1999, when the Japanese publisher Kashiwa Shobô and Basic Books announced the termination of a contract under which Kashiwa Shobô would publish a translation of Chang's book, many in the U.S. press simply assumed that the Japanese publisher had succumbed to a right-wing conspiracy to suppress publication of Japanese crimes. Few questioned Chang's claims that "the Japanese, as a people, manage, nurture and sustain their collective amnesia" about atrocities in Nanjing and that even "respected history professors in Japan" felt a national duty to "discredit reports of a Nanking massacre."[4] Consequently, most media accounts ignored American scholars of Japan who had criticized Chang's book and called for recognition of how researchers in Japan had been documenting atrocities in Nanjing for many decades. Chang either overlooked this research because it was in Japanese or failed to consult knowledgeable American scholars of Japan. Chang's critics also observed that her book fueled the campaign by right-wing deniers in Japan, who seized on factual mistakes in the book as evidence of a conspiracy to fabricate Japanese wartime atrocities to undermine national honor and promote a "masochistic" history.[5] Ironically, Kashiwa Shobô had hoped to translate the book to counter these deniers.

The larger context surrounding the creation of and reception to Chang's book merits the attention of American historians. In 1994 Chang attended a conference in Cupertino, California, sponsored by the Global Alliance for Preserving the History of World War II in Asia and was shocked by large grisly posters of Nanjing victims. She then remembered how her parents, raised in China during the war, had quivered with outrage as they described the horror to her in Urbana, Illinois, and how her "childhood library visits searching encyclopedias and history books turned up little on the carnage."[6] This lack of public knowledge and acknowledgment by Americans played a major role in her determination to use her skills as a journalist to restore Nanjing victims to history. Her research and activism then became part of a much larger campaign by Chinese Americans to make their fellow Americans aware of the history of Chinese suffering at the hands of the Japanese.

Chang's lurid depictions of savagery that included not just mass rapes but also "live burials, castration, the carving of organs, and the roasting of people" inspired many Chinese Americans and other Asian Americans to question why they knew so little about the suffering their parents and grandparents endured in Asia during World War II.[7] Many grew up studying European history and the Nazis but learned little about the war in Asia. Critical of this real gap in the history curriculum and in public consciousness, Ami Chen Mills thanked Iris Chang for inaugurating a "new era of Chinese activism" in the United States.[8] Thanks to the publicity achieved by Chang's book, the Global Alliance became an umbrella federation for more than forty grassroots organizations. Demonstrating both economic and political clout, these groups sponsored campaigns demanding Japan document this history in textbooks, apologize, and pay reparations to wartime victims.[9] In short, Chang's work became a crucial resource for the promotion of Chinese American ethnic identity at the turn of the century.

Chang's contribution to Chinese American solidarity was rooted in a victim narrative in which she claimed that Japan was guilty of two atrocities against the Chinese people, the first being the massacre of 1937 and the second being the denial of that history in the 1990s. Unfortunately, in arguing

for this "second rape," Chang misrepresented the range of Japanese scholarship and activism that affirms that the atrocities did, indeed, take place in
Nanjing.[10] In the wake of the controversy surrounding her book, new scholarship by Daqing Yang and Takashi Yoshida analyzed larger shifts in the circulation of postwar historical memories in Japan, the United States, China,
and Taiwan. These studies provide exemplary models for exploring points
of convergence and divergence.[11] As early as 1967 Japanese historian Hora
Tomio had published a study using military tribunal transcripts and a few
postwar recollections.[12] As Daqing Yang has noted, however, it was in the
early 1970s, shortly before Japanese prime minister Tanaka Kakuei visited
China and established diplomatic relations between the two countries, that
Nanjing sparked public controversies in Japan. Honda Katsuichi, a well-
known leftist journalist, published a series of articles in 1971 in the leading national newspaper *Asahi Shimbun* that included graphic interviews
with survivors and provoked much public discussion and new research in
Japan.[13]

Debate intensified in the 1980s because of publicity surrounding the
Japanese government's screening of history textbooks and because new
evidence, including private wartime diaries, official military records, and
interviews with repentant soldiers, became available. A new emphasis on
national pride and patriotism in the People's Republic of China and increasing publicity about the Japanese textbook controversy generated a new
wave of studies in China (especially after a 1985 memorial was dedicated to
Nanjing victims), and then in Taiwan. The 1990s campaign to deny atrocities by prominent right-wing Japanese, such as politician Ishihara Shintaro
and popular cartoonist Kobayashi Yoshinori, also incited new research. As
Chinese Americans became aware of the textbook controversy and the activities of Nanjing-massacre deniers, they mobilized to combat American
perceptions of Japan as a bulwark against communism in East Asia or a victim of nuclear weapons. Their efforts, exemplified by Iris Chang, however,
sometimes publicized the deniers without also acknowledging the earlier
Japanese scholarship or the ongoing public battles within Japan.

In short, Nanjing historiography, while ostensibly a subject without direct connection to U.S. history, illustrates the internationalization of historical writing in the postwar era and the need to reposition U.S. history
within a broader global context. Few question that U.S. history has been
entangled with histories outside the nation, but as Marcus Gräser noted in
2009, all the calls for transnational and world history have still produced

only a limited amount of empirical research.[14] The accessibility of primary sources from all over the world, especially on contemporary historical topics, provides both opportunities and challenges that can be overwhelming. Mario del Pero has described how "true multinational and multiarchival research requires not just extraordinary linguistic skills, but also a strong knowledge of the histories, cultures, and political systems of the various subjects being studied, a knowledge and erudition that only a selected few seem to possess."[15] Most scholars can barely keep up with new scholarship in their specific fields and lack the training, time, and funding to master multiple historiographies in multiple languages.

Language difficulties probably contributed to the assumption by most U.S. media accounts that Iris Chang's book was not translated because of yet another Japanese conspiracy of silence and attempts to censor her book. Nevertheless, as chief editor Haga Hiraku explained to Doreen Carvajal of the *New York Times*, Kashiwa Shobô made repeated attempts, in English, to inform the public that the contract was canceled because of disagreements about the addition of notes, annotations, and commentary to the translated version. But Carvajal's account only repeated Chang's claims of threats by ultranationalist groups and quoted as evidence an e-mail sent by Haga to Chang in 1998: "As we have indicated before, our publishing company is subject to considerable attack and it's not an exaggeration to say that we have put ourselves in a life-threatening situation in publishing this book."[16] The *Times* story did not include the rest of Haga's e-mail that directly contradicted this impression of a fearful publisher: "But as we stated in the beginning the entire company agreed that it was more important to publish your book for the purpose of exposing the Japanese people to the past war crimes that we are now striving to correct and bring to the consciousness of the Japanese people our responsibility as a nation in this matter."[17]

Kashiwa Shobô issued a press release accusing Chang of sending only "a part of the letters that we had written her, without informing us, to the *New York Times*, while demanding us not to disclose communications between us to the media." Proposing that all communications be given to the public, Kashiwa shobô maintained the contract ended because Chang refused to allow annotations and commentaries to the text to correct "factual errors."[18]

Sonni Efron, of the *Los Angeles Times*, was one of the few reporters to include the publisher's views of "Chang's unwillingness to correct" "significant errors." More important, Efron recognized that the controversy over Chang's book and translation left some Japanese and U.S. scholars "concerned that the increasingly bitter flap will leave Westerners with the mis-impression that little has been written in Japan about Japanese atrocities in Asia." In fact, Efron noted, the National Diet Library contained at least forty-two books about Nanjing and other atrocities. She also described how increasing numbers of former Japanese soldiers were recounting atrocities they committed or witnessed in published memoirs, speeches, and interviews. After years of "government-enforced denial," Efron explained, "Japanese middle school textbooks now carry accounts of the Nanjing massacre as accepted truth." Finally, while other media reviews had simply repeated Chang's claims of Japanese amnesia, Efron quoted a critical review of Chang's book by historian Joshua Fogel, declaring that "we know many details of the Nanjing massacre, Japanese sexual exploitation of 'comfort women,' and biological and chemical warfare used in China because of the trailblazing research" of Japanese scholars.[19]

Efron was not the only U.S. reporter to cite scholarly critics of Chang. In an aptly titled article, "Wars of Memory" in the *San Francisco Chronicle*, Charles Burress challenged Chang's portrayal of Japanese amnesia and her use of "emotion and unrepresentative statements and anecdotes." Burress quoted historian Andrew Barshay's critique that for "decades after 1945, Japanese high school and university textbooks, influential and widely read historical works, to say nothing of magazines and newspapers that circulate in the millions, informed their readerships of the Nanjing massacre in detail." Burress also noted that Chang neglected to mention that "nearly all" of the statements by Japanese deniers "were repudiated by the government" and that "critics say her omission of the mainstream view makes her book misleading and one-sided."[20]

Besides these articles by Efron and Burress, why were so few U.S. media sources aware of a long history of scholarship on Nanjing in Japan? Why didn't more reporters consult American scholars who could assess scholarship in Japan or comment on Japanese public opinion? Even the most cursory review of historical journals or recent newspapers in Japan would have challenged Chang's blanket generalizations about Japanese historical amnesia. Failure to consult these sources reflects not just the lack of influence of scholarship on popular culture but also a general American willingness to accept stereotypes about an unchanging, monolithic, evil Japan that committed war atrocities and then denied this history fifty years later.

This assumed divide in national memories led the media to ignore evidence of collaborative research and activism between groups in Japan,

China, and the United States before Chang's book was published. The publicity generated by the Chang controversy, however, intensified public interest and led to many more transnational collaborations, the English translation of the work of Honda Katsuichi, the English translation of books by
Japanese deniers, and the Japanese translation of Iris Chang's book in 2005.[21]
The circulation of war memories now includes more than just debates about
whether the Japanese committed atrocities in Nanjing but also more complex analyses of the nature of the atrocities, the causes of Japanese behavior,
and the credibility of different kinds of source material. For example, scholars disagree on the number of civilian victims at Nanjing because of chaotic
and incomplete wartime burial records and because some accounts include
victims killed in surrounding provinces outside the boundaries of the city.
The numbers of male civilian victims also can change because of varying
assessments of the Chinese soldiers that shed uniforms and masqueraded
as civilians in a desperate attempt to survive Japanese occupation of the city.
Although scholars now agree that both Japanese military training and the
brutality of the war in China before 1937 contributed to atrocities in Nanjing, they often disagree about the relative impact of these factors. There
are also different views of the reliability of postwar testimony given during military tribunals and confessions elicited from Japanese POWs held in
China during the cold war. Yet perhaps these scholarly discussions about
source materials can help the public understand that even "historical facts"
about Nanjing often reflect the selection and interpretation of postwar data
shaped by global politics, diplomacy, and views of patriotic loyalty.

The Triumph of an American Perspective

Whereas Chang's work condemns the Japanese as renegades, Clint Eastwood's paired films, *Flags of Our Fathers* and *Letters from Iwo Jima*, attempt
to cross the presumed national divide of memory.[22] Yet a close reading of
the films, particularly the latter, suggests that the divide had perhaps been
crossed even before these films were made. Reading these films carefully
in the context of both American and Japanese memory shows again how
interpretations that fail to go beyond a single national memory discourse
can be misleading. *Flags of Our Fathers* was an attempt to replace the iconic
image of the battle generated by Joe Rosenthal's famous flag-raising photograph with a new humanistic image of the struggle. Having encouraged an
American audience to set aside their standard understanding of the event,

Letters from Iwo Jima challenges that audience to explore how that battle looked from the other side. The film devotes substantial time to character development, showing Japanese soldiers experiencing a range of emotions, from joy or longing to fear and grief, thus revealing the Japanese military as an institution with a diverse range of men. Invited to feel sympathy and even identification with many of the Japanese soldiers, the audience is given the opportunity to reach a similar conclusion to that invited by *Flags of Our Fathers*. The basic humanity of the Japanese soldier is paired with that of the American soldier in the first film. The tragedy of the Battle for Iwo Jima produced by the paired films, then, is not just the tragedy of the lost lives of young men, but the senselessness of a war fought between people who can be seen as not at all unalike. If not for the battlefield, one can imagine many of the combatants on both sides becoming friends.

Letters from Iwo Jima represents one of the few attempts by a popular American artist to address a key dilemma of contemporary Japanese war memory: how can the soldiers—personified as fathers, sons, and brothers—who fought for a bad cause, with such a record of atrocities, be mourned? Interestingly, the movie pursues this problem in a way that fits uncomfortably with the narrative of "good soldiers under bad leadership" that has been the preferred solution of recent years. The hero of the movie is Lt. Gen. Kuribayashi Tadamichi, played by Watanabe Ken. Kuribayashi's perspective is joined by two other sympathetic figures: Lt. Col. Baron Nishi Takeichi and Private First Class Saigo. Kuribayashi and Nishi are actual historical figures, while Saigo is a fictional construct, an everyman whose very name is homophonic with the Japanese word for "the last" (he is the last man standing in the film). This trio of characters is infused with American perspectives. Much is made of Kuribayashi's past as an attaché at the Japanese embassy in Washington, D.C., signaling his close familiarity and comfort with American ways. Likewise, Lieutenant Colonel Nishi's ties to the United States are recalled through his participation in the equestrian events of the 1932 Los Angeles Olympics and through his acknowledged friendship with Douglas Fairbanks and Mary Pickford. More important, Nishi plays the key role in humanizing the American enemy to his own soldiers when his unit captures a wounded American, and he insists that the soldier be treated rather than killed. Nishi's facility with the English language enables him to introduce his soldiers to the human side of their captive, as he translates for them a letter the American had been carrying from his mother. The final, fictional component of the sympathetic trio, Saigo, a bread maker before the war, has no ties to the United States whatsoever, but it is this absence of ties that makes his American humanism all the more important.

What is this American humanism? Put briefly, it is defined in opposition to Japanese fanaticism. As we see in *Flags of Our Fathers* (and many other U.S. war films, both celebratory and critical), American soldiers are not anxious to die (even if they are willing). They prefer survival to death and, if at all possible, peace to war. This contrast is highlighted in *Letters* by several characters, both seen and unseen. When Kuribayashi arrives on Iwo Jima to take over the command, he discovers an outpost that is resigned to a hopeless death. Throughout his efforts to redirect defensive plans and preparations, he struggles with an officer corps, best exemplified by Lieutenant Itô, that, in addition to brutalizing its soldiers, seems to actively seek out death. In the midst of a Japanese army now consumed by a vision of heroic deaths, Kuribayashi's struggle is to inculcate in his troops a seemingly American ethos of fighting: fight for a reason, fight to survive as long as possible, and die only when unavoidable. If there is a struggle in the Japanese army depicted in *Letters*, it is this: will the Japanese army fight to achieve glorious death or fight to protect the Japanese people? Kuribayashi constantly reminds his troops that every day they fight on Iwo Jima is another day that the Americans are prevented from firebombing the homeland. This struggle is played out at the level of Kuribayashi and his immediate subordinates, at the level of line officers such as Nishi and Itô, and among the ordinary soldiers such as Saigo. Tragically, the struggle is unresolved because the Japanese garrison is wiped out nearly to the last man, but with the film ending with a wounded Saigo on a stretcher, cared for by the Americans, we are given a glimpse of a future in which American humanism will prevail.

This vision of the ordinary soldier is extraordinarily appealing, especially in Japan, where the film grossed nearly three times more than in the United States. Yet even while the film points to a way to mourn the Japanese war dead (even its officers), there are clear limits. Nishi, the man who rescues the American soldier, is mournable, while Itô, the man who hides himself on the battlefield, booby-trapped to take out more American soldiers, is not. To the degree that the Japanese soldiers conform to a model of soldiery represented in most narratives by Americans, we are encouraged to sympathize and grieve. But that identification is made most possible by the presence of foils, characters who represent a model of Japanese soldiery that is beyond mourning. Thus, *Letters from Iwo Jima* provides a laudable and moving humanization of some Japanese soldiers in the movie but still leaves beyond our reach, even beyond our effort to come to terms with, the unrepentant or fanatical soldiers. The price of admission into postwar consolation is to become like an American. Fanatical resistance to, or rage against, Americans precludes the possibility of being mourned.

We might leap to the conclusion that Clint Eastwood and his scriptwriters, Iris Yamashita and Paul Haggis, imposed an American viewpoint on a Japanese narrative, as Nicholas Barber of the British newspaper *The Independent* assumed in his review of the film.[23] However, the script relies heavily on two Japanese sources, a published collection of Kuribayashi's letters to his children and a biography of the general by Kakehashi Kumiko.[24] Barber's scorn for Hollywood's ability to be "just as mawkish about another country's soldiers as . . . its own" is sprung from the same trap as the praise heaped on Iris Chang's book: an inability to imagine (let alone research) a Japanese discourse, especially one that might be driving in advance of a Western one. Eastwood, Yamashita, and Haggis were not imposing this Americanized portrait of the Japanese soldier. Instead, they were culling it from Japanese sources, not sources published under the pressures of an American occupation, but published immediately prior to the making of the film.

The collection of Kuribayashi's letters to his children reveals a loving and engaged father with a gentle sense of humor who had clearly enjoyed his time in the United States and was the antithesis of the image of a fanatical soldier bent on the slaughter of all members of the opposing nation. Kakehashi Kumiko's biography of Kuribayashi extends that portrait to his conscientious concern for his soldiers and subordinates. She draws particular significance from Kuribayashi's final telegram to headquarters, which ended, as was customary, with a poem. Kakehashi reads Kuribayashi's death poem as a rebuke to the Japanese leadership. "Unable to complete this heavy task for our country / Arrows and bullets all spent, so sad we fall," the poem begins.[25] It is in this expression of sadness, rather than the conventional expression of joy at the opportunity to die for the emperor, paired with the subtle point about insufficient supplies, that Kakehashi uncovers a general who mourns his men and castigates a military command that insists only on death.

We have a chicken and the egg scenario here. Is it the limitations of imagination in Eastwood, Yamashita, and Haggis that results in a movie about the Other in which the others that we are able to identify with are

all like us? Is it the ongoing legacy of occupation-era censorship that results in Japanese authors still unable to portray in affirmative terms an
anti-American character? Or is there an opportunistic mutual misread that
entices postwar authors to read evidence that, in their day and age, is indel-
ibly marked as American, causing the *Letters* team to draw those parts even
larger? Kuribayashi may have expressed sadness to fall in battle, but what
about the subsequent lines of his farewell message: "But unless I smite the
enemy, / My body cannot rot in the field. / Yea, I shall be born again seven
times / And grasp the sword in my hand"?[26] Why discount these lines at
the price of buying "sadness?" In a sense, *Letters* very accurately captures
a Japanese discourse. It is just that it is a discourse of the early twenty-first
century, not necessarily that of 1945. In the twenty-first century, most Japanese understand the meaning of the battle in a way that is much closer
to that of their contemporaries in the United States. The mindset of many
Japanese soldiers on Iwo Jima (and elsewhere) may have, in fact, been more
alien. *Letters* thus offers a window into the ways that Japanese discourse
about the war has changed over the past sixty years.

The Multiple Meanings of an Artifact

Below the visible surface of popular culture, represented in mass media
products such as Chang's and Eastwood's works, there is a reservoir of material culture and family history that sustains, and periodically piques, popular interest in World War II. As the generation that experienced the war
passes away, their children and grandchildren are inheriting their memories through found boxes of memorabilia, containing scrapbooks, letters,
photographs, medals, military service documents, and a class of mysterious
objects obtained as souvenirs of the battlefield. Over the past twenty years
or so, the Japanese media has had many occasions to report on the repatriation of such artifacts, as the heirs of American soldiers have frequently
viewed the souvenirs as objects with a proper Japanese home. Since beginning our work on Pacific War memories, we have received inquiries seeking
assistance in returning flags, diaries, and photos. In some cases we have received the items themselves. These attempts to return battlefield souvenirs
are not necessarily a reflection of a desire to put the past to rest. More often,
they are expressions of a desire to find out what these objects meant to
someone else. If we take a broad view, however, we can approach battlefield
souvenirs as objects at the intersection of complex histories and memories.

Let us take the example of one such artifact in our possession: a rising sun flag covered in writing. At first glance, this is a Japanese object, meaningful only to those residing in Japan. The American owner of the flag could not read the writing on the flag, and many who view it today may not be able to see it as anything other than a symbol of Japanese ultranationalism: the inscriptions covering the white portion of the flag evoke images of mass Japanese fanaticism. But before we consider what the flag meant or means in Japan, let us consider the flag as an American artifact, because that is the way it comes to us today. Acquired on the battlefield and traded vigorously among the troops at the rear, artifacts like this flag testified to soldiers' desires for tangible evidence of their terrifying enemy's imminent demise. Swords were particularly sought after, but objects, such as the flag, that bore the traces of the exotic culture of Japan were also highly valued. If we start with the flag as an American memory artifact, we have an opportunity to consider the significance that military men and women drew from their acquisition, as well as research the marketplace for the goods of the enemy that morphed into a marketplace for goods of a defeated ally in the postwar years. What images of Japan did these objects inaugurate for postwar Americans?

But because our study of memory is about the study of historical consciousness throughout the postwar era, we might also consider how the meaning of the flag could change for Americans over the decades since its acquisition on the battlefield. As more postwar Americans learned to stop fearing and start loving "exotic" Japanese culture, how did their views of these objects change? In the 1980s, as the Japanese economy soared and Japanese corporations purchased American icons such as the Rockefeller Center and Columbia Pictures, did these artifacts acquire renewed ability to evoke menace? Most important, how did these artifacts come to stand in the eyes of so many as a potential route to another family on the other side of the Pacific?

Fortunately, these inscribed flags do give many clues that can enable their repatriation. For historians, they also provide an excellent resource for investigating the changes in war memories in Japan as well. The flag we are considering here was of a genre of gifts given to people going off to the war. The flag might have been acquired at a famous shrine and carry with it, thereby, the talismanic power of the gods. It might also have been purchased more generically. However obtained, the flag would have been inscribed with the name of its recipient, adorned with appropriate slogans, and signed by a community of well-wishers (neighbors, classmates, etc.). The owner of the flag would have then carried it to the front as a memento of home, a reminder of personal ties and national duties. Those who returned from the war alive might have kept the flag in storage or thrown it away. In either case, these flags were not seen as conveying sentiments that were consistent with the new postwar democratic Japan. In more recent years, however, they have found a route to return to public display in museums, community halls, and commemorative spaces. In these spaces, they can be consumed as reminders of a generation that sacrificed itself for the nation, often in disapproving contrast to today's youth who, according to many cited polls, would not defend Japan if attacked. Or, conversely, they may be seen as cautionary tales of how the fascist state inserted itself into even the most private of relationships and, therefore, of the need for vigilance in defense of the postwar Peace Constitution. At a more personal level, for those who receive repatriated flags, the names of lost loved ones on the flags can take on a sacred existence in a society in which writing the names of the dead has great importance.

The particular flag we have, however, opens a window to an often overlooked set of war memories. Against expectations for this class of objects, the recipient was a woman. Instead of being exhorted to summon up "Military Valor and Endurance," the woman was called to "Assist the Prosperity of the Imperial Throne" and "Repay the Country with Charity." In the larger slogans and the smaller personal messages written by her community, we gain insight into both the gendered ways that women were mobilized to war and the fact that women's memories of the war are not necessarily channeled through the experiences of their male kin. Another look at the flag reveals one more surprise. On the right edge of the flag, the recipient is identified as a graduate of the thirty-fourth class of the First Higher Girls' School of Seoul. The woman has a Japanese name, but because Koreans had been ordered to adopt Japanese names in 1940, the name alone is no guarantee that the recipient was Japanese. The First Higher Girls' School suggests that the woman was likely Japanese, but could very well have been from an upper-class Korean family. Whatever her ethnicity, this particular flag has become an artifact of three countries. It is an American artifact, speaking of American memories, by virtue of its postwar routes. It is a Japanese artifact, speaking of Japanese memories, by virtue of its genre and symbols. But it is also a Korean artifact, by virtue of its place of origin. As a Korean artifact, it recalls for many Koreans the coercion and identity theft endemic to the Japanese Empire. More sinister, it may also be a dangerous memento of collaboration. In any case, it is a reminder of the many ways that memories of the war in these places intersect and of the ways these memories change over time, independently and mutually. It is a complex artifact that continuously generates meaning long after the moment of its birth, even in new cultural contexts.

The Opportunity of Digital Technology

But how do we get at this complexity? Although there are a few scholars with the necessary language skills, is it reasonable to expect one researcher to have the English, Japanese, and Korean language skills and historiographical training necessary to unpack the many layers of meaningful memory in an artifact such as this flag? We believe that an answer comes in a fundamental shift in the norms of practices in the field of history and that there is a real opportunity to address these problems directly through digital technology. In short, we call for far more robust habits of collaborative work and an ambitious effort to open up and explore discourses, databases, and archives that reside in different languages.

The Eternal Flames project addresses two major problems for contemporary history: overabundance and the necessity of transnational/translingual research. Working with database and systems engineers, we are designing a prototype website to address language and cultural barriers—a website backed by an innovative multilingual database structure that enables researchers to work in multiple languages. The goal of the site is to enable visitors to acquire information on war memories in multiple languages from more than one society. Staying within just one national memory framework can provide a misleading sense of discursive consistency, even predictability. A strong national memory framework can take even contradictory evidence and subordinate it within a relatively seamless narrative. We hope to destabilize such self-replicating narratives by using new methods. We encourage users to develop understandings that are deeply based on evidence, rather than just abstract ideological imperatives, by making artifacts the point of entry to the website. To do so, we aim to expand the possibility that visitors will encounter unpredictable yet relevant pieces of evidence and narratives. We also need to enhance the ability of users to explore and contribute to constellations of evidence that they might not previously have known to exist.

Let us consider the flag to see how this can work. The archive of the site is available to users to add their own artifacts to the collection, so the flag could be contributed to the site electronically, rather than physically. The page dedicated to it would feature a high-resolution photo of the flag, along with background information. Next to the photo would be a set of tags, key words describing the artifact in ways that would allow others to search and find it. These tags would be in multiple languages, attached to the photo by the original contributor and by users of the site with the appropriate permission level. Along with the photo and the tags would be a space for users to create narrative descriptions of the item in one of four wikis, one each in English, Japanese, Chinese, and Korean. The wiki for the flag (translated for the English, Korean, and Chinese wikis) would include a transcription of the handwriting, data on the flag as of a class of artifacts, and information as available on the path of the object from its original owner to its donation to the digital archive (who had it, when, and why).

At this level on our website, visitors will be able to see information on the object in their own language, as well as ascertain the existence, or not, of a discussion on the object in the other languages. There is an important reason for having parallel wikis in different languages organized around individual objects rather than having the site as a whole exist in parallel sites in other languages, as is the case with Wikipedia. Having the entries in different languages on the same object that exist at only a one-click remove will allow us to utilize the skills of multilingual users to assess, translate, and certify content for monolingual users. Having found the flag and perused the wiki entry in their preferred language, site visitors may quickly ascertain whether this particular artifact is connected to significant cross-cultural debates or controversies.

We are also developing tools that enable users to explore and encounter other artifacts they never intended or expected to examine. Visitors would be able to use timelines to discover other objects that share the flag's key temporal moments. Map tools that allow visitors to locate and follow an artifact's spatial itinerary can also bring up other items that shared its spaces. These multiple contextualizations of the artifact point a visitor toward constellations of objects and information that exist in other places within the archive and within other languages.

The website promotes multiple interpretations of an individual artifact by creating ways to quickly assess the relative intensity and content of discourse about individual objects in their multilingual wikis. For example, the flag could be linked to other items through tags that are visible in all languages on all versions of the page. Consequently, a visitor reading the English page for the flag could see tags in English, Japanese, Chinese, and Korean for the object. Let us presume that the visitor reads only English. How can we entice him or her to explore the trails that lead through the site in other languages? Perhaps the tags could be arranged as rough equivalents. The English "flag" could be paired with the Japanese "hata." Our user could then click on "hata" and see what items come up. A tag cloud tool (a graphical representation that depicts how often keywords are used and which other words they are related to) could show the visitor the other terms most commonly associated with "hata"—in Japanese but also in the visitor's native language. The relatability of terms across languages could be visually represented by something like a Venn diagram that shows at a glance the kinds of meaning constellations that can intersect (and diverge) across languages. This could allow the visitor to continue exploring by clicking related items to see how the range of artifacts changes. The key to either approach is to take advantage of user input, encouraging visitors to not just passively explore but also add content, such as a tag, when appropriate.

Ultimately, however, the key to the site's success is not in finding other artifacts but in finding other people. The digital medium is no panacea or utopia. As in the real world, the passions surrounding memories of World War II that are stirred into protests and even violence can potentially be lethal to digital communication. But the digital medium also offers significant opportunities for forming communities of interest across boundaries that are very difficult to cross in the physical world. As Clay Shirky has observed, these communities can be very resilient when under attack, enforcing community-supported standards of behavior and removing disruptive violators effectively.[27] The problem we want to address here, however, is one that is particularly difficult to resolve in the physical world but that may be within reach in the digital: bringing not just scholars but also war survivors, activists, and the general public into conversation with one another over a shared interest for which they all bring diverse expertise. Forging a community of interest that is not bounded by national discourse (e.g., only Japan scholars studying Japanese memories) requires tackling language barriers.

Building this website has also entailed collaboration between historians and specialists in several other fields, particularly computer sciences and linguistics. The field of digital history is growing rapidly, and there are now a growing number of historians who are also capable of writing software. In our case, however, the original conceptualization of the project, as well as the actual site construction, was possible only through interdisciplinary conversation and collaboration. Colleagues working in digital media, particularly in social networking and social computation, helped us extend our conception of research materials and methods. We are bringing work on social network theory into contact with historians' abiding interest in collective memory, opening avenues for new inquiries into the social formation of memory discourse. At the same time, work in the field of social computation can be employed to dramatically expand the possibilities of collaboration between researchers and the broader public.

We have argued in this essay that in the case of memories of World War II in the Pacific, research should extend beyond the framework of a single nation. Despite the commonsense presumption that memories of the war are still divided along national lines, there are significant ways in which memories circulate, both troubling present relationships and forging deep consensuses. The controversies surrounding Iris Chang's efforts to publicize the history of Japanese atrocities in Nanjing, demonstrate that even events located outside the geographical domain of U.S. history can be mobilized in politics and society and become part of American historical consciousness. Clint Eastwood's efforts to create a pair of movies that might heal lingering wartime divisions ironically succeeded not because he imposed an Americanized memory framework on Japanese materials but because Japanese popular culture had already internalized that framework. Given these kinds of unexpected divergences and convergences, it is manifest to us that the study of global events can benefit tremendously from transnational and translingual research. But demanding mastery of multiple languages and historiographies to properly study the United States in the world is unrealistic. We argue, instead, that it is more productive to aggressively expand the practice of collaborative work and that we can effectively achieve this goal using digital technology. The key to all of this is not erasing the language barrier but making the language barrier visible and negotiable. Our goal, in short, is to help researchers, students, and the public at large find sources in other languages they cannot read, help them make sense of these sources, and thereby expose them to multiple perspectives on the war. In doing so, we hope to engage their participation in the circulation of memory across the globe.

Notes

1. Roy Rosenzweig and David Thelen, *The Presence of the Past: Popular Uses of History in American Life* (New York: Columbia University Press, 1998), 18. Other influential accounts include Susan Porter Benson, Stephen Brier, and Roy Rosenzweig, eds., *Presenting the Past: Essays on History and the Public* (Philadelphia: Temple University Press, 1986) and David Thelen, ed., *Memory and American History* (Bloomington: Indiana University Press, 1990).

2. We are thus trying to heed David Thelen's call to provide collaborative scholarship to "set American history in transnational perspectives." See "The National and Beyond: Transnational Perspectives on United States History," *Journal of American History* 86, no. 3 (1999): 974.

3. Iris Chang used Wage-Giles romanization to refer to the city as "Nanking." Most references today, however, use pinyin romanization to refer to the city as "Nanjing."

4. Iris Chang, *The Rape of Nanking: The Forgotten Holocaust of World War II* (Penguin Books, 1997), 13–15.

5. Fujioka Nobukatsu, *"Jigyakushikan" no byôri* [The sickness of the "masochistic historical perspective"] (Tokyo: Bungei Shunju, 2000).

6. Ralph Kinney Bennet, "The Woman Who Wouldn't Forget," *Reader's Digest*, September 1, 1998, 104.

7. Chang, *Rape of Nanking*, 6.

8. Ami Chen Mills, "Breaking the Silence: The Rape of Nanking," Metroactive, December 12–18, 1996; http://www.metroactive.com/papers/metro/12.12.96/cover/china1-9650.html.

9. For a list of these groups, see "For Justice and Peace: Related Websites," *Global Alliance for Preserving the History of WWII in Asia*, accessed June 9, 2009, http://www.global-alliance.net/related.html.

10. Chang, *Rape of Nanking*, 199.

11. Daqing Yang, "Convergence or Divergence? Recent Historical Writings on the Rape of Nanjing," *American Historical Review* 104, no. 3 (1999): 842–65; Takashi Yoshida, *The Making of the "Rape of Nanking": History and Memory in Japan, China, and the United States* (Oxford: Oxford University Press, 2006).

12. Hora Tomio, *Kindai senshi no nazo* [Riddles of Modern War History] (Tokyo: Jinbutsu oraisha, 1967). All Japanese names are given in the Japanese order, with the family name listed first, followed by the personal name. Exceptions are made for those Japanese whose work in English is analyzed, such as Takashi Yoshida.

13. Honda Katsuichi, *Chûgoku no tabi* [Travels in China] (Tokyo: Suzusawa shoten, 1977).

14. Marcus Gräser, "World History in a Nation-State: The Transnational Disposition in Historical Writing in the United States," *Journal of American History* 95, no. 4 (March 2009): 1038.

15. Mario del Pero, "On the Limits of Thomas Zeiler's Historiographical Triumphalism," *Journal of American History* 95, no. 4 (March 2009): 1081.

16. Doreen Carvajal, "History's Shadow Foils Nanking Chronicle," *New York Times*, May 20, 1999, http://www.nytimes.com/1999/05/20/books/history-s-shadow-foils-nanking-chronicle.html.

17. Yoshida, *Making of the "Rape,"* 174.

18. Chang and Kashiwa Shobô had agreed that the translation "should be certified by a Japanese historian approved by the author." Fujiwara Akira and Inoue Hisashi, historians who had been publishing books and articles on Nanjing since the early 1980s, spent months reviewing the translation and proposed the insertion of bracketed material to correct factual errors. Kashiwa Shobô press release, May 20, 1999.

19. Joshua A. Fogel, review of *The Rape of Nanking: The Forgotten Holocaust of World War II*, by Iris Chang, *Journal of Asian Studies* 57, no. 3 (August 1998): 818–19, quoted in Sonni Efron, "War Again Is Raging over Japan's Role in 'Nanking,'" *Los Angeles Times*, June 6, 1999, http://articles.latimes.com/1999/jun/06/news/mn-44838.

20. Andrew E. Barshay, letter to the editor, *New York Times*, January 4, 1998, quoted in Charles Burress, "Wars of Memory: When Iris Chang Wrote *The Rape of Nanking*," *San Francisco Chronicle*, July 26, 1998, http://articles.sfgate.com/1998-07-26/news/17726046_1_iris-chang-japan-s-responsibility-japan-s-war. Burress also excerpted historian David Kennedy's critique of Chang's reliance on "accusation and outrage, rather than analysis and understanding" of possible causes for Japanese actions in Nanjing. Kennedy, "The Horror: Should the Japanese Atrocities in Nanking Be Equated with the Nazi Holocaust?" *Atlantic Magazine*, April 1998, http://www.theatlantic.com/magazine/archive/1998/04/the-horror/6532/. "When Chang memorialize[d] one of the bloodiest massacres of civilians in modern times," Burress continued, "she wasn't prepared for the firestorm she started."

21. Honda Katsuichi, *The Nanking Massacre: A Japanese Journalist Confronts Japan's National Shame*, ed. Frank Gibney, trans. Karen Sandness (Tokyo: Sharpe, 1999).

22. *Flags of Our Fathers*, directed by Clint Eastwood (Glendale, Calif.: Dreamworks Pictures, 2006), DVD; *Letters from Iwo Jima*, directed by Clint Eastwood (Glendale, Calif.: Dreamworks Pictures, 2006), DVD.

23. Nicholas Barber, "Letters from Iwo Jima," *Independent*, February 25, 2007, http://www.independent.co.uk/arts-entertainment/films/reviews/letters-from-iwo-jima-15-437614.html.

24. Yoshida Tsuyuko, ed., *"Gyokusai sôshikikan" no etegami* (Tokyo: Shôgakkan bunko, 2002), and Kuribayashi Kumiko, *Chiruzo kanashiki: Iôtô sôshikikan Kuribayashi Tadamichi* (Tokyo: Shinchôsha, 2005), translated as *So Sad to Fall in Battle: An Account of War Based on General Tadamichi Kuribayashi's Letters from Iwo Jima* (New York: Presidio, 2007).

25. Kakehashi, *Chiruzo kanashiki*, xxiii.

26. Ibid., xxiii.

27. Clay Shirky, *Here Comes Everybody: The Power of Organizing without Organizations* (New York: Penguin Books, 2008).

PART FIVE

Crafting Narratives

EILEEN BORIS AND JENNIFER KLEIN

When the Present Disrupts the Past

Narrating Home Care

IN 1987 A DEDICATED GROUP OF African American women began to organize in Los Angeles neighborhoods, at polling booths, and in front of the county Board of Supervisors. Home health aides themselves, they sought to reach a vast "invisible workforce" of paid caregivers who labored individually in people's homes, assisting and caring for people with disabilities and elderly persons, often their own parents, spouses, or children. They numbered in the tens of thousands, yet many had little inkling that others out there shared their situation. Although they were funded through a state program, In-Home Support Services (IHSS), their status as independent contractors and elder companions placed them outside the Fair Labor Standards Act, the nation's wage and hour law. Their work "wasn't being recognized as a job," declared rank-and-file activist Lettie Haynes. "We weren't getting enough money, and we weren't being recognized."[1]

In February 1999 the efforts of women such as Haynes paid off when seventy-four thousand home-care workers voted to join the Service Employees International Union (SEIU). "I believe the history books will show that their triumph today will play as important a role in American history as the mass organizing drives of the 1930s," declared AFL-CIO president John Sweeney, who previously had led this powerful union. Berkeley professor Harley Shaiken captured the ebullient mood of the time when he concluded that this victory represented "the new face of labor—women workers, minority workers, low-paid workers, people who have often been so hard to organize."[2]

How was it, we asked, that those who tend to elderly and disabled people for low wages had emerged as the new face of organized labor? What accounted for their triumph? Social scientists, labor strategists, lawyers, and community organizers alike embraced their victory as an inspiring model after years of union decline and stagnation. Caught up in this euphoria, we took on the task of giving home care a history.

As feminists and labor historians, we were confident that we had the tools we needed to write about this recent past. We set out to reconstruct the ideas and interests behind public policies that organized home care into a low-wage job for women of color. We researched back issues of newspapers and professional journals, pored over legal cases and government documents, visited numerous archives, and assembled our own archive of oral interviews, individually held personal papers, and ephemeral organizational materials. We discovered the origins of this occupation in New Deal work relief programs, tracing its development through the post–World War II expansion of hospitals, the War on Poverty, and decades of welfare reform. We reconnected arenas of policy that recent scholarship on the U.S. welfare state had separated: old age, disability, labor, health, and welfare. The state may have organized home care, we learned, but it did not do so on its own. Senior citizens, disabled people, domestic workers, welfare recipients, aides, and attendants participated in forging a system that resulted in unionization.

At first, the story line seemed clear. We would explain how women such as Lettie Haynes, Claudia Johnson, Verdia Daniels, and Beatriz Hernandez—leaders in the Los Angeles campaign—toppled conventional understandings of who was a worker, what was work, and who could be organized. Their victory marked the ascendancy of service-sector unionism in the 1990s, just as industrial unionism had emerged to meet the exigencies of mass production during the 1930s. These low-waged workers stood at the center of a new care-worker economy. It was defined, on the one hand, through the long shift of household labor into commercialized and public service sectors—and especially the explosive growth of the health care and long-term care industries. On the other hand, with the development of more outpatient services, the discharge of patients from hospitals earlier and sicker, and the increasing emphasis on deinstitutionalization in the last quarter of the twentieth century, care work also began to move back into the home. A new type of unionism had to emerge, one that could deal with the distinctiveness of the labor, the complexity of institutional arrangements, the blurred boundaries between public and private, and the perpetual, if often obscured, role of the state. The implication of such unionization was broad, because care work represented some of the fastest-growing sectors of the economy. Moreover, how we as a society arrange care, including long-term care of elderly and disabled people, has become a major challenge of our day.

Looking back, we had initially accepted SEIU's own assessment of its triumph even as we probed the past that had produced it. But, as we discovered, ongoing events have a way of destabilizing neat historical trajectories. The continuing battle over the quality of services, the reorganization of the work, and the unexpected implosion of the unions we were celebrating caused us to pause. So did the politics of a neoliberal moment characterized by continual struggles over state budgets and the conservative push back against public services and public employees.

The book was nearly done, but the present had begun to disrupt the past we were reconstructing. It was not merely that the organization of home care was bound to be an ongoing struggle: a great many "histories" continue into the present, a reality that many authors acknowledge in their conclusions. In our minds, some of this living history easily fit into the story we had crafted. In 2007 the Supreme Court upheld the exclusion of home care from the Fair Labor Standards Act, but left open the door for a legislative remedy. New congressional proposals emerged in response but were not enacted. The passage of a new law or settlement of another union contract we could incorporate into page proofs; such details wouldn't shift the fundamental analysis and might provide the book with a greater sense of closure.

As it turned out, our challenge was greater than that. Just as we were drafting the final section of the manuscript in 2008, schisms within SEIU shook the ground on which we stood. Activist academics saw SEIU as a progressive force in the workplace and beyond and had sent our students to work for it as organizers and researchers. In turn, SEIU had cultivated the support and partnership of academics. Yet even as they sought such allies, SEIU International opened a war on one of its largest locals, with home-care workers at the center of the dispute. As the political situation changed rapidly, it pushed us to rethink not just our conclusions but the building blocks of our historical narrative. Internal labor conflicts affected the sources we had access to but also compelled us to search back through documents we had gathered earlier but had either minimized or overprivileged. To our surprise, we emerged as critics of the International and chose sides in the upheaval playing out in union halls and on the front pages of the newspapers.

We told our editor the manuscript would be late!

Before turning to the events that altered our course, we begin with the narrative we thought we had settled on. We then discuss the cracks that intensified during 2008 and early 2009, as the International and its California health care local, United Health Workers West (UHW), battled over the meaning of union democracy. After presenting key aspects of our readjusted narrative, we end with questions about perspective, permission, and politics that our experience raises for historians of the recent past. At stake is not only the challenge of charting an ongoing struggle but also the relationship between scholarship and activism, and the role that intellectuals can play in politics and public policy.

The Initial Narrative

The existing scholarship in labor studies took it for granted that the victory in Los Angeles offered a model for successful grassroots mobilization.[3] Though our book addresses a long trajectory and a national analysis, our initial articles positioned Los Angeles as the place where SEIU drew on the lessons of previous campaigns and finally got it right. In retrospect, we conflated Los Angeles with all of California, even while noting that Bay Area locals had made larger gains earlier. This focus was logical: we were arguing for the significance of state policy in the development of home care and it was the resistance of LA County, which had half of California's IHSS caseload, that shaped the statewide legal, legislative, and union campaign of the 1990s.[4]

Historians of women, African Americans, and Latinos/as have long grappled with the conceptual and practical impediments to collective action and formal organization among workers who had no shop floor, assembly line, or tangible product. Even in earlier studies of department store, agricultural, and hospital workers, it was apparent who the boss was. Yet in the case of home care that has never been clear—often deliberately so. Although state and local governments funded the service, they denied home-care workers the status of employee, decade after decade. Instead, governments claimed that these workers were independent providers or that the receivers of care were their employers. When home attendants sought to unionize along with other public employees, as they did in New York during the 1960s, local and state governments quickly distanced themselves even further from the employment relationship by contracting out the service to vendor agencies or redefining the mode of payment. Attempts by SEIU to unionize home-care aides persistently ran up against this conundrum, which stymied the union in New York City in the late 1970s. Chicago's dynamic Local 880, for another example, spent years trying to win union recognition for care workers serving the clients of Illinois's Department of Rehabilitative Services. Hence we traced how SEIU developed both an organizing strategy to reach workers dispersed in private dwellings and also a structural one that would finally clarify the employment relationship.

Organizers from several unions (SEIU; United Domestic Workers; and the American Federation of State, County, and Municipal Employees, AF-SCME) and in different locales learned from gains and setbacks elsewhere. In California they knew it wasn't sufficient just to organize workers: the union had to organize the sector and generate new institutional arrangements to make that possible. First, the union asked the courts for a judicial ruling naming the county or state as the employer. The California State Court of Appeals ultimately rejected this argument. Then the union turned to a political and legislative strategy. SEIU legal strategists proposed the creation of a public authority to serve as an employer for collective bargaining purposes. Constituted at the county level, the public authority would set the wage for IHSS care providers in that service area, while consumers (disabled and elderly persons) would sit on the public authority.[5] In crafting legislation, SEIU sought to give IHSS workers the status of public employees, without defining them as civil servants.

Given the other stakeholders in long-term care, such a bill could not pass with the support of labor alone. The union's willingness to enter into a coalition with disability-rights and seniors groups proved crucial. The coalition did not come naturally, however. Consumers had equally strong, long-standing, rights-based movements of their own; their discrete histories mattered too. The Independent Living movement did not want to compromise its painstakingly won gains. To allay worries about unequal power relationships and to bring disability activists on board, SEIU also gave up traditional union prerogatives. Recipients of care would "retain the authority to hire, fire, and direct the personnel."[6] They would make up the majority of the advisory board central to the working of the authorities. Because of such compromises, organized groups of seniors and the disabled lobbied in Sacramento with SEIU, and in 1992 they won, permitting counties to develop these authorities. But counties still had to agree to do it, and their Board of Supervisors had to approve the funds.

Thus, SEIU and the disability groups had to sustain their coalition and political pressure until counties like Los Angeles finally approved an authority. Together, the union and consumer activists drafted an ordinance with LA County in 1997 that created not only an employer for workers but also a consumer-led board. They also prohibited strikes.[7] At the first meeting of the Public Authority in November 1998, the union showed up with enough representation cards to request a National Labor Relations Board (NLRB) election. A decade of organizing and political creativity finally paid off in February 1999, when workers in Los Angeles voted ten to one to join the union in one of the largest mail-in elections ever. It was a breathtaking victory for labor, described in the *New York Times* as "the biggest unionization drive in more than a half century."[8]

Faced with the necessity of increasing state financial support to win over local officials, SEIU repeatedly activated its grassroots networks to support this organizing effort. Through letter writing, picketing, occupations, and other demonstrations, the home-care coalition made it politically feasible and necessary for Sacramento to pass additional bills. In this case, the new public authorities joined the unions and their coalition partners to obtain an additional provision compelling all counties to establish some type of employer for collective bargaining purposes by 2003.[9] The struggle in Los Angeles, it appeared, had set the tone for a statewide political solution to the low wages of care.

Surveying the successful unionization of home-based workers in fall 2007, in an article for *New Labor Forum*, we applauded SEIU efforts as social-movement organizing at its best. We quoted an SEIU official who stated confidently that this case "provided a model that has been duplicated with very minor adjustments in other states," from Washington and Oregon to Michigan. Moreover, we argued that the same story was now playing out in the organization of home-based child-care providers by SEIU and other unions, spreading the success of this new unionism. "These struggles," we wrote in conclusion, "are raising recognition of the value of care work, while re-imagining the home as a dignified place of employment."[10]

But to our dismay, by the time *New Labor Forum* published this piece the following summer, we weren't sure we really believed in it anymore.

Cracks Appear

Our *New Labor Forum* article ended by affirming the deal that SEIU had made with state governments and the contracts it won. No doubt there would be further struggles but, after more than thirty years of experimentation, we concluded that SEIU had established a path to successful unionization for workers who had repeatedly been denied representation. But even within the care-workers movement, there already were deep fault lines underlying that path, ones that fundamentally affected what the contract meant and even the very nature of unionism.

The conflict began as an internal and localized dispute between one of SEIU's largest locals and the International's top leadership. UHW represented a relatively recent merger between Oakland/San Francisco–based Local 250 and a Southern California hospital-worker local, but Local 250 had been a union of hospital and home-care workers at least since the early 1980s. Between 2006 and 2007, the SEIU International Executive Board had decided that all home-care workers in California should be consolidated into one union to achieve "political unity" and statewide bargaining power. By January 2008 the board had grown exasperated that the LA local and UHW were "unable to speak with a unified voice in Sacramento" and that UHW took positions that contradicted the official positions of the International leadership.[11] In turn, UHW leader Sal Roselli had become a vocal critic of the "growth-at-any-cost strategy" of International president Andy Stern.[12] The board directed consolidation to proceed; all long-term care workers would go to the LA local, where the leadership was loyal to Stern.

For several years, the International had implemented a new consolidation program. Its vice presidents had been moving locals and people around, rearranging from above and merging smaller locals into vast megalocals that might span a metropolitan area or even two or three states. Using its centralized authority, the International then appointed new local leadership and reassigned staff. All of this belonged to a larger vision for organizing, a strategic rationale called density. If employers organized as huge multistate or multinational corporations, not bounded by central worksites or states, then labor needed to respond similarly. As SEIU International leader Steven Lerner, the architect of the successful Justice for Janitors campaign, noted, the fate of unions rested on "consolidation, rationalization, and reorganization"; that is, unions had to match the reorganization of capital, which had extended its reach across industries and regions. These dense units would have the resources to crack resistance to collective bargaining and hold politicians accountable.[13]

Only, as it turned out, these California workers did not want to go along with the master plan. In March 2008 UHW sponsored an internal vote, conducted by "an independent third-party," in which long-term care workers unanimously voiced a desire to stay in the union they had built and led for two decades. "I'm not going anywhere," said Rosie Byers, a home-care worker for thirty years, one of the early organizers for Local 250, and a UHW Executive Board member. "UHW is my union. . . . We voted to remain in UHW so all health-care workers can stand together to raise standards for our patients and working families."[14] Stern responded with a barrage of mailers, robocalls, letters, and push polls to UHW members. He threatened to put the local in trusteeship and thereby remove its elected leaders. Density had clashed headlong into workers' autonomy, control, and self-determination— some of the very aspirations for which workers join a union in the first place.

Labor scholars watched with rising concern as the paragon of the new unionism seemed poised to use its authority to suppress internal dissent. Concern turned into dismay in April when SEIU resorted to old-fashioned thuggery, physically attacking attendees at a *Labor Notes* conference in Detroit, where the featured speaker was to be California Nurses Association head Rose Ann DeMoro. The assault was allegedly in retaliation for the nurses' scuttling SEIU's strategy in Ohio. Shortly before, after years of blocking union drives throughout that state, Catholic Hospitals Partners, the employers, had filed for a "snap election" with the NLRB. SEIU alone would appear on the ballot and both the employer and the union would refrain from campaigning. But SEIU had little presence in the hospitals: no organizing committees existed, and no one had contacted workers for years. Thus, when the California Nurses Association entered the fray, charging company unionism, within days the election was off. There were no mobilized workers to defend SEIU.[15]

A handful of academics, as labor supporters, drafted a letter to Andy Stern to register concern that a threatened trusteeship of UHW signaled more troubling issues:

> We believe there must always be room within organized labor for legitimate and principled dissent, if our movement is to survive and grow. Putting UHW under trusteeship would send a very troubling message and be viewed, by many, as a sign that internal democracy is not valued or tolerated within SEIU. In our view, this would have negative consequences for the workers directly affected, the SEIU itself, and the labor movement as a whole. We strongly urge you to avoid such a tragedy.[16]

By the time the letter's authors sent it to Stern on May Day 2008, about a hundred people had signed, including both of us. Stern acknowledged having received and read it.

When the letter ended up in the hands of UHW folks, they were so over-whelmed and impressed by the number and prominence of signatories, they immediately used it in a major ad in the *New York Times*—unbeknownst to any of us. Not all names appeared in the ad, but ours did. Stern and the International Executive Board responded furiously. They immediately shut down discussion and began to pressure signatories to retract, espe-cially those in labor studies programs that relied on union funding. The letter itself, the rebuttals, and defenses spread across the Internet, through left-wing and liberal blogs and the leftist press. Although SEIU's reaction was repression, these incidents, in fact, pried open a wider debate on union democracy, top-down mergers, and the defensive tactics such as neutrality agreements that are characteristic of U.S. unions' adaptations to neoliber-alism. Under neutrality agreements, the union accepts modest wages and benefits, a limited bargaining unit, or other restrictive terms as the price of management refraining from active opposition to representation.

By the 1980s U.S. labor law allowed employers extraordinarily wide latitude to interfere with organizing campaigns and to discourage workers from voting to join unions. Thus, locals sought ways to extend the base where they were organized without having to run a mostly losing gauntlet, a strategy that came to be known as "bargaining to organize." SEIU attorneys proposed a "legal recognition agreement," in which the company consented to neutrality during organizing. Once a majority of workers had signed union cards, the employer either accepted the union (a process known as "card check") or agreed to an accelerated NLRB election.[17] The use of neu-trality agreements and the card check turned into a national strategy within care organizing, as national for-profit chains emerged and captured state contracts. "Bargaining to organize" implemented SEIU's larger strategy to leverage an existing relationship with an employer to reach nonunionized workers in another location—even if it meant trading gains of the already unionized for the right to organize. With hostile employers hijacking the NLRB election process, the neutrality agreement would become the quintes-sential tactic for labor organizing in a conservative age, eventually becom-ing one of SEIU's hallmark approaches.

A tiny regional conflict was out in the open and involved scholars, union members, journalists, labor allies, and activists across the country, expos-ing union compromises to a wider audience. To clarify the issues at stake, UHW offered to conduct a conference call with anyone who had signed the letter. Jennifer was one of about a dozen scholars who agreed to participate, opening a new channel of dialogue with these union workers that would continue through the summer. The first call included UHW staff but also member activists, hospital and long-term care workers who served as shop stewards, and elected bargaining committee members. They articulately and passionately explained their tactical, strategic, and ideological differences with Stern. Having written about medical care, health policy, and insurance politics in her previous work, Jennifer followed up with subsequent phone calls to learn more about how the union created solid footholds in particular workplaces and sectors, how it approached bargaining, and how it won the gains it did through militancy, strikes, trade-offs, and negotiations. Through these conversations, we came to understand that there was something going on here that we had missed.

At the very same moment, in a front-page article, the *Wall Street Journal* reported the existence of a secret agreement between SEIU and three of the largest corporations that specialize in outsourced food, laundry, and housekeeping services: Sodexo, Aramark, and the Compass Group. Given the difficulty of organizing workers under the current NLRB system, Stern had brokered deals that would allow workers to join the union through a card-signing process. In return, the confidential agreements "give the companies the right to designate which of their locations, and how many workers, the unions can seek to organize." Furthermore, the unions surrendered the ability to strike and all control over leaflets or rally plans, which became subject to approval by a committee that represented both workers and management. Unionized workers were barred from making derogatory remarks about employers. Even the conservative *Wall Street Journal* acknowledged that such agreements posed a major debate for organized labor over what kind of trade-offs to make when forging neutrality deals and whether to let union members know of the trade-offs.[18] Stern claimed to have "organized" fifteen thousand workers at Sodexo, Compass, and Aramark. But was there actually a *union*? And what happened in the locations where workers and other allies had been building a union over several months or years if they were not included in the approved company list?

One group quickly found out. Compass, Aramark, and Sodexo are major food-service providers on college campuses. Students at the University of North Carolina in Chapel Hill had begun organizing these workers in 2005—at the urging of SEIU. The students, workers, and union organizers stuck together through persistent intimidation by Aramark management. When summer break came, the organizers packed up and left. As reported in *Inside Higher Ed*, "after weeks of unreturned phone calls, students and workers learned that SEIU leaders had cut a deal with Aramark." The company had not chosen Chapel Hill to be on the list; SEIU agreed and left town. Workers and students were stranded.[19]

These incidents suggested that through such deals, the companies would choose the most marginal locations for unionization, avoiding sites where workers were actually mobilized, shutting down the places where workers had built up some heat. There would be a contract, but there might not be a process of unionization. Clearly, we were going to have to think more carefully about the meaning of brokering such deals and signing such contracts.

As we worked to reconceptualize our argument, the summer of 2008 ended with yet another damaging revelation that caused us to question our analysis. Investigative reporting from the *Los Angeles Times* exposed a pattern of corruption surrounding Tyrone Freeman, the head of the very LA home-care local so celebrated for its inspiring organizing victory a decade earlier. After the 1999 election, Andy Stern appointed his protégé Freeman to run this enormous local. A dynamic young leader, Freeman was fresh from major victories in the South.[20] Late in 2002 Eileen had given a talk to Freeman's staff, when his team still seemed to embody an organizing dynamism and will to improve the lives of home-care workers. In the ensuing years, the LA union had grown through the density strategy, and Freeman consolidated power at the top. The *Los Angeles Times* found Freeman had misused members' dues for personal gain, spent enormous sums on luxuries such as a cigar club and a golf tournament, and had doled out union business to family members and personal friends. Internal democracy and opposition appeared to have been suppressed, while LA home-care workers struggled on with lower wages and benefits than workers elsewhere had won.[21]

Member complaints had arisen before, but the SEIU International ignored them. It wasn't until several more damaging news stories had appeared that Stern finally announced the removal of Freeman. Not only was this a disturbing scandal in the organization everyone celebrated as the harbinger of progressive unionism, but it also happened to be the very local into which SEIU wanted to shift all other California home-care workers. We had to listen more carefully to why UHW home-care workers didn't want to go, and we needed to approach the quandary as scholars.

How could we address that question historically? Our need to revise our own narrative was complemented by the fact that UHW sought some historical perspective on the conflict as well. They also sought allies and outside legitimation. Consequently, they invited two labor historians to speak at their annual leadership conference to be held in September: Jennifer and Nelson Lichtenstein.[22]

As activists engaged with the labor movement, we wanted to see for ourselves what was going on, and the UHW leadership convention became a pivotal moment for us. Jennifer accepted the speaking invitation for political reasons, but we saw it as a research opportunity as well. Eileen would come along and we would spend several days immersed in the culture of a care workers' union. We found the convention itself to be an amazing, inspiring event. Over two thousand rank-and-file leaders and activists attended. Predominantly immigrants, women, and people of color, they conducted training sessions on member organizing and mobilization; understanding the state budget, securing public benefits, and lobbying; collective bargaining; health insurance politics; worker safety and self-protection on the job; coalition politics and community organizing; and race sensitivity. Members from across the spectrum (hospital custodians, nurses' aides, X-ray technicians, and home-care workers) gave speeches and presentations on the main stage in plenaries, with translation offered in half a dozen languages. Sharing their ethnic cultures, they performed songs, skits, and dances, like the International Ladies' Garment Workers Union (ILGWU) of old. They voted on budget allocations, political priorities, and other resolutions. Whether they worked in homes or hospitals, UHW workers displayed their engagement and participation in the union—along with an incredible militancy, solidarity, and willingness to take on a fight. The San Francisco political establishment also showed up, as did several state officials. Mayor Gavin Newsom and others knew that UHW could deliver precinct captains and cash as well as voters.

Observation moved easily into new research that would, we hoped, answer the questions that had been raised for us in recent months. We interviewed home-care workers from a wide array of national and ethnic backgrounds: Mexican, El Salvadoran, Chinese, Hmong, African American, Russian, Bulgarian, Armenian, and white native-born. We met with staff, organizers, stewards, and bargaining committee members at the union hall. We spoke with the African American women who had been leading the home-care workers in the Bay Area since the 1980s. By joining with hospital and nursing home workers, they had come to identify themselves as *health care* workers who "do the same work [and] deserve to earn the same wages and

benefits and enjoy the same high standards of working conditions regardless of whether they work in a hospital clinic, nursing home, assisted living
facility or in someone's home."[23]

Because we interviewed these members at the height of a struggle over
the fate of their union, they were in a particularly self-reflective mood. Compelled to defend themselves against the International's grand strategy, they
had developed forceful arguments about why their union was important to
them and what made it different from other unions. Moreover, they were
quite adamant that the LA local was not the type of union they wanted to be
part of. To them, it represented ghettoization, lower wages and standards,
along with top-down, antidemocratic management. The Tyrone Freeman
scandal had only reinforced their skepticism about SEIU's plans for them.

The die, however, was cast, as Stern and his allies moved forcefully
against these workers in the subsequent weeks. By January 2009, just as
President Obama took office, the union movement was at war with itself.
The International's leadership voted to remove the home and nursing
care workers from UHW and place them in a megalocal of long-term care
workers. The numbers-density calculation, as viewed from the top, over-
rode the workers' own investment in the social world of the union they
had helped to create. SEIU then placed UHW in trusteeship and removed its
elected officials. Immediately, the former leaders and most of its staff left
to form a new union, the National Union of Healthcare Workers (NUHW).
To join the new union, workers would have to vote to decertify SEIU in
their workplaces, an extremely difficult (and risky) task, as it subsequently
turned out.

As scholars, it now seemed incumbent on us to go back to see if, indeed,
there had been different trajectories than those we had initially perceived,
and we now had an enhanced archive to make that happen. Our project had
always taken into account regional differences, incorporating case studies
from New York, California, Oregon, and Illinois, but the current conflict
forced us to take a sharper look at the various stories within SEIU. It pushed
our initial questions further: was a contract the same as a union? What did
it mean to bargain with the state, especially in a period of privatization or
fiscal crisis? What created the real leverage that made bargaining with the
state work? To what degree were home-based workers genuinely participants in the union? Finally, because we had become experts on the policies
and politics of home care, did we have an obligation to take a public role in
the struggle or to stay out as "nonpartisan" observers?

Rethinking the Narrative

We revisited our research and our thesis in at least three particular ways: we looked at specific locals underemphasized earlier, evaluated how initial political victories were won but also maintained or expanded, and thought in broader terms about union strategies in a neoliberal era. It was also clear that our revised history would resist a synthetic narrative. Just as we had learned to separate distinct union stories, we also now understood that we could not conflate union adaptations to service-sector organizing with the perceived constraints of neoliberalism.

We realized that this part of the story had been there all along but had been on the sidelines. We went back and highlighted the experiences of two other unions—Local 250 in California and Local 880 in Chicago. Now the break was clear: Los Angeles no longer could stand for California; we had to write about the Bay Area on its own terms. We had documents gathered a few years earlier, with union permission, from SEIU records deposited in the Walter Reuther Archives at Wayne State University. In addition, Eileen was sitting on a rich archive culled from the personal papers of Karen Sherr, the lead organizer of home-care workers for SEIU 250 in the mid-1990s, whom she had met as part of the California Home Care Research Working Group in 2002.

Our revised narrative highlighted the significance of the Local 250 story. The local had begun seriously organizing agency-employed home-care workers in the 1980s, winning an agreement with San Francisco's major vendor, Remedy. It soon added a home-care division to its nursing home and hospital units. After a triumphant but draining strike in 1986 against Kaiser Permanente and following a short period when the International placed it in trusteeship, Local 250 rewrote its constitution in 1988 to "promote union democracy through the widest possible rank-and-file involvement," including shop steward selection by union members at individual work sites. Under new leadership from rank-and-file activists Sal Rosselli and Shirley Ware, the local valued a vigorous participatory culture and an active shop steward organization. As a result of its strong push into nursing homes, the demographic profile of Local 250 had heavily shifted toward African American and Latina women. Home-care workers, who resembled other Local 250 members, were fully incorporated into the new union structure, becoming member organizers who engaged in thousands of house visits and later acted as stewards.[24]

In the late 1980s, as SEIU began its LA campaign among independent contractors, Local 250—with rank-and-file workers on the bargaining team—won an agreement with a for-profit agency, National Homecare Systems. San Francisco had contracted out most of its home-care services with the agency, which then set out to gut union rights during a new round of collective bargaining. The union's elected bargaining committee, composed of National Homecare Systems workers such as Mabel Davis and Rosie Byers, showed the Chicago-based agency otherwise. When the company stonewalled, home-care workers turned to the allies that Local 250 had built up in earlier hospital and nursing home campaigns. Workers received the support of the San Francisco Board of Supervisors and the city. "Our political clout nailed down this contract and avoided a strike," said Local 250 president Sal Rosselli. Workers won ten paid holidays and up to four weeks of paid annual vacations.[25]

Local 250 built from there. Spreading the word in Spanish, Cantonese, Mandarin, Tagalog, and Russian, organizers reached out to a widely dispersed immigrant workforce. In 1991 the new campaign increasingly turned toward independent providers, now perceived as a workforce far larger than the few hundred employees at any agency. Worker leaders such as Ella Raiford, who not only labored full-time at a nursing home but also cared for a family friend part-time, jumped on board.[26]

Reflecting its particular mixture of progressive politics, community involvement, and history of alliances between the union, advocates, and officials, San Francisco developed the best conditions for home-care workers in the country in the 1990s. For years Local 250 had supported both local and statewide issues, worked in health care coalitions, and promoted big ideas, such as the single payer alternative to President Clinton's plan for managed care.[27] The cross-sector strength of the union was apparent. Home-care workers walked hospital and nursing home picket lines. Said member-organizer Myra Howard, "We supported our fellow union members to unite with them and strengthen the union for all of us. When it comes time to get the public authority and the [Independent Providers] get a contract we will need the help of our brothers and sisters in the other divisions."[28]

The trust that advocates in San Francisco had earned allowed them to organize consumers in ways that never happened in Los Angeles.[29] What resulted, lead organizer Karen Sherr explained, "was more of a social contract—about living together in society—it was about the further organization of society, about political aims and alliances" that would enhance the "vested interest in a continuous and well-qualified care program" by the workers, clients, community, and state social services.[30] Local 250 helped to create a statewide movement but also understood that the county organization of the service necessitated a county-based union.[31]

Given its roots and tendrils, it is not surprising that in 1995, years before the victory in Los Angeles, Local 250 won a public authority.[32] Then, in San Francisco's largest union election in decades, 5,600 independent providers voted to join Local 250 in the spring of 1996, bringing the union's overall membership to more than 40,000. A year later, San Francisco became the first county in California to sign a union agreement for independent providers.[33] Within a decade, with continual improvement in wages and health benefits, turnover among San Francisco's IHSS workers decreased by nearly a quarter. Home-care wages became the highest in the state, topping ten dollars an hour.[34]

Our interviews confirmed how the union at its best transformed caregivers into workers and workers into trade unionists and political actors. In creating its home-care division, Local 250 developed a participatory and democratic union culture that persisted into the next century. To be sure, there were internal disputes and power struggles, but the local prided itself on member involvement. Its elected bargaining committees shaped contracts; bargaining sessions were transparent and open to members. It trained a strong steward's council that was representative of its multicultural workforce. Because aides often couldn't leave the house, stewards used the telephone to maintain contact with their group of workers, circulated information, helped with late checks and unruly clients, and provided advice. They organized home-based meetings with those living or working close to one another.[35] Because of these personal connections and the resulting culture of solidarity, these stewards and member leaders could also turn out their fellow workers, and often clients, for major political actions, hearings, and budget confrontations.

It was only through the phone conferences following the 2008 May Day letter that we learned about the tactical and ideological differences between UHW's form of political unionism and Stern's. UHW members did the work of the union: they sat on the bargaining committees, negotiated directly with management or the public authority, lobbied, and met elected officials. They had dug in their heels to win high work standards, held on to the right to strike, and then worked on modeling their approach for others. On key occasions, Stern or International representatives had flown into California, circumvented the elected bargaining committee, and gone into backroom negotiations directly with the boss, as occurred with Tenet Healthcare and California Nursing Home Alliance, and with Governor Schwarzenegger. According to UHW's then political director Paul Kumar and vice president John Borsos, Stern gave up demands that the workers had already won in order to broker a deal. Those concessions were never discussed with members. Their participation became irrelevant.[36]

Both sides certainly understood that strategic concessions and circumlocutions were necessary in the era of neoliberalism, when the nation's basic labor law essentially no longer protected the right to organize. Growing unions such as SEIU had come to rely on a strategy of "bargaining to organize"—using contract negotiations where the union was strong to win a company neutrality pledge and organizing rights for workers of the same company in a different place or region. For the UHW membership, the union had to build strength and mobilization first by winning real economic gains, security, and power for members. It had to win demands that rooted the union institutionally in the workplace or the sector; it had to involve members in the larger strategic process. Then they could pursue "bargaining to organize" from a position of strength that didn't compromise the reason people stuck with their union in the first place. As they saw it, SEIU had begun to take too many shortcuts. For the International, winning those gains and building the culture of solidarity was too long a process; it didn't grow the union fast enough, the goal of density that promised political clout. The International leadership made quick settlements to get the next neutrality deal; in turn, where the employer was willing, it might be quickly turned around into a prenegotiated deal for the newly "unionized" workers in the agreed-on next locale.

For UHW members and leaders such as Martha Vasquez, Michael Torres, and Ella Raiford, unionizing service workers—especially where the lines between public and private blurred—was about climbing out of a second-class status, not settling for it. The history of Local 250 helped explain the resistance of UHW to the International's dismantling of its homecare and nursing home divisions. Because the story changed, we gained an even bigger analytical payoff from our investigations into its structure. We came to side with UHW under Rosselli in part because we were dubious that putting all home-care workers into one local would work, as long as the state organized home care through county welfare departments. Organizing statewide, we now knew, was both necessary and problematic, given that the legislature set the terms of the program but the counties controlled actual wages.

A bigger interpretative breakthrough came from our new ability to organically connect the historical hybridity of home care as an occupation to competing union strategies. Neither nurses nor maids, home-care workers had a mixed heritage from the occupation's development by both social workers and hospital administrators and its subsequent location in public welfare departments, state health divisions, or hospital-based programs. Its double association with welfare—relying on poor women of color to provide for other dependent people—undermined home care, subjecting the service to politicized charges of fraud and abuse and relegating it to the second tier of the Social Security system with uncertain, and all too meager, state support. Only by moving home care from the arena of welfare to that of the hospital long-term care industry and tapping health care financing, advocates came to believe, might its prestige improve.

We came to understand that what had emerged by the end of the twentieth century were two different care-worker movements: a welfare state unionism, with a core political strategy reliant on creating density within the long-term care sector; and a health care unionism, which contested medical institutions within an aggressive for-profit industry that perpetually sought to reduce costs by off-loading more care work to the home or similarly marginalized spaces. Home-care workers inhabited the lowest rung on the medical hierarchy. For hospital workers, organizing them was essential to counter outsourcing of their labor to the privacy of the home, a space seemingly beyond regulation and outside of the labor law. The only way to fight for dignity and recognition was to morph homemakers and personal attendants into health care workers.

This must be understood in the context of another unexpected event: the largest fiscal crisis since the Great Depression, one whose impact was felt in California almost immediately. Ten years after the Los Angeles victory, the SEIU formula began to implode from the weight of distressed public budgets. As opponents of the union charged, "Stern cannily used political contributions and organizing to reroute welfare dollars into his union and create a whole new class of members." Skeptics wondered whether a union dependent on state funding for and of poor people could ever be democratic.[37] Faced with a massive budget deficit, California governor Schwarzenegger sought to reduce wages in the spring of 2009.[38] In the scramble to balance the state budget, not only did Governor Schwarzenegger pit poor people against one another and welfare against health care, education, and other social services, but his actions highlighted the fragility of the compact that SEIU won from earlier state legislatures and the former Democratic governor. The return of Jerry Brown as governor in 2010 made little difference; he too sought to reduce the state's fiscal debt by slashing home care.

We never believed that the instability of the political compact canceled the potential of political unionism as an organizing strategy, however. We returned to our materials on Local 880 in Chicago. While political deals at the top might fall through, this case showed that a combination of strong grassroots organizing, the development of leadership among the workers, and democratic decision making could sustain the union as a vital institution ready to fight again. Local 880 had deposited its records at the State Historical Society of Wisconsin, along with the Association for Community Organizations and Reform Now (ACORN), but they had not been fully processed yet. We had gone to the archives previously but still hadn't fully culled through this vast, rich collection.

Now, we expanded the Chicago story, according it a new importance. Local 880 emerged from ACORN, which started community organizing in Chicago among home-care workers in the early 1980s. Through its United Labor Unions, the ACORN model cultivated enhanced participation, mobilization, and militancy among low-wage workers. It tied together workplace issues, such as wages and working conditions, with community ones, such as struggles over housing, banking, and living-wage campaigns. Union organizing was one part of a broader mobilization against poverty. The Chicago branch of United Labor Unions, which joined SEIU in 1985 as Local 880, used direct action and political lobbying with agency-by-agency bargaining. It built power by recruiting members through door-to-door canvassing and house meetings, developing leaders for specific actions and mobilizing members for electoral campaigns to gain access to political power.[39] It would *"build an organization* first" that could maintain itself during workplace campaigns, which could take years. Members paid dues from the moment they signed up, well before the union had a contract or certification; for people who made little, paying over that few dollars a month cemented organizational loyalty.[40]

The state of Illinois had two main programs, one organized through vendors and the Department of Aging, the other, through independent providers and the Department of Rehabilitative Services. Local 880 first organized among vendor employees, seeking an NLRB election for each agency. For years, it had only one contract, with National Homecare Systems, but the union grew anyway—because members belonged to it, sustained it, raised the money, and engaged in collective actions together. The local then turned to organizing pressure at the source of home-care funding: the state budget. Year after year, Local 880 pressured the legislature— lobbying, pushing their way into state offices, deploying street tactics, and engaging in mass protests—to increase the rate given to vendors and then demand that the vendors pass on some of the increase to the workers. In the late 1980s the union mounted a major campaign to organize workers caring for clients of the Department of Rehabilitative Services. The state refused to formally recognize the union, but through persistent mobilization, political allies, and militant pressure, the union compelled the state to accede to wage raises and other demands.[41]

Finally, in 2003 Illinois's newly elected Democratic governor, Rod Blagojevich, granted collective bargaining rights to these home-based attendants. Within months, the state legislature responded to massive lobbying and codified his executive order into law.[42] Again, however, we had to emphasize that there was a difference between this situation and the International's prenegotiated deals and neutrality agreements. More than fifteen years of struggle by women deeply invested in their union lay behind the deal with the state in Illinois. Five years later, Blagojevich went down in scandal, opening a wedge for union opponents to try to taint such political, and politicized, unionism. We could speak out with clarity here because we knew the union had a long-standing, hard-won relationship with state actors that well predated Blagojevich. We were able to defend the bargaining rights of home-care workers under assault by the National Right to Work Legal Defense Fund.[43]

Our revised history shows clearly that the state is the entity to bargain with for home health care, but the question remains, what gives those negotiations real sticking power? Is it simply the numbers game—that is, SEIU being able to say it comes to the table representing 100,000 workers in this locale, or 250,000 workers in the state, or a million elsewhere? What kind of deal gets struck if the members are not at the table or part of the process? And when the political deals fall through at the top, is the union there at the ground level to protect the workers? That's why there has to be power at the grassroots—the type of power Local 250 UHW and Local 880 originally built through rank-and-file leadership, member-to-member organizing, social bonds, mobilized political action, elected shop stewards, bargaining committee members, and strong contracts.

We study the past to change the future. Our combination of scholarship and activism has a long tradition and, as the multiple signatories for the 2008 letter show, we are in good company. Perhaps more than most fields, labor history has stood in a symbiotic relationship with the subject of its study, the labor movement. Labor historians believe in unions and, like many radical historians, seek a usable past for current and future struggles. In its emphasis on culture and everyday life, the "new labor history" of the 1960s and 1970s represented not so much of a break with earlier institutional studies, but a continued affirmation of participatory democracy, particularly among those assessing the fate of industrial unionism. African American, women's, Latina/o, and related studies initially turned scholars' attention away from studying unions, seen as discriminatory forces, but the organizing of domestic, farm, and service workers; government employees; and women of all sorts encouraged second looks. So did the apparent renewal of labor when SEIU's Sweeney assumed the leadership of the AFL-CIO in 1995 in the first contested election in a century and Stern's SEIU emerged as the nation's most innovative union.

Radical historians often face the charge that we distort the past by championing the causes of the present. But in our case, the present led us to rethink the past and develop a more robust and complicated portrait of home-care organizing. The fast pace of change saved us from becoming cheerleaders for a time that was proving more mixed and less sustainable than appears if we look at that past only on its own terms. That is, as contemporary historians, we were immersed in the actions and ideas of the last third of the twentieth century. Without a longer-range perspective, we could not step out of that recent past to evaluate the politics of that moment. The past may be another country, but its contours are less fixed than we might expect. It took the upheavals of the past few years to provide an alternative perspective. And it took subsequent skepticism about existing accounts to treat the 1990s and our own time as we would the 1930s: to evaluate documents and contextualize them as historians, not journalists.

We have more knowledge now of how it will all turn out than we did when we began in 2003. But the ground continues to shake: as of 2011 SEIU has retained its members in a series of contentious elections with NUHW, but the now rival unions continue with their bitter contest, as conservative

lawmakers are seeking repeal of the entire edifice of home-care unionism. Moreover, while home aides spent the past decade trying to gain recognition as public workers, the whole array of public workers in human
services—including teachers, nurses, social workers, public attorneys, and
counselors—has been turned into vilified workers by a resurgent right wing
that has found a newly successful tactic to assault the welfare state and yet
again extend the neoliberal agenda. In a 2011 lawsuit filed by Sodexo, a federal district court ordered SEIU to halt its public relations campaign aimed
at getting the company to agree to union organizing based on a card check.
Since the company filed its suit under the federal Racketeer Influenced
and Corrupt Organizations Act, or RICO, the ruling essentially renders this
common strategy, known as a "corporate campaign," equivalent to corrupt
racketeering.[44]

Now our assessment is more sober. To rethink home care requires both
a hard look at the promises of care-work unionism and an assessment of its
welfare state funding. A few years ago, a sociologist, who had gathered her
data while a researcher on a project funded by SEIU 1199 in New York, faced
the ultimate disciplining: the union, she claimed, delayed publication of her
book by charging that she was using confidential information. Their attack
went nowhere but could have hurt the career of an untenured scholar. SEIU
gave us permission to use its archives and to reprint a photograph in our
book. Although we are critical of recent events in this essay, we take the
history of SEIU seriously; indeed, Local 880 provides the moral center of
our tale. But access to information is political. Having to negotiate politics
while passions are high remains one of the perils of writing the history of
the present—one we believe well worth the effort.

Notes

1. "Lettie Haynes," in *Women's Work: Los Angeles Homecare Workers Revitalized the Labor Movement*, ed. Lola Smallwood Cuevas, Kent Wong, and Linda Delp (Los Angeles: UCLA Center for Labor Research and Education, 2009), 31.

2. Jess Walsh, "Creating Unions, Creating Employers: A Los Angeles Home-Care
Campaign," in *Carework: The Quest for Security*, ed. Mary Daly (Geneva: ILO, 2001), 229;
"L.A. Home Care Workers Make History," *SEIU Action* (March–April 1999), 7–9, SEIU
Publications, Walter Reuther Archives, Wayne State University, Detroit; Harley Shaiken,
quoted in Steven Greenhouse, "In Biggest Drive since 1937, Union Gains a Victory," *New
York Times*, February 26, 1999, A1, A18; John Sweeney, quoted in Frank Swoboda, "A
Healthy Sign for Organized Labor—Vote by L.A. Caregivers Called Historic," *Washing-
ton Post*, February 26, 1999, E1.

3. Peggie R. Smith, "Organizing the Unorganizable: Private Paid Household Workers and Approaches to Employee Representation," *North Carolina Law Review* 79, no. 1 (2000): 45–110; Walsh, "Creating Unions," 219–33; Linda Delp and Katie Quan, "Homecare Worker Organizing in California: An Analysis of a Successful Strategy," *Labor Studies Journal* 27, no. 1 (Spring 2002): 1–23; Kristin Jenkins Gerrick, "Note and Comment: An Inquiry into Unionizing Home Healthcare Workers: Benefits for Workers and Patients," *American Journal of Law and Medicine* 29, no. 1 (2003): 117–38.

4. Eileen Boris and Jennifer Klein, "Organizing Home Care: Low-Waged Workers in the Welfare State," *Politics and Society* 34, no. 1 (2006): 81–107; Eileen Boris and Jennifer Klein, "'We Were the Invisible Workforce': Unionizing Home Care," in *The Sex of Class: Women Transforming American Labor*, ed. Dorothy Sue Cobble (Ithaca: Cornell University Press, 2007), 177–93.

5. Jennifer Fleming to Dan Stewart, "Homecare Transition," memorandum, March 11, 1992, Los Angeles County, SEIU Organizing Department, General Organizing, 1984–92, box 42, folder "California Home Care," SEIU Records, Walter Reuther Library for Labor and Urban Affairs, Wayne State University, Detroit, Michigan; Walsh, "Creating Unions," 224. On the use of the public authority, see Gail Radford, "From Municipal Socialism to Public Authorities: Institutional Factors in the Shaping of American Public Enterprise," *Journal of American History* 90, no. 3 (2003): 864, 866–67.

6. Wilma C. to Dan S., Ophelia M., Jennifer F., and Amado D., "Attached Memos Re: Authority," memorandum, December 13, 1990, SEIU Records.

7. Marta Russell, "L.A. County Public Authority: A Zero-Sum Game," *New Mobility* 7, no. 38 (1996): 40, 50–51; Alan Toy, "L.A. County Public Authority: An Empowering Solution," *New Mobility* 7, no. 38 (1996): 41, 55. For the best account, see Walsh, "Creating Unions," 228–30.

8. Walsh, "Creating Unions," 229; "L.A. Home Care Workers," 7–9; Greenhouse, "Biggest Drive since 1937," A1.

9. Walsh, "Creating Unions," 230–31; Janet Heinritz-Canterbury, *Collaborating to Improve In-Home Supportive Services: Stakeholder Perspectives on California's Public Authorities* (New York: Paraprofessional Healthcare Institute, 2002), 13–14.

10. Eileen Boris and Jennifer Klein, "Labor on the Home Front: Unionizing Home-Based Care Workers," *New Labor Forum* 17, no. 2 (2008): 32–41, quotes on 38 and 41.

11. Gerald Hudson to Long-Term Care Division Steering Committee, "Evaluation of the Reorganization of California's Long-Term Care Locals," January 22, 2008, in the authors' possession.

12. Esther Kaplan, "Labor's Growing Pains," *The Nation*, May 29, 2008, 6, www.thenation.com/doc/20080616/print.

13. Steven Lerner, "An Immodest Proposal: A New Architecture for the House of Labor," *New Labor Forum* 12, no. 2 (2003): 12.

14. "SEIU Retaliates against California Caregivers and Democratic Reform Movement," *SEIU Voice*, May 7, 2008, 1, www.seiuvoice.org/2008/05/seiu-retaliates-against-california.html.

15. Chris Kutalik and Mischa Gaus, "SEIU's Disruption Draws Wide Criticism from Union Leaders and Members," *Labor Notes*, April 30, 2008, http://labornotes.org/node/1620; Mischa Gaus, "Quiet Deal Leads to Bitter Fight in Ohio Hospitals," *Labor Notes*, March 27, 2008, http://labornotes.org/node/1582.

16. Letter to Andy Stern, May 1, 2008, in the authors' possession. The letter, as a paid advertisement, appeared in the May 3, 2008, issue of the *New York Times*. For a fuller

account of these events, see Steve Early, *The Civil Wars in U.S. Labor: Birth of a New Workers' Movement or Death Throes of the Old?* (Chicago: Haymarket Books, 2011).

17. Keith Kelleher to Mark Heaney, April 15, 1991, box 11, folder 46, Local 880 Records, Wisconsin Historical Society, Madison; Kelleher to Heaney, July 26, 1993, and Attached Concepts on Accretion, box 11, folder 46, Local 880 Records; on NLRB and employer latitude, see David Brody, "On the Representation Election," in *Labor Embattled: History, Power, Rights*, ed. David Brody (Urbana: University of Illinois Press, 2005), 98–109.

18. Kris Maher, "Unions Forge Secret Pacts with Major Employers," *Wall Street Journal*, May 10, 2008, A1.

19. "Did a Union Double-Cross Its College Activists?," *Inside Higher Ed.*, August 22, 2008, http://www.insidehighered.com/layout/set/print/news/2008/08/22/seiu.

20. Tyrone Freeman, "Biographical Sketch," Instituto Laboral de la Raza, July 5, 2008, http://www.ilaboral.org/dinner2008/tyronefreeman.html.

21. Paul Pringle, "Union, Charity Paid Thousands to Firms Owned by Official's Relatives," *Los Angeles Times*, August 9, 2008; Pringle, "Service Union Bans Former California Local President for Life," *Los Angeles Times*, November 27, 2008.

22. Lichtenstein is Eileen's spouse. He ended up testifying for UHW at the trusteeship hearing.

23. UHW, "Resolution to Build Real Power for Healthcare Workers by Building One Statewide Healthcare Workers' Union," UHW Leadership Conference, San Jose, Calif., September 5, 2008, in authors' possession.

24. Karen Sherr, interview by Eileen Boris, Berkeley, California, May 18, 2005, and June 15, 2006; "Getting from There to Here," *UNITY* 3 (August 1991): 12–15.

25. "New National Homecare Contract in SF Protects Excellent Pay, Benefits," *UNITY* (Spring 1990): 5, SEIU Publications, Local 250, 1984–90.

26. "Local 250 Opens Home Care Campaign," *UNITY* 3 (May–June 1991): 12–13; "Blitz II," *UNITY* 5 (September–October 1993): 12; "We're Young and On the Move," *UNITY* (n.d., ca. 1994): 12; "In the Line of Duty," *UNITY* (May–June 1994): 16; "Local 250 Bulletin: National Homecare Workers" (also printed in Spanish and Chinese), February 25, 1993, SEIU Organizing Department, SEIU Records.

27. Sherr, interviews by Boris, Berkeley, California, 2005–9; Sal Rosselli, "President's Perspective," *UNITY* 5 (September–October 1993): 4.

28. Myra Howard, "Local 250 Members Unite at St. Mary's," *HomeCare Worker* 3 (June 1994): 3.

29. Julie Murray Brenman to Debra Newman, Memorandum on Wages for IHSS Providers, October 24, 1996; "Confidential: Labor Negotiations Information," memorandum to San Francisco IHSS Public Authority Governing Body Members from Staff on Collective Bargaining Team, December 10, 1996, both in Sherr Papers, private collection in Berkeley, California.

30. "Californian Dreams," in *Shadow Economy and Trades Unions* (Duisburg, Germany: WAZ-Druck, 2000), 26.

31. Rosie Byers and Ethel Richardson, "Dear Homecare Worker," n.d., ca. 1995, flyer; "The Collective Bargaining Process," n.d.; both in Sherr Papers; Rosie Byers, "High Marks for Historic Homecare Steward Council Meeting," *HomeCare Worker* 3 (April 1994): 3.

32. "Historic Victory for Homecare Workers," *HomeCare Worker* 4 (Fall 1995); Planning for Elders in the Central City to Supervisors Hallinan and Kaufan, May 3, 1994, Sherr Papers.

33. Peter Fimrite, "Home Health-Care Workers Get Raise," *San Francisco Chronicle*, December 28, 1995; "San Francisco Homecare Contract," *News from the Home Front*, Fall 1997; Sherr, phone interview by Boris, July 3, 2009.

34. "The Campaign to Improve the In-Home Supportive Services Program," Sherr Papers; Candace Howes quoted in Eileen Boris et al., "Workforce Needs in California's Homecare System," CPRC *Briefing Paper*, May 2004, 2. See also Howes's chart, "California IHSS Homecare Workers' Wages and Benefits Negotiated with SEIU and United Domestic Workers Union," May 31, 2004, in the authors' possession.

35. Leon Chow and Juan Antonio Molina, interviews by Boris and Klein, UHW San Francisco Office, September 8, 2008.

36. UHW board members and signatories from May Day letter, May 15, 2008, conference call, notes in the authors' possession; Paul Kumar, John Borsos, and Klein, May 25, 2008, conference call, notes in the authors' possession; John Borsos, "Building a Workers' Movement," *Monthly Review*, July 14, 2008, http://mrzine.monthlyreview.org /seiu140708.html; Martha Vasquez and John Borsos, "Rethinking the Labor Movement," Invited Talk and Discussion, Yale University, New Haven, Conn., February 26, 2009.

37. "A More Perfect Union?," reply to Robert Fitch, post to Portside, e-mail message to authors, August 6, 2005. Paul Pringle, conversation with Boris, Santa Barbara, California, December 17, 2008.

38. Marty D. Omoto, "Judge Blocks IHSS Worker Wage Cut," *California Progress Report*, June 28, 2009, http://www.californiaprogressreport.com/2009/06/judge_blocks _ih.html.

39. We base our analysis on the Local 880 Records, Wisconsin Historical Society. See Eileen Boris and Jennifer Klein, "Organizing the Carework Economy: When the Private Becomes Public," in *Rethinking U.S. Labor History: Essays on the Working-Class Experience, 1756–2009*, ed. Donna T. Haverty-Stacke and Daniel J. Walkowitz (New York: Continuum, 2010), 192–216.

40. "Discount Foundation Application Summary," n.d., ca. 1986, box 2, folder 31, Local 880 Records, 1; Keith Kelleher, "ACORN Organizing and Chicago Homecare Workers," *Labor Research Review* 1, no. 8 (1986): 37–40.

41. Keith Kelleher, "A History of Local 880, 1983–2005" (unpublished manuscript 2005), 39–43, 49–51.

42. See Fred P. Brooks, "New Turf for Organizing: Family Child Care," *Labor Studies Journal* 29, no. 4 (2005): 53.

43. Eileen Boris and Jennifer Klein, "'Not Really a Worker': Home-Based Unions Challenged in Court," *Labor Notes*, October 19, 2010, http://www.labornotes.org /2010/10/%E2%80%98not-really-worker%E2%80%99-home-based-unions-challenged -court.

44. Kris Maher, "SEIU to End Sodexo Campaign," *Wall Street Journal*, September 15, 2011, http://online.wsj.com/article/SB10000142405311190449170457657307416270 0598 .html.

JULIUS H. BAILEY

"Cult" Knowledge

The Challenges of Studying New Religious
Movements in America

IN 1999 A JOURNALIST FROM *TIME* MAGAZINE traveled to
Eatonton, Georgia, to interview members of a controversial new religious
community that had recently relocated to the area. The reporter asked
Minister Marshall Chance, the head spokesperson of the Nuwaubian's Holy
Tabernacle Ministries, whether, as had been widely reported, the community expected the return of a spaceship in the near future. Chance responded, "Some of us do, and some of us don't."[1]

This careful, equivocal, and perhaps alarming exchange exemplifies the
public challenges that new religious movements often face in negotiating
with the outside world: how to simultaneously assuage the concerns of an
often skeptical (and perhaps unnecessarily frightened) public while safe-
guarding the sacred knowledge that binds their community. It also points
to the interpretive challenges that will face those historians who seek to
study such movements. How do historians provide an accurate account of
change over time and the development of new religious movements when
insiders and outsiders approach the evidence from such disparate viewpoints? Those already committed to the community find their claims to
be self-evident, but many outsiders, such as most media, tend to reduce
all new religious movements to "cults." To be described as a cult is to be assigned all the stereotypical qualities associated with such groups: a propen-
sity for "brainwashing"; a controlling, dishonest but charismatic leader; and
systematic manipulation of adherents' trust are but a few.

Yet how can historians, whose access to these communities can be as
limited as any other outsider, construct a coherent narrative out of such
mediated, unreliable public sources and the self-serving and assumption-
driven agendas that produce them? Is there a way to analyze new religious

movements that is convincing for both insiders and outsiders? Can we do so without resorting to oversimplification? Sources that describe the elements of faith constitute the data with which historians of religion, in particular, construct a description of the beliefs and practices of a community.

However unusual those beliefs might seem, we historians also have a commitment to producing accounts of religious communities that the members themselves would recognize and acknowledge as true. Thoughtful works such as Lorne Dawson's *Comprehending Cults: The Sociology of New Religious Movements* (1998), James R. Lewis's *Legitimating New Religions* (2003), and John A. Saliba's *Understanding New Religious Movements* (2003) provide guidance on conceptualizing these religions.[2] However, the central task for historians of analyzing change over time adds challenges that often go unanswered within the context of sociological categorizations of new religions. This seemingly straightforward goal is complicated when we study recently established communities of faith representing alternative belief systems that stretch sensibilities. Some of these sects articulate themselves within an unconventional ancient history that belies their apparent late twentieth- or early twenty-first-century context and origins. To portray such traditions empathetically can be a challenge, particularly when an audience of popular readers is likely to encounter them from within a sensationalist recent history that characterizes new communities of faith as cults.

Must a scholar choose between acknowledging a sacred history and seeking to challenge it with the conventional tools of the historical profession that might serve to discredit a community's own carefully constructed history? Is there a way to be true to both "histories"? These are some of the many interpretive, as well as evidentiary, challenges facing scholars of new religious movements. We who seek to illuminate these recent histories must often situate ourselves between earnest, but controversial, followers of a sacred tradition and a skeptical, often hostile, public that anticipates the worst possible social outcomes for such burgeoning traditions of faith. Within this paradigm, "insider perspectives," while theoretically useful, become less so the more they are culled from difficult, and pessimistic, outsider sources that make statements like Minister Chance's seem bizarre. Historical periodization can also become an issue when the question of origins themselves conflicts with standard chronology or older faith traditions. Where does such a story even begin? Must the Nuwaubian narrative begin in 1993 with the community's arrival in Georgia, or thousands of years earlier as depicted in the Nuwaubians' sacred text?

The solution I propose here is to reframe the "insider/outsider" dichotomy less as opposing forces than as competing frames for evidence that offer, in their own way, potential insights in the construction of historical narrative. In this way, the emphasis is less on the authenticity of the speaker and more on the ways the data put forth fit or dissent from the larger puzzle of the religious community's depiction. This paradigm shift moves new religious movements in from the margins. It articulates them not as unique phenomena but as groups who are undergoing the same historical processes as other "great world religions" that have undergone a process of legitimation. These processes and struggles have allowed some religions to thrive, others to dissolve, and still others to survive but remain marginal or hidden from the view of a larger public. Furthermore, this view allows us to reconfigure competing and sometimes contradictory narratives as varied "strategies" of legitimation that new faith traditions may adopt, either to persuade others to embrace certain positions or to situate themselves in relation to more established religions. In this way, it is the particular approaches and strategies undertaken by individuals and communities that are under critical analysis, not the veracity of the people or their beliefs and practices.

The arrival of the United Nuwaubian Nation of Moors (UNNM) in Eatonton, Georgia, in 1993 provides a case study that allows us to examine the kinds of strategies for self-representation that new religious movements can employ in the face of twenty-four-hour news cycles that often depict their traditions in a negative, and even criminal, light. Spanning the landscape of the nineteenth- and twentieth-century religious movements, historians would be hard-pressed to find one with more diverse beliefs over its relatively brief history than the UNNM: prophetic dates of Armageddon, notions of black racial superiority, elements of UFO religions, and religious narratives establishing Native American and Egyptian ancestry. It is precisely this changing identity and diversity of thought within the movement that reveals the range of options available for many new religious movements as they endure the scorn of outsiders who often label them as "deviant cults" while viewing their own mainstream religion as normal.

Rethinking "Cultness"

In 1993, having purchased 476 acres of land approximately ten miles outside of the town of Eatonton for $975,000, the UNNM moved from Brooklyn to Georgia. They worked hard to transform their land in ways that were clearly alarming, although unintentionally so, to the existing community. By 1997 the Nuwaubians had constructed a forty-foot-high black pyramid, statues of ancient Egyptian gods and goddesses that were eight feet tall, columns with hieroglyphics, a sphinx, and a set of smaller twenty-four-foot pyramids.³ Before much was known about the community, many news outlets, both locally and nationally, speculated that the UNNM would likely be next in the lineage of religious communities such as Jonestown, Waco, and Heaven's Gate that have ended in tragedy. The media, almost from the group's arrival in Georgia, described this small, predominantly African American religious community in ways that were legible only through popular fears about cults and their trajectories toward disaster.

But when the news media rarely define the term, what does the word "cult" mean in the vernacular? To what extent does "cultness" have connotations simultaneously believed to be well understood and actually defying easy interpretation? Framings of these new religions in popular culture often presume that people can know a cult when they see one. However, the pejorative use of this concept to describe the unknown and feared often reveals more about the labeler than denoting any useful knowledge about the community under investigation. Scholars of recent history might feel that they face difficult choices here. They must decide whether the term "cult" can be rehabilitated from its negative use in popular culture, whether it can serve some heuristic purpose, or whether it must be discarded in favor of another concept that they must theorize themselves. In this essay, I propose an additional choice: that we employ the idea of a cult as a category of analysis that allows us to understand elements of the initial relationship between secular and sacred communities. Cult knowledge thus describes the fears and anxieties that the term "cult" invokes for outsiders while also making the strategies that insiders employ to shed and resist the label a central aspect of our investigation.

The media often emphasize the novelty and bizarre quality of new religious movements, but scholars of recent history must cut through those representations to perceive the particular, and often conventional, cultural settings from which new faiths emerge. However, how far back does one go to establish these contexts? For the media, the tragic end of the Jonestown community in 1978 provides all the history they need. Howard Sills, the sheriff of Eatonton, viewed the UNNM as a mixture of Jonestown and Heaven's Gate. "This group here is a combination of all those schools of thought," he observed. Skeptical, he characterized the change over time inherent in Nuwaubian history as a "constantly opportunistic evolving ideology."[4]

Yet historians might come to the conclusion that the UNNM has much more in common with nineteenth-century and early twentieth-century religious communities than it does with these recent, and perhaps tragic, religious formations. William Miller's changing predictions of Jesus's return, Noble Drew Ali's repositioning of blacks as "Asiatics," and the Nation of Islam's glorification of the African American race resonate within the diverse belief system of the UNNM.[5] This does not to diminish its distinctiveness. However, placed in the context of a variety of religious groups in the United States, the UNNM's beliefs are less an oddity than a more recent expression of historical forms of American spiritual creativity.

For every "cult," it seems, there must be a manipulative and charismatic leader who has successfully "brainwashed" a group of followers: if he or she does not exist, the media are happy to recraft a self-identified visionary into that image. News reports cast Malachi York, the leader of the UNNM, in this role. For many media outlets, York's felony criminal record sufficed as background information that undermined his religious credentials and articulated him as an illegitimate, perhaps dangerous, spiritual leader. By meshing his personal history with that of other devious and unscrupulous cult leaders, such accounts sought to discredit him and the UNNM. Popular biographies of Jim Jones of the People's Temple, for example, emphasize his rampant drug use. Accounts of the events at Waco, Texas, in the early 1990s focus on David Koresh's sexual encounters with the female members of the Branch Davidians; other popular narratives speculate about the possibility that psychological impairments affected Marshall Applewhite's vision for Heaven's Gate.[6]

With access to few alternative archives that might provide new perspectives, scholars of recent history must often navigate between insider accounts of past incidents and the media's "official record," which emphasizes instability, petty crime, and abusive behaviors. For example, police reports describe charges of resisting arrest, assaulting an officer, and illegally possessing a weapon leveled against York forty years before he led the community to Eatonton. But some Nuwaubians have described York quite differently: as they view him, he was and is a staunch proponent of civil rights who was unjustly persecuted by the police in the 1960s. Similarly, charisma is often a trait heralded as a marker of a good mainstream religious leader, but in the hands of an individual branded as a cult leader it is regularly framed as a sinister tool for manipulating gullible followers. Both insiders and outsiders have particular motives, conscious and unconscious, for putting forth competing views that depict the past in certain ways. Scholars of recent history need not only to find ways to allow both stories to have a certain status as the "past" but also to abstract them from the moral judgments of the present long enough to establish a new narrative that the community of faith might recognize. Rethinking such narratives as strategies allows us to reflect not only on what the apparent compulsion toward negative portrayals of such leaders in the media tells us about religion in America more broadly but also how the perspective of the believers themselves might be grounded in a legitimate, and different, reality.

Once the cult label is attached to a religion, otherwise innocuous information fed through a suspicious mainstream press to a larger, and in many cases less informed, audience can reinforce this image. The trajectory of the Nuwaubians clearly demonstrates this dynamic. Beginning in the mid-1960s, during their time in New York, the group who would come to be known as the UNNM integrated aspects of Islam into its theology, becoming known as the Ansaru Allah (Helpers of Allah) and Ansaru Pure Sufi, focusing on the mystic aspects of Sufism. Then, in 1969 York took a different turn, encouraging his followers to embrace their true *Jewish* identity. This fluidity in doctrinal approach has resulted in name changes that may impede a simple chronology. York sometimes referred to the group as the Nubian Islamic Hebrews; at other times, he called it the Ancient Holy Tabernacle of the Most High, the Children of Abraham, and the Ancient Mystic Order of Melchizedek. In all these incarnations, the faith blended elements of Judaism and Christianity and, as in some of these traditions, led followers to declare themselves a "chosen people." By the end of the 1980s York's writings also reflected a growing interest in psychology, telepathy, physics, and extraterrestrial life. Just before relocating in Georgia, York incorporated Neteru, an ancient Egyptian deity, in UNNM worship services, emphasizing the glorious history of people of African descent in Egypt.[7]

Newspapers seized on these apparently extreme and seemingly contradictory shifts in philosophy to question the sincerity of the community's beliefs. Yet we might also observe that all religious traditions evolve over time and are rarely practiced precisely as their ancient forebears and founders may have intended. Sometimes sects spin off with new names and make exclusive claims to the original doctrine. In the case of traditional religions, many contemporary adherents presume a timeless and unchanging past. But many mainstream religions have undergone a number of major theological shifts over time yet often downplay the diversity inherent in their traditions. That such transitions have usually been made in a far past beyond the experience of a living audience usually enhances the credibility of such faiths as traditions that embrace related, if different, views. Thus, scholars of recent history must convey the fluid nature of religious belief and practice and argue just the opposite: that nostalgic, timeless portrayals of mainstream religions may mask more dramatic shifts in worldview. Unlike historians of the far past, we have the opportunity to remind our readers how other comparatively recent and embattled religions have come to be accepted. Reframed in this way, the transformative beliefs and practices of new religious movements may be seen less as erratic behavior and more as a resilient characteristic of the nature of religion in America. The emergence of new religions then is firmly situated in particular historical moments. In this way, extreme shifts in ideology over time, even those that occur in shorter increments, become less the exception than the rule.

Reconciling the divergent views of insiders and outsiders into a historical narrative of a religious community is not unique to the study of the Nuwaubians. Scholars of the Latter-Day Saints, such as Jan Shipps, have wrestled with the "prophet puzzle," parsing the testimony of Joseph Smith's neighbors and apostates in comparison to the official church history to create a fuller picture of the founding leader of the tradition. That Joseph Smith rarely spoke about the "First Vision" that he had in 1820 until almost a decade later have led some scholars to conclude that he created the story subsequently to ward off attacks from outsiders who challenged his credibility. Yet to question the reliability of the official church history and then use that same, often conflicting, chronology as the basis to undermine other aspects of the Mormon narrative is problematic.[8] Highly persecuted in the nineteenth century, the Latter-Day Saints are now one of the fastest-growing traditions in the world and in 2012 may produce the first presidential candidate who is an active Mormon. Achieving a sufficiently large membership and social or political power as the Mormon Church has can allow certain relatively recent traditions to define themselves in the public sphere rather than always react to the next slight by outsiders. Differences from other traditions are no longer translated into pathologies. This is not the case for many small, new religious movements whose schisms or reframed perspectives may have occurred in the past decade and not the past century and whose base is sometimes made up of socially, economically, and politically marginalized people. Understanding strategies of repositioning and theological change that have allowed some religions to become unremarkable allows scholars of recent history to understand what is *not* available to even more recent religions. This, in turn, allows us to consider whether each emergent community must be engaged on its own terms or if broader parallels and patterns can be discerned across burgeoning traditions initially perceived as cults.

As with the study of the early Church of the Latter-Day Saints, scholars of recent history in all fields often must navigate events and encounters described by some sources as secular and by others as sacred. Both interpretations deserve serious consideration: to embrace only one is to exclude the other, telling half of the story of a relationship within and between communities. For example, in 1999 the UNNM applied to rezone part of its Eatonton property from agricultural to commercial use, a request that was denied by Putnam County. Specifically, the plan called for the renovation of a hundred-by-fifty-foot building into a worship hall and Ramses Social Club, a structure that had been originally zoned for storage only. Citing several violations, housing officials shut down what the media referred to as a "nightclub," implying a commercial use, but one that the UNNM did not intend. The Nuwaubians claimed they never had a chance to correct the violations before the building was padlocked to prevent their entry. Media accounts framed the tension as a legal dispute in which the UNNM would simply not adhere to the law.

However, the UNNM had a different viewpoint. They viewed their land as sacrosanct and beyond state control. According to their sacred text, the *Holy Tabernacle Ministries*, their ancestors had crossed from the Nile Valley to the Americas before the continental drift. From their perspective, they were the original Native Americans and had a sacred and a political claim to the land. Given this historical identity, the Nuwaubians declared themselves a sovereign nation. They began issuing their own passports and organizing armed security units to protect their property, which further elevated the conflict with the broader community. For the Nuwaubians, their community was not Eatonton, or even the United States, but Tama-Re or "The Land," a sacred site and a native homeland. In contrast, the media commonly referred to the location as a "compound," invoking images of the People's Temple in Guyana and the Branch Davidians in Waco.[9]

The media, which have an interest in promoting consumption as well as knowledge, tend to focus on the most attention-grabbing stories, often forgoing nuance for a concise, uninterrupted narrative. When rumors emerged that UNNM prophesies predicted the arrival of a spaceship, returning from the planet Rizq on May 5, 2003, to ransom the 144,000 true believers prior to the imminent judgment of those remaining on earth, that apocalyptic event produced sensational headlines. However, calculating dates for an imminent supernatural return is nothing new in American religious history. From William Miller's prophesies in the 1840s to Tim LaHaye and Jerry Jenkins's vastly popular *Left Behind* book series, numerous Americans have speculated about and predicted the date of the return of Jesus Christ and what form that resurrection will take. For many Christians, expecting a divine savior who lived in human form two thousand years ago to return is seen as normative, while a similar expectation on the part of a new religion that a spaceship will appear is regularly defined as a deviant belief that confirms its status as a cult. The invocation of extraterrestrials extended UNNM history beyond Egypt and the earliest civilizations to a time before the formation of the earth, allowing the community to be at once new and ancient, uniquely American and transcending humankind, and racially distinctive and supernatural.[10]

Interrogating Insiderness

Given these portrayals in the media and the suspicion often expressed by outsiders to the community, new religious movements are often understandably cautious about the dissemination of information. In many cases, the kind of detailed information necessary to writing a compelling historical narrative is available only to insiders. For scholars of religious history, gaining access to that insider voice without becoming an insider is a difficult task that is, nonetheless, essential to producing an accurate depiction of the faith tradition. However, living human beings in the present are not simply archives of information to be sifted through. They must be contacted and engaged, and trust must be established; historians have some responsibility to write a story that adherents would recognize even if it challenges elements of their own narrative by presenting alternate points of view. To gain insight and access scholars must be willing to shed outsiderness to some extent and be prepared to engage the community's inquiries and suspicions. This process involves choices that a visitor to a manuscript collection will never have to make. Should researchers identify themselves to insiders as historians or merely interested observers? One stance presumably could bring down a social barrier and the other might erect one, regardless of good faith. Can historians sidestep this issue by joining virtual communities that allow anonymous or pseudonymous participation? Websites often allow members to sign up for chat rooms and have access to exclusive information, but is it ethical to do so as a historian doing research? Once in the chat room, must historians identify to all who are online that they are an academic in pursuit of information for an article or book? Perhaps scholars must answer these ethical guidelines for themselves, but each choice has consequences for the type of information that is gleaned, the subsequent work that is produced, and the ethical stance of the researchers.

Monographs of mainstream religions draw on the correspondence of leaders and laity, records of doctrinal debate, and the journals of members, but what constitutes a written archive for new religious movements that do not have extensive records of this kind? Close ethnographic study and a deep engagement with the self-depiction of contemporary communities can produce rich and textured portrayals and understandings of communities that counter, to some extent, misrepresentation or incorrect information contained in sensational media accounts. We can regard such depictions as a kind of public archive of adherents' struggle, not only to express themselves but also to gain religious credibility and political rights in the United States. In this way, the media become less a barrier to an authentic portrayal than one of many competing narratives to be sifted through and analyzed, one in which the insider voices of leaders and members can be heard through careful reading. Yet this is often no easy task. For example, when asked about the existence of an afterlife, Minister Chance, speaking for the UNNM community, stated, "These are the last days and we Nuwaubians have created God's kingdom right here on Earth."[11] These statements point to apparent contradictions and provoke questions not easily asked or answered. If there were to be an expected and impending supernatural event, why would there be a need to construct an elaborate community in Eatonton or seek zoning variances? Alternatively, does the construction of the community itself inaugurate the end times? How representative is this leader's view of the broader UNNM movement as a whole?

Theoretically, a close engagement with members of the community could serve as a way of answering these questions, but not if the participants in such movements are themselves presumed to be "brainwashed" and under the control of a manipulative, unstable, or dishonest leader. Another approach that would allow historians to strip away the barriers to knowledge that the mediated history of "cultness" imposes would be to perform a close textual study of the literature produced and distributed by new religious movements. This too has its challenges and cannot be successfully achieved without some of the methodological interventions I have already described. As with the voices of spokespeople, without membership in the tradition and knowledge about how these texts are understood and related to within the community, historians may go astray or find these documents simply confusing. For example, the *Little Guide Book for Nuwaubians* contains the entire U.S. Constitution. It prohibits disorderly conduct and urges cooperation with authorities, and yet the community regularly turned away county deputies with court orders regarding the zoning violations on UNNM property. In other words, in this document the group at once espoused patriotism and remained suspicious of the intentions of the government. "We did not come as a political threat," Chance stated. "If we were lawbreakers, we would not ask for help from the federal government."[12] Yet is it the duty of historians to reconcile the beliefs espoused in the guidebook and the actions of the community?

There are also unique linguistic barriers that cannot be solved without help from community members. York created his own language, Nuwaubic, a blend of Arabic and English that would require an inside interpreter or instructor to understand. In this way, even a close textual study relies on the leaders and membership of the community with few outside reference points by which a historian might evaluate and contextualize the potential insights they are conveying. Through the examination of the literature of new religious movements, like the UNNM, one can glean an insiderness often not easily translatable to an academic or outside audience.

Although many social historians seek to illuminate the voices of "ordinary people" within religious traditions, nevertheless the tendency has been to focus on the leaders of new religious movements. There are a number of reasons for this, including the prominent role that many leaders seem to play in the construction of the theology and practices of these traditions and the fact that they are more likely to assert an authority to speak for the community. Yet does this approach, perhaps unintentionally, confirm the cult assumptions of a passive constituency? This view articulates leaders such as Minister Chance as skilled manipulators with more fruitful sources of insights and thus the only sites of knowledge.

On the other hand, a religious leader is often physically unavailable to historians of the recent past in a way that followers might not be. Malachi Z.

York, the leader of the UNNM community, rarely granted interviews although he was a prolific writer, penning more than two hundred tracts used in prayer by many of the members as they circle the small labyrinth surrounding the main pyramid. If the theological viewpoints and proscriptions for York's followers are not necessarily the same as his inner workings and thoughts, specific points of conflict might be more difficult to ascertain. Lacking this data, it is tempting to draw conclusions about the religion from the presence or absence of leaders such as York from particular settings where theological views diverge.

Deciphering the statements of spokespeople such as Minister Chance, who is also an ordained Baptist minister, exemplifies the challenge of reading media representations when it is often those very outlets that serve as focal points for resistance by new religious movements. When asked about the source of his authority, Chance said that he had been "ordained and called by God Himself," a statement that does not necessarily preclude hints that York has also dropped that he himself might be a deity. Who, historians might reasonably ask, is Chance referring to in this statement? A subsequent statement made by Chance about York muddied the waters even further. Chance took issue with *Time* magazine's portrayal of York as the "Supreme Being of This Day and Time, God in Flesh." Having studied under York, Chance clarified this point: "He's like a father, mentor, counselor and guide. He was born here and has parents here, though he may trace his culture to the stars."[13]

If few "ordinary" members grant interviews, leaders can become one of the few ways of accessing the community, but such communications need to be read in tandem with other information provided by spokespeople and community members. This offers a broader context for understanding one of the most common sources of scandal for a new religion, and for some older ones: money. This subject, particularly awkward to address among religious communities in general, becomes even more so given the popular perception that many new religious movements are swindling vulnerable people out of their hard-earned funds. When asked how the group could afford the Eatonton property and embark on such ambitious construction projects, Chance responded enigmatically, "We attract people who already have something with them."[14] Translating his beliefs for a skeptical audience, Chance hastened to identify the community and its practices with the Judeo-Christian tradition. "We're all awaiting the coming of the real

Messiah," Chance said. "We are a biblical people. If it's not in the Bible, then we're not concerned with it."[15]

Appealing to the preservation of and necessity for racial and ethnic concerns, or heritage projects, can also insulate new religious movements from persecution, if only temporarily, while they establish themselves. Chance framed the Nuwaubian movement a "cultural renaissance" for its members. "We can feel and get a sense of our own cultures here," he said. "We're comfortable for and with everybody." Ultimately, establishing the community's "Americaness"—embracing both diversity and American exceptionalism— can be a key hurdle in a religion's survival in the United States. Chance did this zealously. "We're looking at the greatest country, the greatest land, the greatest place," he said. "America's a great country." Yet, as has been the case with other new religious movements, the UNNM also laid claim to its own Zion: "We're building a place that's something better" and "People have encountered miracles here." Not only were Nuwaubians Americans, but they also understood themselves to be one of the first indigenous peoples on the continent. "These are tribalistic lands," Chance insisted. "It's home for us."[16] In this case, Chance downplays the "strangeness" of the community without seeking to directly refute the charges against it.

Scholars of contemporary movements must often sort through conflicting understandings of patriotism and the possibilities for the supernatural. But without access to the larger community, it is difficult to assess how widespread such beliefs are, gauge the intensity with which they are felt throughout the tradition, or understand how they impact events. For example, another community spokesperson portrayed the Nuwaubians as an open-minded and welcoming community. "We are very particular about giving people their space and letting them be what they want to be," she insisted. The community had, she said, plans for a theme park and the gates of the community were opened daily to visitors during certain hours. Yet how members felt about these developments remains just as absent from the record as the views of the average Nuwaubian about theology, patriotism, or the apocalypse.[17] Ironically, the actions of the county made it even harder for dialogue and exchange to occur. Many of the structures and businesses that were operational or under construction were padlocked by authorities during the conflict, which prevented the Nuwaubians from returning to their shared community and led to the demise of many public facilities, including a health food store, bar, recording studio, and a taxi company.[18]

Secrecy and the Sacred

As is true in most historical fields, "facts" do not exist in a vacuum but are subject to interpretation. Historians who write about new religions must make a significant commitment to interpretation and to the methods that ground interpretation in what evidence can be obtained. New religions can be placed in multiple alternative contexts that might shift the perspective of historians and readers. An organization's need to guard facts about itself, however, can make ordinary information difficult to access for reasons beyond even the adherents' or leaders' control. Legal problems leveled against new religious movements can inhibit their ability to speak, either publicly or for possible publication, about the allegations until the matter is resolved (if in fact it is resolved, or the resolution does not preclude confidentiality). The shadow of a 1993 FBI report that linked the UNNM to welfare fraud and extortion during the group's time in New York followed it to Georgia, and although this information was reported in the media, for legal reasons members of the UNNM could not always speak for themselves or defend the church against such allegations. Similarly, the media regularly reported that York was a convicted felon, without necessarily saying what he had been charged with or why. In rare instances newspaper outlets noted that York had served three years in prison and relayed his specific crimes. Yet, these "facts" could easily be woven into a broader Nuwaubian narrative that established York as a courageous leader fighting against a corrupt police force.[19]

Many new religious movements are also caught between the perils of secrecy and the potential shock value of what is hidden being revealed. The *Macon Telegraph* obtained copies of the applications to both the Holy Tabernacle Ministries and the Ancient Mystic Order of Melchizedek. According to these documents, the Mystic Order required a twenty-five-dollar membership fee and a vow of silence that prohibited discussing information about the community. The application also asked for a medical history, an HIV test, and copies of birth certificates and Social Security cards. In return, members were given passports and license plates that allowed them easy access to the community through the main gate.[20]

As even this outsider report suggests, if these requirements were true, members of the UNNM could have disclosed their membership process, but only by potentially violating sacred traditions and practices and risking new questions about the criteria for admission to the community. As current and former members came forward to level charges of abuse, sexual assault, and financial malfeasance against York, media scrutiny of their ongoing legal troubles increased, revealing more information that outsiders regarded as suspicious. York, it turned out, had a $528,000 home in Athens, where officials found $125,000 in cash. Sacred knowledge complicated York's trial, because the leader refused to let the court officials say his name during the proceedings because he was "secured." Some Nuwaubians gave members of the media a "copyright notice," stamped with "Received, Jan. 08, 2003" by the "Clerk of Federal Moorish Cherokee Consular Court, USA." The notice stated that York's name and aliases could not be used without permission and that there would be financial penalties for "unauthorized" use of his name.[21]

Despite the members' best efforts to control information, some court outcomes can nonetheless be definitive for these religions. On January 24, 2003, York pleaded guilty to two counts of having sex with children as part of a plea agreement that would give him fifteen years in federal prison and three years of supervised release, a decision that seemed to herald a turning point, and perhaps even an end, for this religion.[22] The challenges of doing recent history include uncertainty about whether York's conviction marks an artificial end point to the narrative. The loss of a leader, although significant, does not necessarily halt the development and transformation of a socially and theologically evolving community and tradition. Declaring the demise of new religious movements is a dangerous prognostication, given their history in America and groups such as the Church of the Latter-Day Saints that overcame seemingly certain extinction.

Concluding the narrative of the UNNM feels particularly arbitrary, because religious communities, ideologies, beliefs, and practices are likely to continue evolving past the date of publication. York's incarceration, for example, was a significant marker in the trajectory of the UNNM, but it allowed other stories to begin. His daughter, Hagar York-El, has sought to propel the movement forward in her father's absence, by gathering the remaining members back together, seeking new adherents, and proving her father's innocence. In addition, the act of publishing may put scholars in an enhanced dialogue with the community and can lead to new developments for historians. Community members may be moved to talk back and question whether the portrayal is "right." If insiders confirm the historians' analysis, does that make the account somehow more "true"? Not necessarily, but it might pry open the doors for further research.

In many ways, thinking about contemporary religions and how we as historians choose to frame our subjects says much more about us than it says about those we study. This chapter suggests that, whether acknowledged or not, historians can easily make problematic judgments about new religions at the outset of the research, gathering information that confirms suspicions under the guise of objectivity. Indeed, if scholars truly believe that a community is dangerous, there could be a moral imperative to alert authorities to the potential danger before its story ends in tragedy as others have.

Outside this either/or proposition is the possibility for what we value as historians: a close reading of the available sources to examine the diverse viewpoints of such communities, the strategies they employ to survive in the United States, and how they change over time. In their ideology, the Nuwaubians demonstrated a flexible capacity to adapt their beliefs and practices, a malleability that allowed them to attract different constituencies and provide a sense of distinctiveness. This strategy worked to greater and lesser degrees with eighteenth- and nineteenth-century movements such as the Shakers, the Latter-Day Saints, and the Oneida Community. Although contemporary newspaper accounts were not always kind to these groups, modern religious movements face additional obstacles in an information age where ideas and opinions circulate globally at unprecedented speeds. With Jonestown, the Branch Davidians, and Heaven's Gate as templates, most new movements are presumed guilty by outsiders until proven innocent. With twenty-four-hour news coverage and websites devoted to establishing new religions as cults, and where modern science seems to fly in the face of sacred narratives, what does it mean to safeguard knowledge that falls outside the mainstream?

This volatile atmosphere is a part of the context in which contemporary historians write. Rather than having to make a moral judgment about the tradition under investigation, studies can be reframed in ways that do not call the legitimacy of a new religious movement into question or reproduce unfounded prejudices. For example, unusual or contradictory claims might be rearticulated as strategies to address the dilemmas of being labeled and stigmatized as a cult. Such a history might ask, how does a community prove that it is *not* a cult? At the same time, invoking the term "cult"—at once elusive and seemingly self-explanatory—might actually become another weapon to be employed against the "weak."

Even with that risk, such histories also provide an opportunity for astute scholars to examine what is at stake for mainstream traditions in labeling other communities as cults. What would it mean to acknowledge that York and the Nuwaubians have ambitions that are possibly not so different from those of the Puritans or the early Christian church? What do the binaries invoked in the media tell us about religion in America? The payoff for this could be considerable, as historians rescue new religions from obscurity and honor their claims to the realm of the sacred. The Nuwaubians alone present crucial opportunities. Rather than a redemptive figure who went to prison for his beliefs, Malachi Z. York is currently figured as simply a convicted felon; rather than a devout community waiting for the advent of a supernatural spiritual event, the Nuwaubians are understood as "Space Invaders" looking for UFOs; and rather than a sacred text, the *Holy Tabernacle Ministries* is viewed as a tool for manipulating and brainwashing misguided followers. It remains to be seen if the Nuwaubians can weather this scandal as other groups have sought to do, with leaders such as Elijah Muhammad and his relationship with female followers and Aimee Semple McPherson and her alleged abduction.[23]

Rather than a problem, the gap between the skeptic and the committed provides an opportunity and a framework to analyze the evolution of American identity in the contemporary United States. The distance between insider and outsider provides a useful space to examine how each community can lay claim to the role of victim and label the other as a persecutor, each reading evidence through a lens that supports its own stance. It is in this interplay that we glimpse something of how each group imagines the contours of normative religion in America. One also gains an understanding of the frustration that new religious movements experience as their own secrecy causes suspicion rather than devotion. Conversely, movements that have a visible public presence can be equally agitating to the larger community. In defending their right to remain in Eatonton, the Nuwaubians have navigated a challenging position between maintaining distinctiveness and embracing assimilation. Although the veracity of the charges and future of the group remain in doubt, the Nuwaubians present perhaps the most compelling contemporary example of a new religious movement that embraced its "strangeness" and sought to make it "familiar." The close and creative examination of the location of historians in relation to their contemporary subjects could open up a whole range of inquiry about burgeoning new religious communities in America.

Notes

1. Sylvester Monroe, "Space Invaders," *Time*, July 12, 1999, http://ynam.org/articles /07-12-09.htm.

2. Lorne Dawson, *Comprehending Cults: The Sociology of New Religious Movements* (New York: Oxford University Press, 1998); James R. Lewis, *Legitimating New Religions* (New Brunswick, N.J.: Rutgers University Press, 2003); John A. Saliba, *Understanding New Religious Movements* (Walnut Creek, Calif.: Altamira, 2003).

3. Monroe, "Space Invaders."

4. Patricia J. Mays, "Georgia Sect Alarms Neighbors," Associated Press, July 27, 1999, http://news.google.com/newspapers?nid=1955&dat=19990727&id=UyoiAAAAIBAJ&sj id=naYFAAAAIBAJ&pg=3573,7365565.

5. Dawson, *Comprehending Cults*; James R. Lewis, ed., *The Oxford Handbook of New Religious Movements* (New York: Oxford University Press, 2004); Sean McCloud, *Making the American Religious Fringe: Exotics, Subversives, and Journalists, 1955–1993* (Chapel Hill: University of North Carolina Press, 2004); Saliba, *Understanding New Religious Movements*.

6. Robert Endleman, *Jonestown and the Manson Family: Race, Sexuality, and Collective Madness* (New York: Psyche, 1993); Brad Bailey and Bob Darden, *Mad Man in Waco: The Complete Story of the Davidian Cult, David Koresh, and the Waco Massacre* (Waco, Tex.: WRS, 1993); Mariana Georgacarakos, *Notorious Killer Cult Leaders: Marshall Applewhite, Bonnie Nettles, Jim Jones, David Koresh, Charles Manson, and Jeffrey Lundgren* (n.p.: Webster's Digital Services, 2011); Walter Martin, *The Kingdom of the Cults* (Minneapolis, Minn.: Bethany House, 2003).

7. Theodore Gabriel, "The United Nuwaubian Nation of Moors," in *UFO Religions*, ed. Christopher Partridge (New York: Routledge, 2003), 150–54; A. A. B. Philips, *The Ansaru Cult in America* (Riyadh, Saudi Arabia: Taweed, 1988).

8. Jan Shipps, "The Prophet Puzzle: Suggestions Leading toward a More Comprehensive Interpretation of Joseph Smith," in Bryan Waterman, ed., *The Prophet Puzzle: Interpretive Essays on Joseph Smith* (Salt Lake City: Signature Books, 1999), 25–47.

9. Tom Lassete, "Tensions Simmer around a Black Sect in Georgia," *New York Times*, June 29, 1999, http://ynam.org/articles/06-29-09.htm.

10. Susan J. Palmer and Steve Luxton, "The Ansaru Allah Community: Postmodernist Narration and the Black Jeremiad," in *New Trends and Developments in the World of Islam*, ed. Peter B. Clark (London: Luzac Oriental, 1998), 361; William Miller, *Evidence from Scripture and History of the Second Coming of Christ about the Year 1843* (Boston: Dow, 1841); Tim LaHaye and Jerry B. Jenkins, *Left Behind: A Novel of the Earth's Last Days* (Carol Stream, Ill.: Tyndale House, 2011).

11. Lassete, "Tensions Simmer."

12. Hilary Hilliard, "Accusations of Racism," *Macon Telegraph*, August 8, 1999, http:// ynam.org/articles/08-08-99.htm; Malachi York, *Little Guide Book for Nuwaubians* (n.p.: New Babylon, 1992).

13. Matthew I. Pinzur, "Eatonton Site Raises a Lot of Questions," *Macon Telegraph*, August 8, 1999, http://ynam.org/articles/08-08-09B.htm.

14. Lassete, "Tensions Simmer."

15. Mays, "Georgia Sect Alarms Neighbors."

16. Pinzur, "Eatonton Site."

17. Ibid.

18. Jim Thompson, "Religious Sect Plans Gala Event," *Morris News Service*, December 31, 1999.

19. Ibid.

20. Pinzur, "Eatonton Site."

21. William Osinski, "Sect Leader Promised Salvation via Sex, Teen Says," *Atlanta Journal Constitution*, June 2, 2002; Robert Peecher, "Lawyers Argue Details in York Case," *Telegraph*, January 18, 2003, http://www.religionnewsblog.com/page/1431.

22. Peecher, "Nuwaubian Leader Pleads Not Guilty," *Macon Telegraph*, May 9, 2002; Peecher, "Lawyers Argue Details"; William Osinski, "Nuwaubian Leader Pleads Guilty on Child Charges," *Atlanta Journal Constitution*, January 24, 2003.

23. Karl Evanzz, *The Messenger: The Rise and Fall of Elijah Muhammad* (New York: Pantheon Books, 1999); Matthew Avery Sutton, *Aimee Semple McPherson and the Resurrection of Christian America* (Cambridge, Mass.: Harvard University Press, 2007); Daniel Mark Epstein, *Sister Aimee: The Life of Aimee Semple McPherson* (New York: Harcourt Brace Jovanovich, 1993).

Index

SINCE 1970: HISTORIES OF CONTEMPORARY AMERICA

Jimmy Carter, the Politics of Family, and the Rise of the Religious Right
by J. Brooks Flippen

Rumor, Repression, and Racial Politics: How the Harassment of Black Elected Officials Shaped Post–Civil Rights America
by George Derek Musgrove

Doing Recent History: On Privacy, Copyright, Video Games, Institutional Review Boards, Activist Scholarship, and History That Talks Back
edited by Claire Bond Potter and Renee C. Romano